THE COMPLETE MALTESE

The Complete

MALTESE

By Nicholas Cutillo

First Edition

HOWELL
BOOK HOUSE
New York

Howell Book House
Macmillan Publishing Company
866 Third Avenue, New York, NY 10022

Collier Macmillan Canada, Inc.
1200 Eglinton Avenue East, Suite 200
Don Mills, Ontario M3C 3N1

Library of Congress Cataloging-in-Publication Data

Cutillo, Nicholas.
  The complete Maltese.

  1. Maltese dogs. I. Title.
SF429.M25C88   1986   636.7′6   86-20881
ISBN 0-87605-209-X

Macmillan books are available at special discounts for bulk purchases for sales promotions, premiums, fund-raising, or educational use. For details, contact:

> Special Sales Director
> Macmillan Publishing Company
> 866 Third Avenue
> New York, NY 10022

10   9   8   7   6   5   4

Printed in the United States of America

To Aennchen Antonelli, whose love of and dedication to the Maltese graced the fancy for decades. There was a very special quality about Aennchen, hard to define, and found in very few. The Maltese and its fancy were fortunate to have been touched by one such as she. Her death has left a void that shall never be filled.

Contents

Preface

THE GROWTH in the number of Maltese in the United States and several other nations over the past few decades has been astounding. There are, therefore, great numbers of newcomers to the Maltese fancy. These newcomers are charged with the responsibility of keeping the Maltese the same aristocratic little dog he has been for centuries. It would be tragic for the Maltese to go the way of some other breeds which have attained "popularity."

Many fanciers are eager for any information regarding the breed. Up to now, the only *major* work published on the Maltese was a complete history by Mrs. V. Leitch in 1952.

THE COMPLETE MALTESE is intended for all those who love the Maltese. It is a history, and a practical guide to the many aspects of caring for and enjoying one or more Maltese.

The hours spent in compiling this book have been fraught with moments of frustration and distress. However, these were far outweighed by the moments of joy and satisfaction. It is my wish that what follows brings pleasure and increased knowledge to all those who read this book.

NICHOLAS CUTILLO

Acknowledgments

SINCERE THANKS and appreciation are extended to:

Mr. Timothy Lehman, without whose help this book would not be a reality.

Riders on the Wind, for unearthing such wonderful treasures.

Mr. William Blair, for all his help and encouragement.

Mr. Cord Hamilton, for his assistance with the photographs.

Dr. Paul Sova DVM, for expending his time and for his sincere interest in the Maltese.

And most of all, to those of the Maltese fancy who so generously supported this endeavor by sending pictures, photographs and information.

THE COMPLETE MALTESE

1

The Origins of "Ye Ancient Dogge of Malta"

THERE IS LITTLE DOUBT that the Maltese is one of the oldest of dog breeds. Darwin himself placed the origin of the breed at 6000 B.C. An aristocrat of the canine world, the Maltese has been known by a variety of names through the centuries. Originally called the *Melitaie Dog*, he has also been known as *Ye Ancient Dogge of Malta*, the *Roman Ladies' Dog*, the *Comforter*, the *Spaniel Gentle*, the *Bichon*, the *Shock Dog*, the *Maltese Lion Dog* and the *Maltese Terrier*. Finally, approximately within the past century, he has come to be known as, simply, the *Maltese*.

Malta of Old

Melitaie Dog, the name by which he was known to the Greeks and Romans, was derived from the Island of Melitaie, the ancient name for the Island of Malta. Malta is one of the most ancient sites of civilization. Settled by the Phoenicians at about 1500 B.C., Malta incorporated several other Mediterranean peoples who had inhabited the island as far back as 3500 B.C. Civilization on the island grew and prospered. There are numerous historical accounts of the magnificently opulent Maltese civilization. It was within this celebrated society of the ancient world that the tiny Maltese dog was prized and nurtured by its citizens. A leader in the crafts and arts, both domestic and military, in that era, Malta became one of the most important ancient centers of trade. It was from here that these highly prized dogs found their way throughout the world.

Original Roots

Historically there is no evidence to suggest that the Maltese is indigenous to the Island of Malta. He is descended from a Spitz-type dog, bred for turf and marsh, by the peoples inhabiting south central Europe and the area which is now Switzerland. It is likely that the dog was carried south by these people as they migrated down the Italian and Greek peninsulas. Eventually, the dog was found throughout the Mediterranean region. It is believed that the dog came to the eastern Mediterranean via the ancient island trading center of Malta, as Malta was a major supplier of goods to the area. The Maltese dog was included among the exotic Maltese articles of trade and was a highly prized diplomatic tribute. Arriving in the Middle East, the Maltese dog soon populated the area.

Eventually, the dog found himself even farther to the East. Carried by trade caravans loaded with occidental merchandise and tribute, the Maltese dog migrated as far as Tibet and China. Indeed, he was taken to Japan and the island areas, such as the Philippines off the Asian coast. In the Middle East and the Far East he was sometimes known as the *Fu Lin* dog, possibly, as noted by Mrs. Leitch in her book, *The Maltese Dog,* a name which was transliterated from the Greek *E Po Lin.*

The Maltese had a strong influence on the type of dog developed in Tibet. Historical evidence leads one to believe that the Maltese is part of the gene pool of the Lhasa Apso and the Tibetan Terrier. Specimens of both these breeds now bred in the United States are a great deal larger than earlier dogs. The Lhasa, for example, should measure nine or 10 inches at the shoulder for males, females slightly smaller. This is quite a small dog. Further, white does occur in the Lhasa Apso, albeit less frequently than colors. The pure white Lhasa Apso has black points. The Tibetan Terrier and Tibetan Spaniel are also ancient breeds, and the Maltese dog may have been introduced at some early point in their histories.

The Maltese may have also served as a foundation for the toy-type dogs in China. Early Western ceramic and porcelain representatives of the Pekingese bear little resemblance to the dog we know as a Pekingese today. They are higher and straighter of leg, and longer in muzzle: a definite Spaniel-type. These early representations of the Pekingese bear strong resemblance to ancient illustrations of the Maltese. Indeed, the first Pekingese brought to England from the Chinese Imperial Palace do not bear any resemblance to the modern Pekingese at all. They more closely resembled a dog of Maltese type.

Artifacts and Documentation

The first known representation of a Maltese-type dog is dated 600–300 B.C. It was unearthed in a dig at Fayum, near Cairo, Egypt. From evidence such as this, it is concluded that the Maltese was among dogs worshiped by the ancient Egyptians.

Maltese are featured on Greek vases found at Vulci, dated about 500 B.C., which are now part of the Bassegio collection. The ancient Greeks are known to have held their Maltese in great esteem. They were fed the choicest of foods from golden bowls. They were known to command great sums in the marketplace. Indeed, they were highly prized, especially among ladies of the upper classes and people of influence, such as governors and statesmen.

Tales of the undying devotion of the Maltese for his master are numerous in ancient Greek texts. Specific instances are recorded where the Maltese's devotion was so great they were known to have willingly followed their masters to the grave. The Greeks, in return, were equally devoted to their Maltese dogs. They erected elaborate shrines and tombs in honor of their dogs. The written tribute to the breed was elaborate, as well. It came in the form of both prose and verse, penned by some of the most noted men of the epoch. Among them was Aristotle (384–322 B.C.), who wrote a short history and account of the breed. He noted that the place of origin was the Island of Malta. He made note of their small size, about that of a weasel or rat, and their perfect proportions.

Timon in 280 B.C. wrote describing the Sybarites and their luxuriant lifestyle. Included among their prized possessions were the little white dogs imported from the Island of Malta. These little dogs attended the Sybarites at all they did, including luxurious baths and banquets.

In 264 B.C., Callimachus wrote in some detail of the very small dogs imported from Malta. He noted that the dogs were kept mostly by women, as a source of amusement and pleasure. Because of their function, he observed that the smaller they were the better. Women were known to have carried Maltese dogs in their bosoms and easily in their arms. The Maltese was indeed a very pampered pet, as it is recorded that they were even taken to bed with their masters. Callimachus is the first writer to make note of the use of the Maltese dog for medicinal purposes. The dog was laid upon the stomach or chest of the afflicted, in order to draw and ease pain.

Others among the ancient writers to mention the Maltese were Aelian, Artimidorus and Epaminodus. Aelian wrote: "Epaminodus, on his return from Lacedaemon, was summoned to a court of law to answer a charge involving the penalty of death, because he had continued the command of the Theban army four months longer than he was legally authorized to do . . . . The judges were ashamed of themselves, and acquitted him, and let him go. As he was leaving court, a little Maltese came and fawned upon him, wagging his tail. 'This animal,' said Epaminodus, 'is grateful for the good I have wrought, but the Thebans, to whom I have rendered the greatest service, would put me to death.'"

By the time the Romans had taken control of the Mediterranean, a definite Maltese-type was well documented. The Romans were great record-keepers and statisticians. They classified the Maltese with the group of dogs they named *Catelli*—small dogs kept as pets. It was recorded in Roman history that the Maltese had been imported into Rome and the Italian peninsula. Historically, the Romans claimed that the Maltese was the same kind of dog that had been popular in Egypt and Greece for centuries. The descriptions of the Maltese of the period have him as a very small dog, most suitable as a lap dog. Physically, the Maltese was described as possessing a long, silky coat and a feathered, curly tail.

Roman Emperor Claudius is recorded as being the owner of a white Maltese. It had continued to be the fashion for people of power and wealth to possess Maltese. Another such person was Publius, the Roman governor of Malta. Publius ruled the Island of Malta at the time of the Apostle Paul. Publius owned a tiny Maltese named "Issa" of which, it was recorded, he was extremely fond. He was so taken by the exquisite beauty of the little Maltese that he commissioned a portrait of the dog to be painted. The painting was of such quality and so lifelike that it was difficult to distinguish the real dog from the painting.

The poet Martial (A.D. 40-104) used Publius' Maltese, Issa, as a subject when, in part, he wrote:

> Issa is more frolicsome than Catulla's sparrow. Issa is purer than a dove's kiss. Issa is gentler than a maiden. Issa is more precious than Indian jems.

The epigram ended:

> Lest the last days that she sees the light should snatch her from him forever, Publius had her picture painted . . . .

There were numerous other Romans who discoursed upon the endearing and enduring qualities of the Maltese. Noteworthy among those is Strabo (63 B.C.–21 A.D.), who described the Maltese as being the smallest kind of its species. He noted that the owners of the dog included the wealthy and socially powerful. He gave the name *Canis digno throno* to them, because princes held them in their hand while sitting upon their thrones. They were kept to provide amusement and pleasure. They were the favorites of the ladies of the period, who tenderly nurtured them, and kept them as they would precious jewels. Of the physical nature of the dog, Strabo noted that they were bright and devoted, despite their small size. He compared their size to that of a ferret or weasel.

Another Roman to include the Maltese as subject matter was Pliny the Elder (A.D. 23–79), who noted their small size. He ascribed their origin to Malta. In one of the first descriptions of the dog being a color other than white, Pliny allowed that the Maltese could also be black and black and white.

Saint Clement of Alexandria, in the second century A.D., included reference to the Maltese in his prose.

As with other things central to Roman society, there is no doubt that the Maltese was spread to the far reaches of the Roman empire.

After the Fall of Rome

Gradually, as with all civilizations that had preceded it, the power of Rome began to fade. The empire began to weaken. It was plagued by foreign invasions, especially by nomadic tribes from the East, which plundered across the eastern European plain. The empire that was Rome was eventually divided into two seats of power, forming the Eastern (Byzantine) and Western (Rome) Roman Empires. The popularity of the Maltese endured through this transitional period, as there is documented evidence of his existence in both capitals.

Following the fall of Rome, the Maltese continued to be popular in Byzantium. In the West, the invading tribes dispersed Roman culture, and no further evidence of the breed may be documented. It is doubtful, however, that the breed perished. It is more likely that the Maltese was carried off by the new invaders. They continued to breed and crossbreed the dog, and carried it East with them, as they eventually abandoned their Roman conquests.

As Europe entered the Dark Ages, the written record of man ceased, as did that of the Maltese. As had been true of the dog's history to that point, the Maltese enjoyed times of great popularity; at other times it became quite a rarity. Despite all, the breed managed to endure and survive. Toward the end of the Dark Ages in Europe and the dawn of the Renaissance, the Maltese reappears and is once again included in the recorded history of man in both Eastern and Western Europe. In addition, there are definite records of the Maltese in China and the Far East at about A.D. 1400.

The Maltese and the Renaissance

The emergence of Europe from the Dark Ages brought with it, among other things, a renewed interest in things genteel. Life became brighter. There was once again time for pleasureable pastimes and pleasant repasts. With the reemergence of the finer things in life, the Maltese once again appears upon the scene in Europe.

In the East, the dog breed had never really been lost. There are records of Maltese kept by the Sultans of the Turkish empire. Recorded delegates and embassies arrived in Rome from China and the Far East. With them they brought along with their silks, gold and jewels, small pet dogs favored by Eastern royalty and ladies of the royal courts of the East. It is likely these

This statute of a Maltese dog was unearthed at Fayum, Egypt.

The British Museum

The fourteenth-century French tapestry, "Lady with a Unicorn," has a Maltese dog represented.

Cluny Museum, Paris

The Maltese was a popular subject in fourteenth-century French tapestries.

traders and ambassadors returned to their far-off countries with rare goods from Europe, including rare pet dogs.

At this time Lyon, France, had become much as Malta had been so many centuries earlier: a major center for world trade. During this time, the origin for the Maltese was ascribed to Lyon. Because of Lyon's prominence in commerce, most authors took it to be the original place from which the breed sprung.

With the renaissance, the Maltese again appears in the art and literature of France, Germany, Spain, Italy and the Netherlands during the thirteenth through fifteenth centuries. It is recorded that the Maltese dog, as described by the ancients, was nonexistent at this time on the Island of Malta.

The Maltese Comes to England

Recorded history places the arrival of the Maltese in England during the reign of King Henry VIII (1509–1547). According to Leighton's *New Book of the Dog,* the most ancient of all lap dogs of the Western world were probably imported into England at the time of his rule from Lyon, France.

It is not until the reign of Henry's daughter, Elizabeth I (1533–1603), that extensive interest in the breed throughout the British aristocracy is documented. It is known that Elizabeth, herself, was the owner of a Maltese. The Sultan of Turkey presented her with a specimen in 1583.

Personal physician to Elizabeth I, Dr. Johannes Caius, wrote a volume in Latin, which classified all dog breeds known in England at the time (1570). Among the many breeds, he included the Maltese. He assigned it the Latin name *Canes delicati* and classified it as a "Spaniel Gentle." Reporting that the dog's history and origins had been recorded by the ancients, he wrote, in part:

> That kind is very small indeed, and chiefly sought after for the pleasure and enjoyment of women. The smaller the kind the more pleasing it is, so that they may be carried in their bosoms, in their beds and in their arms while in carriages.

Dr. Caius also recorded the dog's believed medicinal powers. It was thought that through its body heat, the Maltese was able to draw out pain and illness from the chest and stomach, when applied to those areas. Because of this practice, in addition to the warm and affectionate nature of the dog, the Maltese came to be called the "Comforter," a name that lasted for several centuries.

In 1576, British author Fleming translated the Latin of Dr. Caius, which follows, in part:

> Of the delicate, neat and pretty kind of dogs called "Spaniel Gentle" or "Comforter," in Latin *Melitaie* . . . there is besides another sort of gentle

A fifteenth-century portrait of an Italian lady and her Maltese dog. Lorenzo Costa is the artist.

St. James Palace, London

The Maltese was used as subject matter in paintings done by the Flemish School. Hans Memling (1425–1500) included a Maltese dog in his portrait of Vanity.

The Maltese dog is present in this painting of Tobias and the Archangel Raffael. Painted by Piero Pollaiuolo (1443–1496).

Sabauda Gallery, Turin, Italy

Holy Roman Emperor Charles V (The Bold), 1500–1588, pictured with his Scribe and dogs, including a Maltese seated at the foot of his desk.

Royal Brussels Library

dogges in this our English soyle, but exempted from the order of the residue, the dogges of this kind doth Callimachus call "Melitaie" of the Island of Melita (now Malta) in the sea of Sicily, an island indeed famous and reknowned. These dogges are little, pretty, propper and fyne: and sought to satisfie the delicatnesse of daintie dames and wanton women's wills . . .

Mary Queen of Scots (1542–1587) was a great dog fancier, who kept many breeds. She imported several Maltese into Scotland from Lyon, France. Mary was persecuted and eventually beheaded by Elizabeth I of England. Tradition has it that when Mary went to the block her Maltese was with her, beneath her skirts. Upon her death, the little dog was said to have grieved the loss of her mistress so much that it eventually died.

During this same period (1500–1600), extensive trade routes were being developed between the European nations of Spain, England, Portugal and the Netherlands and the countries of the Far East, including China, Taiwan and the Philippines. The British were especially involved in the trade of dogs. British dog expert V.F.W. Collier established that the Maltese dog was one of the five types being bred in China at that time. In addition, there are records to evidence the fact that the Maltese dog was still being kept by the women of the Turkish empire.

In England, several authorities recorded information on the breed. In the late 1500s, just before his death in 1607, Aldrovandus wrote an early history of the breed, in Latin. He is recorded as having said that there were two varieties of the Maltese: one with a comparatively short coat, the other with a long one. As he was unable to ascertain which was correct, he illustrated both varieties in his volume. By the illustrations, it would appear that both were close in type, except insofar as the coat is concerned. The variety with the longer coat appeared to be much the same as the breed today.

Aldrovandus is quoted as having seen a Maltese sold for the equivalent of $2,000. In today's terms, the price paid would approximate five figures.

Naturalists and the Maltese

E. Topsel, in 1607, described the Maltese of his day as being about a foot long, the smaller and more delicate the more precious. To achieve that end, it is reported, the bodies of the dogs were confined, to prevent natural growth and development. Their diets were also restricted for the same purpose. The same practices were being employed in the East, with the same results in mind.

Topsel made special note of the luxurious silken coat, which was a great feature of the breed. Like many earlier authors, he noted the gentle, yet fearless, nature of the breed.

From this point in recorded history, details of the breed began to be

Engraving of a Maltese Lion Dog executed by Gessner (1516–1565).

The Maltese dog, as it appeared in the 1500s. This sixteenth-century engraving appeared in *The New Book of the Dog*, by C. Ash.

A sixteenth-century German engraving of a Maltese dog. Notice the relationship in size between the man's foot and the Maltese.

Aldrovandus (1522–1605) described two types of Maltese dog. At left is an engraving of the long-coated variety, at right is the short-coated variety.

A seventeenth-century French painting of a smooth-coated, parti-colored Maltese dog.

Bibliothique Nationale, Paris

A seventeenth-century German portrait by Cranach of Catherine of Mecklenburg, wife of Henry the Pious, with her Maltese Lion Dog.

The Museum of Dresden

Portrait of Elizabeth, Queen of Bohemia (1596–1662), with a Maltese dog at her skirts. By Gerard Van Honthorst.

Woburn Abby, England

23

better documented than before. Although crossbreeding was a common practice at the time, a consistent type continued to be recorded as the "Maltese dog."

The great Swedish naturalist Linnaeus, in 1792, established the bionomical method of naming animal and plant species. He gave the name *Canis familiaris melitacus* to the Maltese. His notes on the breed stated that the dog was quite tiny, "being about the size of a squirrel." He also allowed that the dog should possess a long silky coat.

Perhaps the earliest pictorial evidence of the Maltese dog, pictured nearly exactly as he appears today, may be seen in a 1763 painting of Nellie O'Brien by Sir Joshua Reynolds. The portrait shows Ms. O'Brien with what is unquestionably a Maltese in her lap.

The French naturalist, Buffon, included the Maltese in his *Book of Natural History,* published in 1777. The name he gave the breed was *Chien de Malte* and *Bichon.* He personally preferred the later. He noted in his text that the Maltese had become quite rare at that time. He even had to rely upon an engraving of the dog he found in the King's library to sketch from in order to illustrate his book. He described the dog as being small. It was so small, in fact, that it became fashionable for ladies to carry the Maltese in their sleeves. Because of his size and weight, this could be done with ease. Eventually, the fashion of carrying one's Maltese in the sleeve was abandoned. Buffon reported that the inherent filth of a long coat, especially a white one, was found to be distasteful and fell from fashion.

The court of Louis XVI remained loyal to the Maltese. Queen Marie Antoinette owned a pet Maltese named "Thisbee." Unfortunately, both came to untimely and tragic ends. The little Maltese leaped to its death from the Saint Michele Bridge over the river Seine in Paris on the day the queen was beheaded, October 16, 1793.

The "Shock" Dog and the Lion Dog

Still another name especially popular in England for the Maltese during this period was the *Shock* dog. It came to be used because of the dog's rather untidy appearance much of the time. There was a certain amount of "filth" inherent in the long white coat. Bathing was not a popular custom among people at that time. It is highly unlikely that the Maltese got bathed with any more frequency than their masters bathed themselves. Not being attended to properly, the coat of the Maltese would tend to stick out in "shock." Possibly the Maltese coat at that time was somewhat curlier-textured than that of later specimens. This texture would add greatly to the "shock" appearance, as well.

It was popular to trim the Maltese to make him look like a lion. The body coat was shaved from the rear quarters, up to the ribs. The legs and tail, except for pompons, were shaved close as well. A large pack or mane

The "Chien de Malta" or "Bichon" as pictured by the French naturalist Buffon in his *Book of Natural History*, 1777.

Sir Joshua Reynolds's portrait of Nellie O'Brien holding a Maltese dog.
Wallace Collection, England

Black and white Maltese Lion dog owned by the Marquise de Pompadour (1721–1764). From the eighteenth-century French School of Dr. Mery.

was allowed to remain about the ribs, neck and head, much as a contemporary Poodle clip. Trimmed in such a pattern, the Maltese was called the *Maltese Lion Dog* and the *Little Lion Dog.* There are a great number of representations of the Maltese trimmed in this manner in paintings of the period.

In the Same Gene Pool

By the 1800s breeding purebred dogs had become quite fashionable. The Maltese was one of the breeds in which dog breeders all over Europe had an interest. The Maltese was now thriving. So too were several breeds that are direct descendants, cousins if you will, of the Maltese. These resemble the Maltese in many respects, but have certain distinguishing characteristics. It is likely that earlier these characteristics were evident within the Maltese itself. These certain characteristics must have popped up in the breed often enough to create interest among some breeders.

A breed that traces directly from the ancient Maltese dog is the Curly-haired Bichon, or *Bichon a Poil Frise,* as he is called in France, where he was developed. Here the breed is known as the Bichon Frise. The major difference between the Bichon Frise and the Maltese, from which the breed sprang, is the curly coat. The Bichon's coat is loosely curled rather than straight and flat. The Bichon in France may be 12 inches at the withers—slightly larger than the Maltese. In addition, lemon and grey spots are permitted in the body coat, whereas, in the Maltese, a pure white coat is most desired.

The Little Lion Dog or Bichon Petit Chien Lion, is a small dog prevalent in France, but rarely found elsewhere. Several have been bred in England, and recently some have been imported from there into the United States. This dog was developed in France at the same time as the Bichon Frise. It exactly resembles the Bichon Frise, but for his slightly smaller size. His height is 8 to 14 inches at the shoulder, and can weigh from 4½ to 9 pounds. He is much the same dog as the Bichon, but for a trimmed coat which gives the dog a lion-like appearance. As noted earlier, this had been a custom popular in times past, within the Maltese breed.

The rare Havanese Bichon, or the Havana Silk Dog, is also a direct descendant of the Maltese. He was developed from Maltese brought by the Spaniards to Cuba and the West Indies. In appearance he is quite similar to the contemporary Maltese, but for slight variations. He is slightly larger than the Maltese, weighing up to 13¼ pounds. His coat, while being silky, like that of the Maltese, may be colored. Rarely pure white, it may be beige, more or less dark or "Havana" brown. It may also be white broadly marked by those colors. The face and feet may or may not be trimmed.

The last breed recorded as being a direct descendant of the Maltese dog is the Bolognese. He was popular in Italy, especially in the city whose

The Bichon Frise.

The Shock Dog, In an 1843 engraving.

The Havana Silk Dog.

Little Lion Dog.

The Bolognese Dog.

name he bears, Bologna. The earliest record of these dogs was in the late 1600s. In 1668, Cosimo de Medici, a breeder of the Bolognese dog, was recorded as having sent several specimens of the breed to a leading personage in Brussels. The Bolognese is somewhat larger than the Maltese, being 5½ to 9 pounds. His height is from 10½ to 12 inches for males and a slightly smaller 10 to 11 inches for females. As with his Maltese progenitor, the Bolognese should be pure white, without markings, not even simple shading. The points are black. The Bolognese is similar in appearance to the Bichon Frise, as his coat does not lie flat to the body, but rather stands away. However, he does not possess the corkscrew curly coat of the Bichon Frise.

Into the Nineteenth Century

A modern type Maltese dog had reestablished itself upon the Island of Malta. In a book published in 1833 by a Maltese man, Mr. Simelli, there are scenes depicting Maltese people accompanied by their dogs. These dogs are unmistakably the same as the Maltese as we know it. Despite proof of his existence, the Maltese had once again become quite rare. In 1830, the noted English painter, Landseer, documented the near extinction of the breed in England in the title of one of his paintings, which was a portrait of the then rare Maltese.

Noted dog author of the time, Richardson, also known as the great "Stonehenge," gave evidence that the Maltese dog was still being bred in England, although not on a grand scale. He described the Maltese as a "small Poodle, but with silky hair rather than wool, and the short turned up nose of the Pug."

Because of the great rarity of the breed at the time, a Maltese dog and bitch were purchased for Queen Victoria of England in Manila, the Philippines, in 1841. An account of this transaction was recorded by Richardson, and following is part of what he published with regard to these Maltese in 1859:

> Cupid (dog) and Psyche (bitch) were brought from Manila in 1841, and bought there at a high price by Captain Lukey of the East India Company's service. They were intended for the Queen [Victoria of England], but after being nine months aboard ship, were found upon their arrival in England, not presentable, their coats having been entirely neglected during the voyage.
>
> Psyche, a descendant from Captain Lukey's Cupid and Psyche, is now [1859] 20 months old, pure white, weight 3¼ pounds, measures in length of hair across the shoulders 15 inches (7½ inches long on each side) and when in her gambols presents in appearance a ball of animated floss silk, her tail falling on her back like spun glass.
>
> Of all the canine pets, this breed (Maltese) is the most lovable, being extremely animated and sagacious, full of natural tricks, and perfectly free of

the defects of the Spaniel, viz., snoring and an offensive breath, being naturally cleanly and capable of instruction.

As noted earlier, because of their poor condition upon arrival in England, presentation to Queen Victoria was impossible. The Maltese were given, eventually, to Captain Lukey's brother, a breeder of Mastiffs. His brother was also the breeder of the litter described in the preceding paragraphs.

Some other gleanings from the writings of Richardson pertinent to the Maltese are as follows:

> The dog should not exceed five pounds in weight, although some good specimens have weighed as much as 6½ pounds. Although Victoria was not the recipient of the Maltese intended for her brought from Manila, some Maltese dogs eventually did become part of her kennels.

It is also recorded that Queen Victoria was the owner of not only Maltese dogs, but also a breed called the "Maltese Skye Terrier."

Richardson made reference to a painting chronicling the perilous progress of the Maltese dog when he wrote:

> The breed was so scarce some time ago as to induce Sir E. Landseer to paint one of *The Last of His Race*.

Idstone, another English authority on dogs, wrote in 1872 that the Maltese Terrier, as it has been called by some writers, had probably been a domestic pet for more centuries than any other specimen of the dog family. He also wrote:

> There is little doubt that he [the Maltese] was a favourite with the ladies of Ancient Greece, and imported by their nation as one of the luxuries of the rich. I, myself, have seen a very good model of the head of one of these little animals carved upon a knife or dagger handle, by no "prentice hand," and one of the date of the Grecian Empire. Throughout the Roman period, he was still a favourite, as appears from the writings of Strab.
>
> As though aware of their beauty, Maltese pets are most remarkable for cleanliness and freedom from stain or smell, but they require washing and combing.
>
> A beautiful specimen of the Maltese is painted by W. Powell Frith, R.A., in the arms of an old lady, in his celebrated painting of *The Railway Station*. The eminent artist, whose quick observation nothing escapes, had evidently noticed that the Maltese had been recovered from oblivion, and would become, as he must become when more readily obtainable, deservedly popular with our wives and daughters.

Beginning during the mid 1800s, and continuing into the early 1900s, there were great debates among noted dog writers and dog authorities of the era. One of these debates centered around the question of which family of dog the Maltese belonged. A large group, especially in England, thought

Maltese engraving, circa 1890–1900.

French Maltese, Floss and Lulu, owned by C. Pettit, as they appeared in De Bylandt's book, *The Races of Dogs.*

Portrait of the Duchess of Alba, with a Maltese dog at her skirt. Painted by Goya (1746–1828).

the breed to be of terrier origin. They based their judgment upon the feisty, terrier-like temperament the Maltese dog possesses. As with the English terrier breeds, the Maltese of the period was an excellent ratter and exhibited great fearlessness, despite his small size. This group called the dog a "Maltese Terrier," a misnomer that has persisted to this day.

Other noted authorities of the era disagreed. They insisted that both the body and coat type of the Maltese are spaniel in nature. These experts noted, too, that the terrier traits of the Maltese could as easily be attributed to the spaniel. A great deal of crossbreeding had occurred over the years. It is likely, therefore, that there were several different types of Maltese dog extant. Accordingly it is not surprising that debate raged among nineteenth century dog authorities.

Ultimately, in the early 1900s, it was concluded that the "Maltese dog" was neither terrior nor spaniel. Rather, he should correctly be referred to as, simply, the "Maltese dog."

Beginnings of Dog Shows

As the nineteenth century closed, the great interest in crossbreeding to create new breeds diminished. The great interest and fashion of the time swung to established breeds. From that era to this, the interest has continued and grown.

Meanwhile, interest in the purebred Maltese was once again sparked, although the dog itself was quite rare. In 1862, 20 Maltese were exhibited at a show in London.

The Kennel Club (England) was established in 1873. One of the first functions of that body was to establish a stud book. The first English stud book has twenty-four Maltese registered between 1859 and 1873. The first dog show licensed by the Kennel Club was held in 1873, and Maltese were in competition.

The descendants of Psyche and Cupid, brought from Manila for Queen Victoria, were owned by a prominent breeder of the time, Lady Giffard. Most famous of her dogs were four-pound "Hugh" and his litter sister, three-pound "Queenie." Her dogs were noted for their long silky coats. Lady Giffard's famous kennel was active from 1875 to 1885. By engravings and photos of the period, we know that the English Maltese of the era were rather small—considerably smaller than has come to be the fashion there. They had wavy coats, and earsets that were both high and low.

Interest in the Maltese grew scantly. At about 1880 the breed reached a modest zenith: it held its own until about the time of World War I, when interest began to fade. The Maltese once again had come close to extinction, especially in England. James Watson wrote in his book, famous at the time (1909):

32

Such a thing as a good Maltese Dog is all but unknown in this country [England], and few seem to care about taking up the fancy. . . .

At about this same time, the Kennel Club began offering classes for Maltese dogs, other than white. Such classes were offered from 1902 to 1913. The first entries made under this classification were made in 1908. The last were made in 1913. The colored Maltese differed from the white variety. The English standard for the Maltese called for the white variety not to exceed 12 pounds. The colored variety could not exceed 8½ pounds. All colors were admissible into the colored classes. The white variety was required to be "pure white." Besides the size difference, there were other variations between the two varieties. The colored coats were coarser textured than white coats. The head of the colored Maltese tended to be shorter muzzled and broader skulled than those of the white Maltese.

The Maltese Comes to the United States

During the modest zenith of the breed between 1900 and 1914, many English dogs came to the United States, and especially to Canada, where the breed was thriving and extremely popular.

The origins of the Maltese in the United States is obscure. It is certain that original breeding stock arrived here from England, Canada, Germany, France and Italy. The earliest known Maltese on record in the United States was born in 1873. He was entered at Westminster in 1879, and was also the first colored Maltese shown here. Entered as a "Maltese Skye Terrier," he was described as being white with black ears.

There was great interest in colored Maltese in the United States. Some crossbreeding was done here, as in England. One such recorded crossbreeding used a Maltese and a black Pomeranian. The resultant litter produced black Maltese, identical in type to the white variety.

The first Maltese to be exhibited in the United States were entered in the Miscellaneous class. The Maltese was later moved to the Nonsporting Group, and finally to the Toy Group, where they remain.

The first white Maltese exhibited was entered at the first Westminster show (1877) as a "Maltese Lion Dog." Born in 1875, his owner was from New York City. Maltese dogs were shown regularly in the United States throughout the 1880s and 1890s. The annual Westminster show consistently drew large Maltese entries. There were many Maltese fanciers located in New York City at the time.

The first Maltese to be registered in the American Kennel Club's Stud Book were two bitches. They were: "Snips"—origin unknown, and "Topsy"—an import. The year was 1888.

From 1900 through 1910, there were numerous Poodle kennels throughout the American midwest involved in Maltese. Crossbreeding between these two breeds was frequent and it is likely that the Maltese was used to lock in small size, color, and pigmentation. White Toy Poodles were among the first to be acclaimed in the show ring. Some of the undesirable results of these crossbreedings have lingered to this day. The Toy Poodle has difficulty with a "round" eye, as has the Maltese, rather than the "almond" eye called for in their standard. On the Maltese side of the issue, an incorrect "Poodle-like" coat texture can be found in some Maltese.

In 1901, two more bitches were entered into the American Kennel Club Stud Book. In 1902, six Maltese were entered, four dogs and two bitches. It was not until the 1950s that 50 Maltese had been registered in the American Kennel Club Stud Book.

In 1950, the breed ranked 76th among all breed registrations for that year. There were seventy-three Maltese registered in 1950.

The Numbers Start to Swell

By 1960, the breed was 50th in total registrations for all breeds. There was a total of 2,995 Maltese registered with the American Kennel Club between 1950 and 1960. The increasing numbers of Maltese being bred is apparent, comparing the rise from only 73 Maltese registered with the American Kennel Club in 1950 to the 490 individual registrations in 1960.

By 1970, the number of individual registrations for the year had soared to 4,197. The breed had moved up in popularity, taking the number 41 spot in number of registrations that year. The total number of Maltese registered between 1960 and 1970 was 21,777.

By 1980, the breed had risen another ten notches in the rankings— Maltese were then in the number 31 spot. A total of 60,718 Maltese were registered with the American Kennel Club between the years 1970 and 1980. By 1980, an astounding 7,324 Maltese were registered with the AKC.

The number of Maltese bred and registered with the American Kennel Club continues to increase, as the breed has increased in popularity. Between 1980 and 1982, there have been an additional 15,825 Maltese registered. In 1982, with 8,050 Maltese registered, the breed had inched its way up another notch to number 30 among all breeds.

The total number of Maltese registered with the American Kennel Club from 1950 through 1985, by which time the breed was 26th among all breeds, is an astounding 128,504 dogs. With this sort of growth in popularity, it seems certain that the "New Golden Age of the Maltese Dog" is truly upon us.

We, as dedicated members of the fancy, must seek to maintain very high standards, for ourselves and the breed. This is necessary if we are to insure that these great days of popularity are indeed kept "golden."

2

The Maltese Fancy in America: 1896–1979

AS MENTIONED EARLIER, the origins of the Maltese in America have been clouded with time, as few exact records were kept in the early days of the fancy. Owners of Maltese exhibited in the late 1800s are recorded, but the breeders and pedigrees are usually unknown. For the most part, the Maltese of the period were individually owned. There were very few breeders or kennels of note rearing particular lines.

Good specimens of Maltese of this period are at the American Museum of Natural History in New York City. These mounted examples had been presented to the Museum over the years, and may be seen upon request. They were originally part of a mounted exhibit of the different dog breeds, dismounted shortly after World War II.

One mounted Maltese of the period is Nellie Bly, a gift to the Museum of Mrs. E. C. Seaman. Another, a male Maltese dog named Bijou, was a gift of Mrs. A. M. Good of New York City in 1896. It is interesting to note the similar characteristics of these specimens as compared to the Maltese of today.

Early Breeders and Dogs

At the turn of the century, and in the first decade of the new century, Maltese breeders had begun to establish themselves, primarily in the Midwest. Many of these breeders owned pet and toy dog kennels. Many also bred Toy Poodles, and crossbreeding Maltese and Poodles probably occurred at this point.

35

The origin of most of the breeding stock used by many of the early breeders is unknown. An exception is that of Mr. W. P. Farmer's Union Park Kennels of Chicago, Illinois.

In 1896 Mr. Farmer imported four Maltese from Europe. With these four, Mr. Farmer established his breeding program, which was to become the most prolific of the time. Two of Mr. Farmer's bitches, Da Da and None Such, were top winners at the Chicago shows, as well as at the World's Fair Show held at St. Louis, Missouri, in 1904.

Early registrations in the AKC Stud Book were made on the basis of show wins. Of the six registrations for 1902, five dogs were owned by Mr. Farmer. Eventually, Mr. Farmer had sold Maltese dogs to breeders and fanciers in all parts of the United States and Canada, thus helping to establish many new Maltese kennels and breeding programs.

Other early winners in the show ring included Cupid, Girlie, Queen, Cupid Jr. and Dottie Dimple. These dogs were owned and bred by another outstanding breeder of the time, Miss Josie Newman of the Travilla Kennels, Kansas City, Missouri. Another early Maltese breeder to import European stock into this country was Mrs. E. W. Clark, of the Few Acres Kennels.

American Maltese breeders, from the earliest times until present, imported dogs from Canada, England, Italy, France and Germany. These imports have strengthened the quality and character of our dogs.

Another famous breeder of the era, whose top-winning Maltese competed with those of Mr. Farmer and Miss Newman, was Mrs. Gertrude Ross Phalen of the Rossmore Kennels, Chicago, Illinois. She was active from 1901-1911. One of her most prized stud dogs, Baby Boy, a six-pound dog, was considered to be an excellent Maltese at that time. He won in Chicago shows, and also in New York City and the Canadian show rings.

Mrs. Phalen also bred and showed one of the smallest studs at the time, Ch. Sonny Boy, just 3¼ pounds. Ch. Tiny Boy, Sonny Boy's kennel mate, was also extremely small. Both dogs were sold to Mrs. Koerlin, of New York City, an active Maltese breeder from 1905-1919. Mrs. Koerlin was one of the first to put championship titles on Maltese in the United States, namely Ch. Sonny Boy and Ch. Tiny Boy.

Roy B was one of several top stud dogs being shown in the United States around 1900. He was owned by Mrs. L. Boll, of the Archer Kennels, Chicago, Illinois. Roy B, at seven pounds, was considered to be the best coated dog in the United States.

Other outstanding studs of the time were Curley, owned by G. E. Safell, Hoosier Kennels, Indianapolis, Indiana and five-pound Prince Cupid, owned by Mrs. M. I. Gander of the Domus Kennels, Wichita, Kansas.

The years between 1905 to 1930 were prolific for the Maltese. There were a number of seriously dedicated people working to attain the highest

A Maltese dog, "Nellie Bly," owned by Mrs. E.C. Seaman in the United States, mid-1800s.

Courtesy American Museum of Natural History

A Maltese dog, "Bijou," owned by Mrs. A. M. Good, New York City, 1896.

Courtesy American Museum of Natural History

A Maltese dog at 14 years of age, owned by La Condesa Beatrice de Tavara, July 29, 1914.

Courtesy American Museum of Natural History

quality Maltese possible. Mrs. Virginia Leitch in her book, *The Maltese Dog,* called these years the "golden age of Maltese." Not until the present time had there been so many people striving hard for the promulgation and betterment of the breed.

The Stinzings

Of the many people involved in this "golden age of Maltese," several had outstanding achievements. Miss Kate Stinzing and her mother, extremely involved and active breeder-exhibitors, from New York City, used Italian imports in breeding seven champions. Many of the Stinzing dogs, which were bred between 1902 and 1925, are behind the dogs of today. Some of their most outstanding were Ch. Dido, Snow Flower, Beauty Girl, Ch. Fido II, Lotty Girl and Snow Cloud's General Major.

The Koerlins

Perhaps two of the most motivated and enthusiastic fanciers of the period were Mrs. M. Koerlin and her husband. In 1906, Mr. Koerlin founded the first Maltese breed specialty club, called the Maltese Terrier Club of America. He also worked with the American Kennel Club to establish the Maltese standard, which was in effect from 1906 to 1963. Both Mr. and Mrs. Koerlin were enthusiastic exhibitors, often helping new-comers to the show ring; many had been introduced to dog shows by the Koerlins.

Their stud force consisted of Ch. Sonny Boy, considered to be the most outstanding American Maltese at the time, weighing just 3¼ pounds, and Ch. Tiny Boy which they received from the Rossmore Kennels. Both were tiny and possessed superb coats. These studs were much in demand by Eastern fanciers, and were very instrumental in the development of the smaller type Maltese in the United States.

Studebaker

The successful breeding program of Mrs. Helene Studebaker Henderson was cut short by her untimely death. In 1914, using English and Canadian stock, she founded her Studebaker Kennels at New Rochelle, New York. One of her notable dogs, Am. & Can. Ch. Studebaker Namur was later sold to Mrs. Anna R. Judd. In an entry of 17 Maltese, Studebaker's Wee Sister was Winners Bitch at the first annual specialty show held by the National Maltese Club on November 30, 1917 at the Waldorf-Astoria Hotel in New York City.

Normacot

The famous English Normacot Maltese were imported into the United

States by Mrs. J. Arbuckle of Chicago, Illinois. She called her kennel here after the kennel in England from which she obtained her breeding stock. Both her American and English bred Maltese carried the Normacot prefix. In addition to her English imports, several dogs bred by Mr. W. P. Farmer complemented her breeding program.

Melita

Mrs. Anna Judd was the reknowned breeder of the top-winning Melita Maltese. Her kennel was located in Seattle, Washington. Mrs. Judd purchased her first Maltese, Melita Romeo, from Mrs. Rosswag in 1908. Her bloodline was based upon three English bloodlines, namely, Esperance, Normacot and Brixton, combined with her Melita Romeo dog. In 1915 she imported the English Ch. Impy, a winner at Crufts in 1914.

Mrs. Judd was an outstanding success in the breeding of the smaller type Maltese. Her Maltese were not only successful in the show rings of the Western United States, but also in Canada. She registered a number of her dogs in Canada. In 1919, Ch. Melita Snow Dream was the first Maltese to be awarded an all-breed Best in Show in Canada.

Mrs. Judd came East several times. In 1918, she exhibited at the Westminster Kennel Club show, taking Winners Dog with her Melita Cupid. She returned to Westminster in 1929, bringing with her 12 entries out of a total of 17. She was again awarded Winners Dog, this time with her Prince Melita.

Dyker

In 1908, Mrs. Carl Baumann established her Dyker Kennels in Brooklyn, New York. She purchased her first Maltese, Dyker Dolly, a dog of pure Rossmore breeding through Mrs. Phelan, of Chicago. She added other Maltese of superior bloodlines to her breeding program occasionally, as well as using the services of the outstanding stud dogs of the era. Her first stud dog, purchased from Mrs. Koerlin, was Yankee Boy.

The Dyker Kennels became the largest and finest of the Maltese kennels in the East. Yankee Boy was the sire of her famous Dyker Dolly II, who was undefeated, and won all honors until defeated in the ring by her son, Sweet Sir of Dyker.

Mrs. Baumann and her Dyker Maltese won the Newbold Challenge Cup for the Best Maltese in Show, awarded at the Westminster Kennel Club show in 1915; the Maltese Club of London's award for Best American-bred Maltese; the bronze plaque for the most outstanding Maltese of the year offered by the *Canine Societe de Savoie, Ais Les Baines, France.*

Dyker Maltese were in demand by other breeders of the era. Stock from her kennel formed the foundation for several Maltese breeding programs of the era.

Other Dyker Maltese of note include Ch. Dainty Maid of Dyker, owned by Mrs. Rossman; Ch. Dyker's Snow Shell of Esperance, an English import from Mrs. Horowitz of London; her famous stud dog Ch. Dyker Major Mite, who was bred by Mrs. Rossman. Ch. Major Mite, born July 21, 1915, was sired by Mrs. Baumann's Jollo Jiffy and out of Mrs. Rossman's Ch. Putsee Girl.

Arr

Perhaps the most influential bloodline of this era on our present-day Maltese are the dogs of the Arr bloodline. Arr Maltese were known the world over for tiny size, conformation, gorgeous coats and numerous other typical qualities.

Mrs. Agnes Rose Rossman was the breeder of this line, to whom the present-day American Maltese is so indebted. Mrs. Rossman was the breed's greatest authority, having spent an enormous amount of time in research of the breed.

At 19 years of age she married Mr. James G. Rossman. Mr. Rossman gave her the dog that won her heart, Ch. Sweet Sir of Dyker. Mr. Rossman paid Mrs. Carl Baumann $650.00 for Ch. Sweet Sir, an almost unheard of price for a dog at the time.

Mrs. Rossman became so enthralled by the breed, she soon purchased other Maltese which were to become the foundation of the Arr bloodline. They were: Ch. Dainty Maid of Dyker from Mrs. Baumann; Ch. Putsee Girl and Little Peanuts from Mrs. Quackenbush; Beauty Girl, Lotty Girl and Ch. Dido from Kate Stinzing; and Studebaker Princess, an English import from Mrs. R. Porker and sold to her by Mrs. Helene Studebaker Henderson. She later added other Maltese to her kennel.

Some of the more famous Maltese dogs of the Arr bloodline include Ch. Lady Anna of Arr, whelped November 12, 1916 (Little Peanuts × Beauty Girl), who finished at Westminster in 1918, in an entry of 15 Maltese; and Ch. Lady Issa of Arr, named after the legendary pet of the Roman Governor Publius. Ch. Issa's show career began when she was 11 months old. Her career was impressive, even by today's standards, and included several Best in Show wins. Issa died October 17, 1922, after which her mounted skin was presented to the American Museum of Natural History, in New York City.

As mentioned earlier, Maltese of the Arr bloodline were noted for their small size. Lady Ido of Arr was one of the smallest Maltese ever bred, weighing just 1¼ pounds as an adult. Lady Rhea of Arr (2¼ pounds) and Sir Soma of Arr (4 pounds) were lovely smaller ancient-type Maltese owned by Mrs. Garms, bred by Mrs. Rossman.

The mounted skin of Ch. Lady Issa of Arr,
owned by Mrs. Rossman of the Arr Kennels.
*Courtesy American Museum of
Natural History*

A portrait of Mrs. Rossman holding her
famous Ch. Lady Clio of Arr.

One other Maltese of note from the Arr bloodline was Ch. Lady Clio of Arr (Sir Bobo of Arr × Ch. Putsee Girl) whelped August 17, 1921. She was considered to be the finest Maltese at that time. Judging from her photo, one could easily see that she would be as highly admired today. The American Kennel Club chose Ch. Clio to represent the breed in *The Complete Dog Book.* She was the mode for over 40 years, until she was replaced by one of her descendants, Ch. Aennchen's Shikar Dancer in 1963. Ch. Clio's mounted skin was presented to the Hall of Fame at Cornell University, Ithaca, New York, after her death.

At one time, Mrs. Rossman had 60 Maltese in her Arr Kennel. Some of those worth note were Ch. Sir Bobo of Arr, Ch. Sir Mark of Arr and Ch. Sir Paul of Arr.

Her entry at the 1930 Westminster show was one of the largest in the history of the breed and Westminster. In a total entry of 26 Maltese, 20 were owned by Mrs. Rossman, and several of the others were of her breeding.

In later years, Mrs. Rossman served as honorary president of the Maltese Dog Fanciers Association, in the late 1940s.

Boro

Using first the Boro and then the Amador Star prefix, Mrs. Charles Boro of Jackson, California, bred Maltese from 1921 to 1935. She was one of the first American breeders to import Invicta bloodline from England. These dogs were Invicta Juliette, Invicta Pilgrim and Invicta Frolic, bred by Miss M. M. Neame. Her first dogs were Lady Dolly of Dyker, bred by Mrs. Baumann and Melita Cherie, bred by Mrs. Judd. The first dog of her own breeding was Boro's Prince Meneris. Six of her Maltese finished: Lady Dolly of Dyker, Boto's Lady Meneris, Invicta Cherub of Amador Star, Amador Star's Major Mite, Amador Star's Snow Dream and Bob Snow White of Amador Star.

Hale Farm

The reknowned Hale Farm Maltese were bred by Miss Eleanor Bancroft and her mother, Mrs. Robert Hale Bancroft. They took their prefix from the Bancroft's historic home in Beverly, Massachusetts. Built in 1621, the farm had continuously belonged to the Hale family until the death of Mrs. Bancroft in 1937.

The first Maltese owned by the Bancrofts were English imports which were never registered with the American Kennel Club. The daughter of these two imports, Ch. Sheila of Hale Farm, whelped May 1, 1927, was registered with the American Kennel Club based upon her show record.

Their two most influential dogs, Sir Toby of Arr and Snow Flurry of Hale Farm, were purchased from Mrs. Rossman. Ch. Sheila was bred to Sir

42

Toby, resulting in a litter of two champions, Ch. Bob Snow White of Hale Farm and Ch. Circe of Hale Farm. The next Hale Farm champion, White Wings of Hale Farm, resulted from breeding Snow Flurry to Ch. Circe.

With the purchase of Amador Invicta of Hale Farm (Boros Duke Maneris × Juliette of Amador Star) in 1932, the Bancrofts introduced the bloodlines of Melita and Dyker as well as the English Invicta bloodline into their breeding program.

The dogs enjoyed the good life at Hale farm for many years and the Bancrofts were avid, active fanciers. After the death of Mrs. Bancroft, Miss Bancroft sold all but a few dogs. Most went to Dr. Vincenzo Calvaresi and his wife, Maria Pardo de Calvaresi, breeders of the Villa Malta bloodline, from which descend many of the Maltese bred in America.

The number of Maltese registered with the American Kennel Club between 1902 and 1918 steadily increased. Then came a steady decline in Maltese registrations. Finally, by 1939 the Maltese was nearly extinct in America. One major reason given for this tragic decline was a horrendous outbreak of distemper during the 1930s, before the advent of modern drug technology, and the perfection of an effective distemper inoculation. Many kennels and breeding programs were wiped out or halted by this dread disease.

Thankfully, there were enough concerned and dedicated fanciers in the United States interested in saving the breed from extinction. From the very limited numbers of Maltese surviving in the United States and Canada, these few made a valiant effort to re-establish the breed in North America. From that point, registrations once again began to increase.

Hannah Mee Horner

A breeder-judge with a peerless reputation was Miss Hannah Mee Horner from Upper Darby, Pennsylvania. Her two original Maltese, Skytop Lassie and Skytop Sunrise, were Canadian imports of the Hale Farm bloodline. They were purchased from Mrs. Andrews of Halifax, Nova Scotia. Miss Horner was a strong advocate of line breeding.

During the late 1940s, Miss Horner was the noted breeder and owner of Ch. Skytop White Flash, the first of the breed to win the Toy Group in those years.

Miss Horner was president of the Maltese Dog Fanciers Association when it held its first two match shows. The first was held on the grounds of Mrs. Virginia Leitch's Jon Vir Kennels in Riverdale, Maryland, on October 16, 1948. The second was held at the Belvedere Hotel in New York City, on April 16, 1949.

Villa Malta

No history of the Maltese could be complete without an accounting of

A lovely example of Miss Eleanor Bancroft's Hale Farm Maltese, Ch. White Wings of Hale Farm. This dog was eventually given to Dr. Calvaresi, Villa Malta Kennels.

A well known portrait of Villa Malta's famous Italian import, Int., Am. Ch. Electa Brio.

Another Italian import to Villa Malta was Int., Am. Ch. Electa Laila.
Courtesy AKC Library

A later import to the Villa Malta Kennels was multiple BIS Ch. Electa Pampi.

44

Dr. Calvaresi and his multiple Best in Show team, shown taking Best Team in Show at the Eastern Dog Club show in 1952. Team members included Ch. Electa Brio and Ch. Electa Pampi. The other two dogs are unidentified.

BIS Ch. Musi of Villa Malta. Dr. Calvaresi, breeder, owner, handler. *Courtesy AKC Library*

the achievements of Dr. and Mrs. Vincenzo Calvaresi of Bedford, Massachusetts. Dr. Calvaresi was a professor of language and an attorney. His title of Doctor had been conferred upon him by Mussolini in the 1930s. He had a great interest in the cultural arts, especially classical music. Dr. Calvaresi was a quiet, dignified man, with an air of self-assurance. His manners were like those of a diplomat.

Mrs. Maria Pardo de Calvaresi, an elegant woman, had been an operatic singer in Spain. She met Mrs. Hale Bancroft and her daughter when arrangements were made for Mrs. Calvaresi to coach Miss Bancroft in conversational Spanish.

To open conversations, Mrs. Calvaresi would always begin by asking about the Bancrofts' Maltese dogs. The Calvaresis and the Bancrofts soon became close friends. Mrs. Calvaresi was eventually presented with their first Maltese, a gift from the Bancrofts. The Doctor also bought a pair of the dogs as a gift for his wife. With these dogs commenced the Villa Malta bloodline. The Calvaresis were soon to become avid exhibitors and breeders. The dog show ring was soon to become very familiar with this superb showman and his lovely white dogs. He kept his Maltese in print, and on television throughout the many years of his involvement in the breed. Thus, he made the Maltese dog more familiar to the American public than ever before.

The Calvaresis inherited a good deal of their original stock from Miss Bancroft in 1937, after the death of her mother. From that time until 1947, all Villa Malta Maltese were of pure Hale Farm breeding. Many of these dogs were shown to their championships under the superb direction and showmanship of Dr. Calvaresi. These included Ch. Hale Farm Hermanita, who finished in 1946 at ten years of age, Ch. Cupid of Hale Farm and Ch. White Wings of Hale Farm.

Dr. Calvaresi struggled, with a handful of others, to keep the breed alive. However, with the rapid disappearance of American bloodlines, it became necessary for Dr. Calvaresi to augment his breeding program by importing Maltese from Ireland and Italy. In 1947, he imported four Irish Maltese. Two came from the Suirside line, bred by Mrs. J. Felice. The other two came from Mr. J. B. Farrell, one of which was American—Ch. Jill of Shady Lane.

While visiting Milan, Italy, in 1948, he made the acquaintance of Nadya Colombo, breeder of the Electa line of Maltese. The Electa dogs were larger than our American dogs, but possessed superb coats and large round, dark, beautiful eyes. He returned to the United States with Int. Am. Ch. Electa Brio and Italian Ch. Electa Laila. He later imported Italian Ch. Electa Pampi, whelped November 8, 1949. Int. Ch. Brio's show record in this country included 15 Group 1sts, 24 other Group placings and 41 Bests of Breed. Ch. Pampi was equally successful in the show ring. Both dogs lived to be nearly 15 years of age.

When Dr. Calvaresi began to exhibit his Maltese, he noted that most, including his own, were shown in an unkempt manner. With time, he learned by trial and error the best ways to prepare a Maltese for the show ring. The following are his observations on preparing a Maltese for the show ring:

> The Maltese young or mature must have been taught good ring manners before being shown. The Maltese is very intelligent and obedient, and is always willing to please its master. I think that the Maltese coat will look its best, with a beautiful sheen, if it is washed two to three days prior to a show. The grooming, first with a fine brush and then with a steel comb, should begin with the legs, always using downward strokes. The part goes from the nose to the tail, and should be a well-marked straight line. Of course you must have his ears and teeth clean and his toenails clipped. If these suggestions are carefully followed we will not only improve the appearance of our dogs, but will also determine the Best in Show dog from a runner-up.

The Villa Malta Kennels had several Best in Show dogs to its credit, but was most renowned for the spectacular Maltese teams, trained and shown by Dr. Calvaresi. His teams were the first Toy teams to go Best in Show in the United States, which they did on numerous occasions. These teams were great favorites on many television programs, as well. His original team used his Italian imports. However, over the years the dogs used in the teams were frequently changed. At the 1952 Westminster show, Villa Malta won its 18th Best Team in Show. The dogs in that team were Ch. Tanelline, Ch. Talena, Pixie and Fida, all of Villa Malta.

In 1958, after having bred Maltese for over 20 years, Dr. Calvaresi was awarded the Gaines Fido for his many years of dedication to the Maltese dog. He had bred over 80 champions and the Villa Malta Kennels were known the world over.

Dr. Calvaresi was president of the Maltese Dog Club of America, located in the Eastern United States, when that club and the Maltese Dog Fanciers of America, the other Maltese club in the country, merged. The merger of the two clubs formed what is today the AKC-recognized parent club, the American Maltese Association. He was elected the first president of the newly formed association in 1962, serving in that capacity for a year.

When his wife died, his involvement with the breed began to diminish. In 1966, he exported 18 champion males to Japan. In May 1969, he announced his intention to retire from breeding. At this point he disposed of all his Maltese, many of which went to his associate, Mrs. Margaret Rozik of Belle Vernon, Pennsylvania. Mrs. Rozik now carries on the Villa Malta name.

Dr. Calvaresi then relocated in Trenton, Florida, for a time. Eventually, he returned to his native Italy, and now resides in Portugal.

Dr. Calvaresi in his breeding program had stressed certain qualities which he felt were essential to the breed. He was especially concerned that Maltese not be made into pampered pets, in the foolish way many Toy dogs are characterized.

The qualities of paramount importance in the Maltese, according to him, were that the dog be small and sturdy but, most of all, bright and energetic.

He felt Maltese could play in the snow, and should. He believed that the natural personality should not be inhibited, nor should any one part of a Maltese's beauty be placed above his basic strengths.

He dealt with people in a very business-like manner and in a very precise way. He was a master showman who made an impact upon everyone with whom he had contact.

Ch. Electa Pampi was one of the more famous Villa Malta dogs. One of this dog's first get was the famous Remmo of Villa Malta. He was a larger dog, though not huge. He had excellent pigment and a profuse, straight coat. Others included Ch. Mimino of Villa Malta, owned by Halia Taylor; Ch. Talia of Villa Malta; Am. Int. Ch. Villa Malta Carlito, owned by Louise Carlsen; Ch. Rico of Villa Malta; and the noted Ch. Diavolini of Villa Malta MMA (Maltese Merit Award), sire of Ch. Schallino D'Lacy, Ch. Marietta D'Lacy, Ch. Anmore's Imp of Satan, Ch. Non Vel's Weejun of Cameo, Valley High First Mate and Ch. Ricco of Villa Malta.

Merrilynn

The Merrilynn Maltese Kennels, located near Cleveland, Ohio, was owned by Mrs. Agnes Benson. Mrs. Benson had owned Maltese since 1903, first as house pets. She later bred and exhibited them. Her bloodline was based upon the Hale Farm Maltese. The Merrilynn Kennels were very active in both breeding and exhibiting of the Maltese, as well as the promotion of the breed in the 1940s.

Noteworthy among her dogs were: Ch. Hale Farm Clytie; Ch. Merrilynn Malta; Merrilynn Mikita, whelped April 17, 1944 (Ch. Merrilynn Malta × Hale Farm's Clytie) and Merrilynn Mot, whelped January 18, 1946 (Merrilynn Malta × Ch. Hale Farm's Clytie).

Mrs. Benson served as vice-president of the Maltese Dog Fanciers association, and was active in the early formation of the fancy. Her hobbies included modeling charming Maltese figurines in clay.

But for a tragic turn of events, there may well have been many more Merrilynn Maltese champions. Mrs. Benson ceased breeding and exhibiting after the untimely death of her husband.

Jon Vir

"The grand lady of Maltese" is the title which the Maltese fancy has affectionately given to Mrs. Virginia Leitch, breeder of the Jon Vir

48

The "Grand Lady of Maltese," Mrs. Virginia Leitch, in a portrait with her famous Ch. Jon Vir's Tiny Boy.

Jon Vir's first English import, Harlingen Sun Ray, was bred by Mrs. C. Roberts.

Maltese. Mrs. Leitch was an attorney in Washington, D.C. for over 30 years, and was qualified to handle cases brought before the Supreme Court of the United States.

At one time Jon Vir Kennels, located in Riverdale, Maryland, was one of the Maltese showplaces of the country. It was constructed with the comfort of the Maltese who would live there as the prime requisite. After its construction was completed, the Jon Vir Maltese spent a few nights in the kennel. However, Mrs. Leitch could not live with the idea of having her Maltese live outside in the kennel. The kennel then remained empty, but for the few occasional boarders.

After the control of distemper, which was the scourge of the breed before the advent of a vaccine, Mrs. Leitch was responsible, along with a handful of other breeders, for keeping the breed from becoming extinct in the United States. She banded together with Dr. Calvaresi, Mrs. Watkins, Mrs. Agnes Benson, Daisy Miller and several others in order to strengthen the numbers of the breed in the United States. To these few pioneers goes the credit for the foundations of today's beautiful Maltese. Due to the efforts of Mrs. Leitch, along with the others, the breed was once again on its way to reaching the great popularity it had enjoyed at the turn of the century.

The zenith of Mrs. Leitch's involvement with the breed came during the 1940s. Second to her concern with firmly re-establishing the breed in America was Mrs. Leitch's ultimate goal of breeding the very small type. She was active in the show ring, finishing several champions and having pointed others to near championships.

The first two dogs she owned were Ch. Toby of Villa Malta and Cupid's Powder Puff, which were purchased from Dr. Calvaresi. She then added a bitch from Mrs. A. Benson, Judy of Merrilynn. She soon made arrangements for the importation of stock from the British Isles, with hopes of improving and strengthening her stock. Because of the negative effects of World War II on European and American air transport, arrangements to bring these dogs to the United States were fraught with trouble and delay. Ultimately, in September 1946, Harlingen Sun Ray, from Mrs. C. Roberts, Harlingen Kennels, England, and Show Man of Suirside and Blossom of Suirside from Mrs. J. Felice, Suirside Kennels, Ireland, arrived here. Still later, after air travel and importation became less troublesome and restricted, Mrs. Leitch imported one other dog from Ireland, Rosabelle of Suirside, and two others from England, White Queen of Sigroc from Mrs. Davies and Invicta Silver Fret from Mrs. Shears.

Finally, Mrs. Leitch located and used at stud the last of the famour Arr dogs, considered to be the greatest of their time. Skipper of Twelve East, whelped June 18, 1937, was sired by Sir Soma of Arr, out of Lady Dido of Arr, two dogs bred by Mrs. Rossman. Skipper, bred and owned by Mrs. P. Garms of Huntington, New York, was brought out of retirement to sire a

50

Mr. and Mrs. Jack Leitch (right) and Mrs. Elizabeth Melgaarde. Mrs. Melgaarde is holding Skipper of Twelve East. The puppies are by him, out of Lady Irel of Arr.

Jon Vir's Felice of Suirside.

Pix Jester of Jon Vir and Pix Bright Star of Jon Vir, pure Jon Vir bred dogs owned by Lee Pickett. This photo appeared on the cover of *Pure-Bred Dogs—American Kennel Gazette* in December 1968.
Courtesy AKC Library

51

litter at age 12 years. This breeding brought Arr bloodline back into pedigrees and also enabled Mrs. Leitch to realize her ultimate goal. With the introduction of Arr bloodline into her breeding program, she was able to breed many three to four-and-a-half-pound beautiful Maltese. These dogs possessed many of the same characteristics and were similar in type to Ch. Lady Clio of Arr.

Visitors to Mrs. Leitch and her dogs at Jon Vir always remarked upon the beauty of the lawns which rolled gently down towards the kennel from the house. It was a charming sight to see her little Maltese let out to play on the green lawns, leaping and frolicking in the grass. The late Dr. Frederick W. Seward delighted in telling of his visit to Jon Vir, where "Maltese hopped about in the green grass like so many popcorn balls."

All the freedom and the extensive playful exercise allowed her tiny Maltese to develop sound movement and well-conditioned bodies without increasing size. The Jon Vir dogs epitomized the current standard for being fearless, despite their size. They were vigorous without loss of their gentleness.

Mrs. Leitch was a world traveler, having made many visits to Europe and the Mediterranean. There she studied the probable birthplace of the breed, referred to in the Bible as the Island of Melita. After years of research and travel abroad, interviewing foreign Maltese breeders and collecting pictures and histories, her book, *The Maltese Dog,* was released in 1953. It was the most comprehensive volume assembled to that date dealing with the Maltese. The book won instant acclaim, and is now a collector's item.

Mrs. Leitch sold her home in Maryland, and retired to Coconut Grove, Florida, in 1959. With her, she brought her famous Ch. Jon Vir's Tiny Boy, his son and a female pet of her deceased husband.

The first American Kennel Club sanctioned match held by the Maltese Dog Fanciers Association was held on the grounds of her home in Maryland. Maltese fanciers came from near and far to attend this event.

Skipper of Twelve East was shown in the veterans class at this event, for which Mrs. Leitch, Ann Jones and Daisy Miller served on the show committee. Mrs. Leitch's husband, Jack, served as publicity director for the show.

However, by the time of the second sanctioned match held on April 16, 1949, in New York City, Mrs. Leitch had become uninvolved with the Maltese Dog Fanciers Association. As she expressed in her book, she had become disillusioned with dog clubs and recommended against participation in such organizations.

However, she lent encouragement and support in 1959 and 1960 to the movement to promote and organize the breed fanciers into a new National Maltese Association destined to be the American Kennel Club's Maltese parent club.

52

After organization of the American Maltese Association had success-fully been completed, it was decided by the membership of the fledgling club to express their gratitude and admiration for Mrs. Leitch by offering a trophy dedicated in her honor. The trophy, called "The Virginia Leitch Memorial Trophy," was to be presented to the breeder of the winner of the American Maltese Association national specialty on March 30, 1968. It was won by Tony Aennchen Antonelli for Ch. Aennchen's Poona Dancer.

Mrs. Leitch died on September 7, 1969, at a nursing home in Homestead, Florida. The proof that she had become one of the greatest Maltese breeders of all time lies in the fact that her Jon Vir Maltese are behind many present-day pedigrees.

Daisy Miller

Daisy Miller was born Daisy Orr, in Mississippi. She lived most of her adult life in New York City and Chicago. Her early ambition was to be an animal sculptor.

She entered the business world in Chicago, where she worked for five years at the Chicago Tribune. In New York, she was associated with newspapers, magazines and the music trades. While program director of WABC Radio, and then later CBS Radio, she talked "dogs" on the air to fill a 15 minute spot. Response to succeeding talks on what proved to be a popular subject broke all known radio records.

That resulted in the formation of the Animal Protection Union, an association of breeders and owners of purebred dogs, best known for having traced over half a million dogs.

Organizing anything from a Theodore Roosevelt presidential cam-paign to the Maltese Dog Fanciers Association was a form of relaxation, according to Mrs. Miller. Mrs. Miller was known to thousands of dog fanciers, via her radio spot, which was broadcast for 13 years.

Mrs. Miller owned Merrilynn Mot (Ch. Merrilynn Malta × Ch. Hale Farm Clytie), bred by Mrs. Benson, was Secretary-Treasurer of the Maltese Dog Fanciers Association, and was active in the breed ring.

Other noteworthy Maltese fanciers and breeders active in the fancy in the 1940s and 1950s include Mrs. Bertha Watkins, Miss Ann Jones, Mrs. Elizabeth Melgaard, Mrs. Evelyn L. Irones, Commander Harold C. Shaw and Mrs. Ralph Loudon, among many others.

Eloise Craig

Eloise Craig and her husband Robert established their Good Time Kennels in Normal, Illinois. Eloise had a lifelong interest in the breed and was a positive, motivating force. In the mid 1940s, she was most responsible for the healthy re-establishment of the breed in the Midwest.

53

Because of her vast journalistic background, she was the breed columnist in *Pure-bred Dogs—American Kennel Gazette* from 1930 to 1981. In addition, Mrs. Craig was editor and publisher of *The Maltese Rx,* official publication of the American Maltese Association, from the inception of the American Maltese Association in the early 1960s until the time of her death in 1982. Mrs. Craig was listed in "Who's Who Among American Women" for her newspaper work and for authoring two books, including *Maltese Puppies.*

Good Time Kennels went from Saint Bernards to Maltese in 1945 after Eloise broke an ankle and leg in 1940 and could no longer run with the Saints. After many years of attempting to buy a female in this country, Matt Smith of Vancouver, B.C., Canada, let them have a Best in Show bitch, which they showed to her championship when majors were almost non-existent. While showing in conformation she was in the obedience ring as well, earning a C.D., becoming Ch. Valletta's Princess Norma, C.D.

After waiting years for a female, they had one dumped in their laps: Eve Apple Blossom (also Canadian breeding) who presented them with a first litter of five females and two males. They then added Am. Can. Ch. Bechi of Villa Malta, Leon Big Bold (Canadian) and Ch. Bacco of Villa Malta, C.D., showing both Villa Malta dogs to their championships.

A Maltese puppy that later became Ch. Bechi of Villa Malta, was a favorite with the children in Bob and Eloise Craig's junior kennel club. The young people all wanted to show him in their junior shows because he was being trained for the show ring and was easy to handle. One nine-year-old girl showed him to Best in Show in a children-only dog show.

Two juniors later trained two of the Craig's Maltese to their obedience degrees. They were Ch. Bacco of Villa Malta, C.D. and Ch. Valetta's Princess Norma, C.D. Ch. Bacco later became top winner in a Chicago obedience trial with a junior handler.

An Eve daughter, Good Time Eve of Independence, became the foundation stock of Dr. and Mrs. F. W. Seward in Goshen, New York, while another from that first litter went to start Boyd and Pat Clark's Cla-Mal Kennels. Yet another daughter went to Herb and Marge Kellogg, to give them their first Maltese.

The trio was joined by Frank and Lorena Dodge of Fran-Rena Kennels, who had a Jon Vir Maltese and together they broke the stranglehold of Eastern breeders who would sell males only. Ch. Bacco of Villa Malta, C.D., known as Tuffy, "had crate and would travel." A very prepotent stud, he spent much of his time traveling between Normal, Illinois, Jackson, Mississippi, Goshen, New York and Indianapolis, Indiana. He was to be used at stud by the Dodges, Sewards, Clarks and in Joliet, Illinois, by the Kellogs, until all had almost the same bloodlines.

While showing at the old Morris & Essex show in New Jersey, Eloise and Mary Van Epps became very close friends. Mary had combined Villa

Christmas card from the late 1940s sent by Daisy Miller, featuring Merrilynn Mot and her puppies.

Ch. Invicta Nicker, noted for his beautiful head, was the third BIS Maltese in United States history. Shown on the West Coast in the early 1950s he was by Int. Ch. Invicta Dime × Sigroc's White Dimity.

Group winner Ch. Nita of Villa Malta, took her first major on the day she turned six months old and finished five months later. Bred by Dr. Calvaresi, and owned by Eloise Craig.

Courtesy AKC Library

55

Malta, Jon Vir and Skytop breeding into her Pine Oak line, which excelled in coat. When Mary moved to Arizona, her Pine Oak Druann joined the Good Time Maltese, where she was shown to her championship at the same time the Craigs' Ch. Nita of Villa Malta was winning Groups, as well as producing a Group winner.

Eloise Craig held membership in and had been an officer of, usually secretary, every Maltese organization except the very first.

With Aennchen and Tony Antonelli and Helen Poggi, Eloise was a co-founder of the American Maltese Association at a meeting in New York City. Eloise was the first American Maltese Association secretary. She had served as vice-president, Midwest, and had been treasurer from 1975 until her death.

Her interest and devotion to the Maltese continued long after she ceased breeding. Her activities to promote the breed did not wane, until the day she died—January 27, 1983.

Other Good Time Maltese of note are Ch. Good Time Christmas Eve, whelped Christmas Eve 1959, returning home a champion Christmas Eve 1960; Ch. Good Time Hilda, owned by Dr. R. Berndt, author of *Your Maltese;* Ch. Good Time Terry Lynn, owned by past American Maltese Association president, H. Kellogg; Ch. Good Time Zita, finished by Jane Simpson; Ch. Good Time Chatter Box, Ch. Good Time Issa, C.D., owned by Marilyn Jensen.

Fairy Fay

Union City, Michigan, was home to the Fairy Fay Maltese, owned and bred by Elvira Cox. Miss Cox began breeding in 1952, at which point she purchased five Maltese from Mrs. E. Ferguson's Tamalene Kennels, Seattle, Washington. Later she also purchased from Mrs. Ferguson Am. Eng. Ch. Leckhampton Larkspur, who was a Group winner both here and in England. He was shown here at quite an advanced age, which did not deter him from his American Championship and a Group 1st. His outstanding features were his head and superb long coat. Also purchased from Mrs. Ferguson were English import Am. Ch. Invicta Nicker, noted for being the third Maltese in United States history to go Best in Show, which took place in 1952, and another English import, Am. Ch. Invicta Chione, a bitch. The two aforementioned English males became the primary stud force at Fairy Fay.

Ch. Scipio of Villa Malta, C.D., came to Fairy Fay in 1956. He has the distinction of being the obedience trials winner at the first American Maltese Association "A" match. He was a multiple Group winner, as well. Also from Villa Malta came the bitch Ch. Tulio of Villa Malta, one of the dogs which had been part of Dr. Calvaresi's famous team.

Miss Cox's breeding was the foundation for a number of kennels.

Some noteworthy dogs of the Fairy Fay Kennels are Ch. Tammy of Tamalene; Fairy Fay's Nicker, sire of many champions; and Ch. Fairy Fay's Figaro, foundation stud of Dorothy Tinker's Al Dor Maltese. Mrs. Tinker owned Ch. Fairy Fay's Kapu (Ch. Fido of Villa Malta × Fairy Fay's Rosita), a half brother to Ch. Fairy Fay's Figaro. Ch. Kapu was among the top ten Maltese in America when he was being shown.

Lester

Mrs. Alfreda Lester was the breeder of Lester's Maltese in California. She was especially active during the 1940s and 1950s, when very little knowledge of the Maltese was available. Mrs. Lester was affectionately known to her many friends as "Freddie."

Her first two dogs, Jon Vir Penelope and Jon Vir Sensation, which were some of the last few Jon Vir dogs bred, were received from Mrs. Leitch. She carried on her pure Jon Vir breeding single-handedly on the West coast for many years. Her dogs are behind most West coast Maltese, and especially those of California. Most notably, Miriam Thompson's illustrious Sun Canyon Kennels trace back to Lester breeding.

"Freddie" Lester was a charter member of the Maltese Dog Fanciers Association and the American Maltese Association, as well.

She died in August, 1982. Her charm and knowledge are greatly missed, especially by the West coast fancy.

Cecil

Another breeder of note on the West coast was Mrs. Gladys B. Cecil. She was born in March 1901 in Kansas City, Missouri, but she lived in Santa Maria, California for 25 years. It was there that she established her Cecil's line of Maltese.

Her first Maltese was acquired from Mrs. Lester in 1957, Ch. Lester's Lilly Lady of Cecil MMA, a bitch of pure Jon Vir breeding. Ch. Lilly eventually produced four champion offspring. Eleanore Frost sold her what she considered to be her finest stud dog, Delta's Cluri Chaun of Silver, a dog of Invicta breeding. These two dogs produced the first dog owned by Miriam Thompson. Four other Maltese from Mrs. Cecil were later added to Ms. Thompson's Sun Canyon Kennels, as well.

Mrs. Cecil was an active breeder-exhibitor for a number of years. She was a charter member of the American Maltese Association, working extensively over a period of years on the constitution and by-laws for that association.

Some noteworthy dogs bred by Mrs. Cecil are Group placing Am. Jap. Ch. Cecil's Don Figaro III, who was sold to Japan; Am. Can. Ch. Jay's Contessa Felice D'Figaro, who weighed just 3¼ pounds at maturity; Group placing Ch. Cecil's Donna Katie Isle D' Malta and Ch. Cecil's Don Luigi Isle D' Malta, owned by her sister, Mrs. Mildred Boggess.

Mrs. Cecil died at 75 years of age on June 30, 1977.

Mado

Another lady of note in the Maltese fancy on the West coast was Margaret Douglas. She owned and bred Maltese for over 30 years in San Francisco, California. She used several prefixes, most familiar of which was Mado. Forming an association with Dr. Helen Poggi, Reveille Maltese, the prefix became Mado Reveille. Still other dogs bore simply the Douglas prefix. Mrs. Douglas co-owned several dogs with Mary Walsh.

Born in Tasmania, Australia, before the turn of the century, she was a great lover of the Maltese dog. She became involved in the breed quite by accident, when she met a gentleman who was a member of the Golden Gate Kennel Club.

There were very few Maltese in the San Francisco area at that time. She acquired a male from the Villa Malta Kennels, the only Maltese in the city of San Francisco at that time.

Mrs. Douglas was always first with her generous contributions to further the cause of the breed. She held charter memberships in the Maltese Dog Fanciers Association, the American Maltese Association and the first chapter club under the American Maltese Association, the California Maltese Club, later known as the Bay Area Maltese Club.

Although Margaret loved the show ring, she did very little exhibiting herself. However, she became so much a part of all Maltese functions that after her death on July 29, 1972, her absence left a huge void whenever Maltese fanciers met.

Mrs. Douglas was so well respected that the official California Maltese Club medallion was offered in her memory at the Golden Gate Kennel Club spring benched show in 1973.

Some noteworthy dogs of Mrs. Douglas' breeding were Ch. Mado Reveille Lilli Bit and Ch. Douglas' Gaminia, sired by Dr. Helen Poggi's Ch. Lester's Morning Reveille.

Some of the dogs Mrs. Douglas co-owned with Mary Walsh were Ch. Mado Reveille Little Alfie, Ch. Mado Reveille Nellie Blye, a Group placer, Ch. Mado Reveille Play Girl, Ch. Mado Reveille Snow Man and Ch. Mado Reveille Little Bam Bam.

Kellogg

Herbert W. Kellogg and his wife, Marjory, of Joliet, Illinois, were ardent Maltese fanciers. They bred and showed the Kellogg Maltese in the 1950s, and were a leading force in helping form the American Maltese Association into a national organization.

58

Ch. Douglas' Gaminia.

Ch. Mado Reveille Nicholas, owned by Margaret Douglas.

Ch. Kellogg's Princess Feather, finished her title in 1964.

Mr. Kellogg had been a lifetime dog fancier. He began breeding Cairn Terriers, then Maltese. Mr. Kellogg exhibited extensively both in the conformation and obedience. He finished both conformation champions as well as C.D. and C.D.X. dogs. Mr. Kellogg was the first person to finish an American, Canadian C.D.X. Maltese, Kellogg's Beau, C.D.X.

Mr. Kellogg was an American Kennel Club licensed obedience judge as well as a conformation judge of Toy breeds.

He served as president of the American Maltese Association for several years, and was serving the association as treasurer at the time of his death. Mr. Kellogg was born August 31, 1910 and died August 23, 1975. His wife died in 1974.

Kellogg champions of note were Ch. Kellogg's Princess Feather, owned by Juanita Lewis, and Ch. Good Time Terry Lynn, bred by Eloise Craig.

Kismet

Mrs. Rose Sloan was the breeder of Maltese of Kismet in Union, New Jersey. She was active in the 1950s and 1960s, using Good Time and Aennchen bloodlines to produce many winners. Her dogs were exceptionally prolific. Among them, Aennchen's Dancer of Kismet, C.D., produced a litter of four females and three males, all of which survived, in 1960.

Mrs. Sloan was very active in the fancy, being a charter member of the American Maltese Association. She served as secretary of that association. She also wrote numerous educational and informative articles for the official publication of the American Maltese Association, *The Maltese Rx.* She wrote articles for other dog publications as well.

Noteworthy Maltese of Kismet include one of their top sires, who was a Toy Group winner, Ch. Shabudi of Kismet; Ch. Deebu of Kismet, a Group placing dog; Ch. Dai Khan of Kismet; Jinnivah of Kismet (Good Time So Fancy, C.D. × Aennchen's Manipuri Dancer), who attained the age of 15 years; and Ch. Deebu Gidget of Kismet, C.D.X.

Oak Manor

The Oak Manor Maltese, bred by Wilma Stahl from Lumberville, Pennsylvania, were known in the 1950s. Many Oak Manor champions were produced.

Mrs. Stahl was a woman of strong opinion. She thought Maltese that weighed four pounds or less to be quite useless. She stressed that the dog under the coat should be of prime concern to breeders. She maintained, "We are emphasizing the coat too much, and not paying enough attention to the rest of the Maltese." She also thought the idea "the coat makes the dog," a false notion. She suggested Maltese breeders consider limiting the coat length to five-and-a-half inches, without credit for extra length.

60

Sadly, despite her concentration on a larger, more robust dog, her kennel was wiped out by hard pad distemper. At that time, 26 champions were lost, in addition to as many puppies and champion-producing brood bitches. The Oak Manor Maltese never recovered their former prominence, and in a few years disappeared altogether from the Maltese scene in the early 1960s.

Ariel

Marcia McMillin of Ariel Maltese has a 33-year association with the breed. As of this writing, she has curtailed her showing activities, but continues to keep her line going by breeding a few litters a year. She now resides in Chattanooga, Tennessee, with nine adult Maltese and puppies, occasionally.

She purchased her first Maltese as a puppy from Dr. Calvaresi in 1950, Ch. Floria Tosca of Villa Malta, and showed her to her championship. During the 1950s and 1960s, Marcia was a very active breeder, exhibitor. In addition to Ch. Tosca, she bred and showed Ch. Ariel Zinka and Ch. Ariel Graciella, as well as pointing several others.

In founding the Ariel bloodline, Miss McMillin bred to champions owned by Dr. Calvaresi, Mrs. Leitch and Mrs. Stuber.

Alpond

An ardent breeder of the late 1950s and 1960s was Alice Pond from Youngstown, New York, where she still resides. No longer very active in the breed, Mrs. Pond bred several lovely winners bearing her Alpond prefix.

Most notable among these were Ch. Alpond's Sky Rockett, owned by Mr. Francis Geraghty, and Ch. Sky Rockett, Winners Bitch and Best of Winners, from the puppy class, under judge William Kendrick at the first American Maltese Association Specialty held in 1966.

Another bitch of her breeding, with the call name Bright Eyes, was Am., Can. Ch. Alpond's Shine Little Star. She was top Toy dog in Canada in 1967 and 1968, winning numerous Toy Groups and was a Best in Show winner in the United States, as well. Bright Eyes was owned and shown by Virginia Fredericks.

Mrs. Pond owned Ch. Folklore Minute Mame, sired by Ch. Mimino of Villa Malta and bred by Halia Scott Taylor.

For the American Maltese Association, Alice Pond served as treasurer for several years, while active in the fancy.

Other notable Maltese bearing the Alpond prefix were Ch. Alpond's Scamperino, who was sold to Evelyn Schaefer, and Ch. Alpond's Bright Little Star.

Ch. Sussi of Villa Malta, shown winning the Toy Group at Huntingdon Valley Kennel Club, September 1959. Owned by Wilma Stahl.

Courtesy AKC Library

Am. & Can. Ch. Alpond's Shine Little Star finished with Group wins from the classes in both countries. She was bred by Alice Pond and owned by V. Frederick.

Pendleton

Ann and Stewart Pendleton were noted breeders, but especially exhibitors of Maltese. They became active in the fancy in the 1950s and were very prominent in the show ring through the 1960s. Their interest continues, though in a limited way.

Their Ch. Brittigan's Sweet William was one of the first top-winning Maltese in the history of the breed here. By 1962, Ch. Sweet William had five all-breed Bests in Show, 20 Group 1sts, 30 Group 2nds, 11 Group 3rds and five Group 4ths. He held the record for the largest number of all-breed Bests in Show, until a new mark was set in 1966 by Ch. Aennchen's Toy Dancer.

Another top-winning dog owned by the Pendletons, Ch. Brittigan's Dark Eyes, won eight all-breed Bests in Show. This record was eventually tied by three Aennchen dogs, and was finally broken by Ch. Aennchen's Poona Dancer.

Maltese bred by the Pendletons include Ch. Pendleton's White Knight (Ch. Pendleton's Wee Magic × Brittigan's Tiny Teena), Ch. Pendleton's Dreamy, Ch. Pendleton's Bewitchin Lola, Ch. Pendleton's Short and Sweet, Ch. Pendleton's Try Baby and Ch. Pendleton's Adohra.

Mrs. Pendleton was the second president of the American Maltese Association, being elected after Dr. Calvaresi left the post. She served as president for three consecutive terms. She did a fine job of coordinating club activities and leading the new club through the maze of regulations necessary for American Kennel Club recognition so that specialty shows could be held.

Mrs. Pendleton organized the necessary match shows, as required by the American Kennel Club, prior to the holding of point shows. The first sanctioned match was held on the grounds of her lovely home in Louisville, Ohio. Maltese fanciers flocked there from both coasts, as well as from the Midwest.

The Pendletons have since retired from Maltese activities. Mrs. Pendleton became an AKC approved judge in 1971. The couple have retained their interest in the breed, being current members of the American Maltese Association.

Alma Statum

Alma Statum was a fancier most active through the 1950s and early 1960s. Her breeding was mostly of the Villa Malta bloodline. Although she bred and showed several lovely Maltese, fame came through Int., Am. Ch. Lacy of Villa Malta. Lacy is distinguished as being the very first Maltese in the modern (post American Maltese Association) history of the breed in America to be awarded an all-breed Best in Show. Ch. Lacy was honored for her history-making win by being used as the illustration on the cover of

Ch. Brittigan's Sweet William shown going BIS at the Lima Kennel Club show in 1957 under Alva McCall. Wynn Suck is handling. Mrs. Pendleton is to the far right in this photograph. *Courtesy AKC Library*

Ch. Brittigan's Dark Eyes, a noteworthy winner of the 1950s.

Courtesy AKC Library

Mrs. Pendleton's Group-winning brace.
Courtesy AKC Library

Ch. Pendleton's Boy's Boy, a Best in Show winner, bred and owned by Anne and Stewart Pendleton.

Ch. Nimino of Villa Malta, owned by Halia Scott Taylor, 57th champion from Villa Malta Kennels. He finished with Group placements from the classes and five majors.

the official American Maltese Association booklet containing the newly approved standard of 1963.

After years of dedication to the breed, Mrs. Statum died in April of 1974.

Folklore

Folklore Maltese were bred by Mrs. Halia Scott Taylor. Mrs. Taylor had been retired from a singing career for ten years when she met Dr. Calvaresi at the Eastern Dog Club show in Boston, Massachusetts. Being a lover of dogs and things of beauty, the Maltese dog seemed to perfectly suit her. From Dr. Calvaresi she purchased her first Maltese, a five-month-old puppy, Mimino of Villa Malta (April 11, 1956-September 5, 1970). Mimino was a Ch. Ricco of Villa Malta grandson.

Mrs. Taylor had re-established her career as a singer and had moved to Panorama City, California. In June of 1958, after relocating in California, she finished Ch. Mimino of Villa Malta. Soon after Ch. Mimino was sent to Mrs. Marge Lewis, of the Al Mar Maltese, in Independence, Missouri. While with Marge (1959-1961) Ch. Mimino established an impressive show record, amassing 30 Bests of Breed, four Group 1sts, six Group 2nds, six Group 3rds and five Group 4ths. He proved himself well as a stud dog while with Mrs. Lewis, siring seven champions. After his return to California, Ch. Mimino remained Mrs. Taylor's constant companion, until his death in 1970.

After moving to California, Mrs. Taylor initially aligned with Mary Irvine of Irvine Maltese. In association with Mrs. Irvine and her daughter, Pat Irvine, Harriet began to breed her Folklore bloodline.

Ch. Mimino sired three champions out of Ch. Irvine's Contessa: Ch. Irvine's Little Goody, which remained with the Irvines; Ch. Folklore Count Me Too, which was sold as a puppy to actor Edmund O'Brien, who later sold him to the breeder of Maltese, Dorothy O'Connell, who used him as her foundation stud; Ch. Folklore Minute Mame, sold as a pointed bitch to Alice Pond (Alpond Maltese), who finished her. Ch. Mame is the grand-dam of Best in Show winner, Am., Can. Ch. Alpond Shine Little Star.

By breeding Ch. Mimino to Ch. Irvine's Angel, two dogs were whelped, Folklore Too Much and Mi-No-Angel, which was sent to Dr. Calvaresi.

In 1962, Ch. Mimino was bred to Ch. Tanita of Villa Malta, owned by F. Weiner, producing Ch. Tamaritta of Folklore. Ch. Tamaritta was bred to Ch. Lock's Little Joe, producing the noteworthy Ch. Enrico, shown by Lenard Reppond and owned by F. Weiner.

When Mrs. Taylor sent Ch. Mimino to Mrs. Marge Lewis to be specialed and used at stud, Mrs. Lewis in return sent the notable Ch. Patrick Al Mar of Villa Malta to be used at stud in California. Ch. Patrick

66

sired six champions during this time (1959-1961), one of which was Ch. Lock's Little Joe.

During the years of her involvement with the breed, Mrs. Taylor was very active within the fancy. In 1965 she organized the California Maltese Club located in the San Francisco Bay area. This club later became the Bay Area Maltese Club.

It was Harriet's dream that the California Maltese Club should one day become an AKC recognized specialty club. It was through the California Maltese Club that Harriet Taylor came to have an impact upon the fancy.

In 1965, Mrs. Taylor also founded the *California Maltese Club Reporter,* together with the aid of a long-time member of the fancy, Verna Reed. The *California Maltese Club Reporter* was the vehicle by which the membership of the club was kept aware of Maltese activity in the Western United States.

Harriet inspired people to show their Maltese, and to work together for the advancement of the breed and fancy. Her ever-helping hand in training and grooming resulted in many new champions.

Mrs. Taylor designed and presented the Virginia Leitch Memorial Trophy, which was won by the Antonellis of Aennchen's Dancers.

Bejune

B. June Pozzi (Bejune Maltese) of Santa Rosa, California, was most active in the fancy during the 1960s and 1970s. Her breeding program was originally based upon Ch. Aennchen's Shikar Dancer. She blended the Aennchen, Jon Vir, Reveille and Lester bloodlines.

She acquired a co-ownership with Roberta Harrison of the Bobbelee Kennels. The dog bred by Mrs. Harrison, Ch. Bobbelee Brag-A-Bout, was a Ch. Shikar son. This dog was an important force in her breeding program.

She also acquired a Ch. Shikar daughter, Am., Can. Ch. Fiddle Dee Dee Igloo (Ch. Aennchen's Shikar Dancer × Lamsgrove Melody, an English import). Ch. Igloo was bred by Margaret Shives. Ch. Brag-A-Bout to Ch. Igloo produced her outstanding stud dog, Ch. Bejune's Potentate of Malta, a Ch. Shikar double grandson.

Ch. Brag-A-Bout to Fiddler's Green Snow Cloud produced Ch. Bejune's Lolle Pop, a top West coast winner, and two outstanding littermates, Am., Can. Ch. Bejune's Top of the Mark (June 21, 1964-October 26, 1969), a champion at less than ten months, and his brother, Am., Can. Ch. Bejune's Maxim of Llonee Lane, American and Canadian Group placer. Ch. Bejune's Poetry in Motion was out of a repeat of this breeding. The BIS winner, Ch. Bejune's Tomfoolery, also came from this establishment.

Maltacello

Ginni Sunner Evans was the original breeder of Maltacello Maltese in Bethel Park, Pennsylvania. She began breeding in 1961, combining the Villa Malta and Duncan bloodlines. Her dogs included Ch. Timpo of Villa Malta and Ch. Duncan's Kimberly.

A noteworthy dog of her breeding is Ch. Valentino of Maltacello, who was WD and BW to finish his championship at 11 months, at the 1967 Westminster show.

Mrs. Evans was president of the American Maltese Association and was an enthusiastic, motivating force for the short period of her activity. She bred six champions, including Ch. Snow Dancer of Maltacello, by the time she retired from the fancy in the early 1970s.

Eve-Ron

A most active and enthusiastic breeder and exhibitor would well describe Mrs. Evelyn Schaefer, of the Eve-Ron Maltese in Ohio. Mrs. Schaefer was active in the breed and an American Maltese Association supporter from the late 1950s until the day she died, June 26, 1981.

Some of her many winning Maltese include: Ch. Boreas Non Pariel, son of Ch. Joanne-Chen's Teddy Bear Dancer; Ch. Eve-Ron's Jendi from Oak Ridge MMA, producer of five champions; Ch. Eve-Ron's Sno Kist Cherub, a 1976 top producer; Ch. Eve-Ron's Tiddly Wink, owned by Alice Pond; Aennchen's Mecca Dancer, bred by Aennchen Antonelli; Group winning Ch. Mac's Apache Joray of Eve-Ron, owned by Peggy Lloyd; and Ch. Eve-Ron's Johnny Be Good, sired by Ch. Mac's Apache Joray of Eve-Ron.

Starward

Messrs. Frank Oberstar and Larry Ward of Euclid, Ohio, began their Starward Maltese with English imports in 1960. Mr. Ward had seen a Maltese for the first time in the arms of a little girl at the Farmers' Market in Los Angeles in 1959. From that point on, an effort was made to procure quality Maltese.

In July 1960, Vicbritta Claire was purchased from Mrs. White's Vicbritta Kennels in England. These two gentlemen used Claire to learn the proper care and presentation of a Maltese, having had no previous experience with the breed.

They showed Claire at the 1961 Westminster show; their first time showing at the "Garden." Their efforts were well rewarded as she was WB enroute to her championship.

Several other English imports came to Starward. Among them were Am. Ch. Amphion Prince of Gissing, a Group winner who was the top

Ch. Aennchen's Poona Dancer, winning the Toy Group at Westminster, 1966, under Edith Nash Hellerman. Poona was owned by Frank Oberstar and Larry Ward and handled by Mr. Oberstar.

Courtesy AKC Library

Ch. Invicta Leckhampton Cinderella, an English import bitch, owned by Starward Kennels.

rated male Maltese in 1963, and a bitch, Cherub of Gissing, both purchased from Mrs. Hunter's Gissing Kennels. In addition, Am. Ch. Invicta Leckhampton Cinderella, a bitch with superb coat and pigmentation, was purchased from Miss Neame and Mrs. Brierly.

Starward's first homebred champion, Ch. Starward's Girlfriend, was out of Ch. Cinderella. Ch. Amphion proved to be a worthwhile stud, siring several litters of good quality, including Ch. Starward's Comet (our of Ch. Vicbritta Claire), owned by Ruth Roath of Illinois.

In February 1964, Starward acquired Aennchen's Poona Dancer (by Am. & Bda. Ch. Aennchen's Siva Dancer) from Mr. and Mrs. J. P. Antonelli. Mr. Oberstar and Poona broke all previous Maltese records. They are still record holders for the largest number of Group 1sts won by an owner-handled Maltese. As of this writing, Ch. Poona remains the top-winning bitch of all time. She was BB 242 times, had 131 Group 1sts, 54 Group 2nds, 26 Group 3rds, 18 Group 4ths and was BIS 38 times.

Ch. Poona was among the top ten Toy dogs in 1965 and 1966, and was Best Toy at Westminster, 1966. She was among the top ten dogs, all-breeds in 1966-1967, and received awards from Quaker Oats and Kennel Review in 1967 for Top Toy. She was the American Maltese Association Specialty winner in 1967 and 1968. In addition, Ch. Poona was named official mascot of the Navy's *U.S.S. Lenawee.*

In 1968, Ch. Poona was retired with a BIS at the Livonia (Mich.) KC. She died in August 1974 and remains at this writing the second top-winning Best in Show Maltese in United States history.

After Ch. Poona's retirement, Starward had several other winners, including Ch. Starward's Gulliver, who was BW at six months, for five points at the 1969 AMA Specialty; Ch. Aennchen's Pipal Dancer; and Ch. Shareen's Captain Starward, BW at Westminster, 1968, owned by M. Spilling Innman.

Soon after, Starward Maltese were retired and Mr. Ward was elected president of the AMA for a term. At this writing, both gentlemen continue their memberships in the AMA. Mr. Oberstar now pursues an active judging career.

Stentaway

Mary Hechinger bred the Stentaway Maltese through the 1960s and 1970s. The Stentaway line was based upon Sun Canyon, Bobbelee, Cotterell and Starward bloodlines. Her dogs enjoyed some success in the show ring, and Ch. Sun Canyon Drummer Boy became a champion at seven months, one of the youngest champions of record.

Maltese owned and/or shown by Mrs. Hechinger included Cotterell's Topper's Frosty, sire of Ch. Al Dor's Little Rascal; Ch. Starward's Prince Valiant and Bobbelee Gay Echo.

Noteworthy dogs bred by Mrs. Hechinger of the Stentaway line include Am, Can. Ch. Stentaway's Sonny Boy (Ch. Sun Canyon Drummer Boy × Ch. Sun Canyon Sunshine Girl), Am., Can., Bda., Mex., Intl. C.A.C.I.B. Ch. Stentaway's Drummer Boy, owned by Ruth Roath, and the famous multiple Group Winner, Ch. Stentaway's Brag-A-Bout.

Malone

Malone's Maltese, bred by Jennie Malone of Lexington, Kentucky, were active in the show ring during the 1970s, until the very early 1980s, when Mrs. Malone died. Her kennel originally bore the prefix Jen-C. It was based upon the Sun Canyon, Le Grand, Villa Malta and Casa Remmo bloodlines. Eventually, her kennel was named Malone's Toys.

Early Malone dogs include, Ch. Enchantonio of Casa Remmo, a dog; Jen-C Jette, a bitch; Sun Canyon Jack of Hearts; Le Grand's Don Quijote of Malone; and Pashes Jen-C Jownsee Juliette.

Mrs. Malone's first owner-handled Maltese champion was Ch. Malone's Tamarsk Rose, sired by Ch. Enchantonio of Casa Remmo. Other noteworthy Malone's Toys include: Ch. Villa Malta Olivia and Ch. Villa Malta's Jen-C Sable, bred by Margaret Rozik; Ch. Malone's Chris-Ter-Fer and Ch. Malone's White Satin Melissa.

Mrs. Malone's most noted homebred was the bitch, Ch. Malone's Snowie Roxanne, a multiple BIS winner. She was BB at Westminster, 1979 and also in 1982. Ch. Roxanne was also Best of Breed at the Greater Houston Specialty in 1981. She was owned by Nancy Shapland and shown to her impressive record by the professional handler, Peggy Hogg.

Boreas

Mrs. Patricia Howell of West St. Paul, Minnesota, was an avid fancier for a number of years. She began with her Boreas Maltese in the late 1960s. She still maintains her membership in the AMA, but no longer shows. She is especially noted for her book, *The Modern Maltese,* published in 1967.

Her first Maltese were Kismet Pasteirk and Deebu Gidget of Kismet, purchased from Rose Sloane. Her first champion was Ch. Boreas Rex, who proved to be a prolific stud. Ch. Rex's litter brother, Am., Aust. Ch. Boreas Bonitatis, was sold to Mrs. Pamment of Australia. After quarantine, Ch. Bonitatis was BIS the first time shown in Australia at the Casterton championship show, January 24, 1970. He was also Group 1st at the Croydon North Agricultural Society show. This was the first BIS dog bred by Mrs. Howell.

Caramaya

Robert and Ollie Stewart were active breeders and exhibitors of the

Caramaya Maltese in the late 1960s and the 1970s. While no longer active in the fancy, their dogs were noted winners for about a decade.

Most notable of their dogs was Ch. Caramaya's Mister (Ch. Caramaya's Bojangles × Sugar Cane of Pierce Lane), who was BB at the 1974 AMA Specialty. Ch. Mister was owned and shown by Shirley Hrabak of Florida, later shown by Darlene Wilkinson of Illinois.

Moderna

Jari Bobillot of Moderna, Washington, was most active in the fancy during the 1960s and 1970s. The Moderna Maltese were successful in the ring and were used by several other breeders in forming their own breeding programs.

A top-producing bitch at Moderna was Twinkie Tu of Moderna. In 1969, she produced three champions sired by Am., Can. Ch. Floriana Mdina, owned by the Olvers of Canada. These were Ch. Moderna's Breeze, Ch. Moderna's Punch and Ch. Moderna's Bold.

Mrs. Bobillot bred Ch. C & M's Snow Flame of Moderna (Ch. Romeo of Maltacello × Moderna's Chiffon) who finished from the puppy class at just eight months. Ch. Flame was co-owned by Carol Thomas and Faith Noble of Florida. Mrs. Bobillot also bred Ch. Fantasyland Baby of Moderna, owned by Carole Baldwin of Fantasyland Kennels.

Nyssamead

Susan Edstrom Webber of Connecticut bred the Nyssamead Maltese. An active breeder and exhibitor during the 1960s and 1970s, her line was based upon Ch. Aennchen's Shikar Dancer.

She purchased her first Maltese from Mrs. Deaner, a bitch, Cashmere's Zoe of Mignon. She later purchased Ch. D'Arlene's Meringue.

The first dog to carry her kennel name, Nyssamead's Tesspainia, a bitch, came in the first litter she bred. Tesspainia was a documented top producer in 1969.

Among the champions she produced are littermates Ch. Nyssamead's Chloe (bitch) and Ch. Nyssamead Cicero (dog), by Ch. Winddrift's Sharazad, a Ch. Aeenchen's Shikar Dancer linebred stud. Ch. Nyssamead's Chloe went Best of Breed over multiple specials from the puppy class, on the way to her championship.

Because the results of the first breeding of Ch. Sharazad to Tesspainia were so successful, Mrs. Webber repeated the breeding. The resulting get were Am., Can. & Bda. Ch. Nyssamead's Dhugal, owned and shown by Claudette Le May of the Sugartown Kennels and Am., Can. Ch. Nyssamead's Disa, owned by Sharmion Aune Foucault from Montreal, Canada.

Mrs. Webber showed Ch. Disa to her American title, putting several

Group placements on her along the way. Ch. Disa was then sold to Mrs. Foucault, who put the Canadian title on her. Ch. Disa became a consistent winner in Canada, named #2 Maltese in Canada in 1972 and #3 in 1973.

Another litter of multiple champions was sired by Ch. Nyssamead's Jonah of Tenessa, owned by the Feldblums of Tenessa Maltese. The dam of this litter was Nyssamead's Fabrienne, owned by Mrs. Webber. The resulting get were Ch. Nyssamead's Iago and Group winning Ch. Nyssamead's Meggin.

Mrs. Le May, owner of Ch. Dugal, also owned Nyssamead's Fazid.

Mrs. Webber has retired from breeding and the show ring, and presently lives with one housepet, Nyssamead's Kirsten.

Gwenbrook

Dr. and Mrs. John Holbrook, originally from Long Island, New York, bred and showed Maltese for several years using the Gwenbrook prefix. Their initial stock was Aennchen, later adding Michael Wolf's Mike Mar breeding. During the late 1960s and early 1970s, they enjoyed success in the show ring with several Group winners and two BIS dogs.

When Dr. Holbrook retired, he and Gwen moved to Arizona, where they continued to exhibit for several years. Dr. Holbrook served as delegate to the AKC for the AMA for several years before his retirement.

Some of the Gwenbrook Maltese worth noting are Ch. Aennchen's Sita Dancer and Ch. Aennchen's Teej Dancer, bred by the Antonellis; BIS Ch. Aeenchen's Imp of Gwenbrook; Ch. Gwenbrook's Deidre; BIS Ch. Mike Mar's Gwenbrook (Ch. Mike Mar's Devil Dancer × Alpond's Shine on Little Star); Ch. Gwenbrook's Elena (Ch. Mike Mar's Gwenbrook × Aennchen's Teej Dancer) and Ch. Gwenbrook's Modesty (Ch. Mike Mar's Gwenbrook × Ch. Gwenbrook's Melissa).

De Tetrault

Miss Virginia Davey had the De Tetrault Maltese and was active during the 1960s. Miss Davey combined the Joanne-Chen, Boreas and Villa Malta bloodlines to form her strain.

She co-owned several dogs with William Cunningham, a professional handler and friend who showed several dogs for her. Miss Davey was an avid and dedicated Maltese fancier until her untimely death.

Some De Tetrault Maltese of note are Ch. De Tetrault's Captain Star, Ch. De Tetrault's White Majic, co-owned with Mr. Cunningham, and Ch. De Tetrault's Mr. Victor.

Seafoam

Seafoam Maltese were bred by Kathy Clifton of San Francisco. Kathy

Ch. Nyssamead's Dhugal, bred by Mrs. Webber, owned and shown by Claudette LeMay.

Ch. Nyssamead's Meggin.

Ch. Caramaya's Mister, an AMA national Specialty winner, owned by Mrs. Hrabak.

Multiple BIS-winning Ch. Bobbelee Apr Love, bred by Mrs. Harrison and owned b M. J. Chaisson. *Courtesy AKC Librar*

became involved in the fancy in 1956, but did not begin showing Maltese until 1960. Her first champion was Group winner Ch. Joanne-Chen's Indi Dancer (Ch. Joanne-Chen's Siva Dancer × Mars Top Tip Topper), bred by Joanne Hesse. Seafoam Maltese figured in the breeding programs of several San Francisco Bay area fanciers. Seafoam Maltese are not retired from all activity.

Maltes'a

Maltes'a Maltese were bred by Judith O'Brien Carrick of Chicago, Illinois. She maintained high quality breeding on a very limited scale from the late 1950s through the 1970s. For many years, she bred lovely dogs, and is now retired from the fancy. Dogs of note from the Maltes'a bloodline include Ch. Maltes'a Ballerina, Ch. Maltes'a Miracle Match, Ch. Maltes'a Empress, Ch. Maltes'a Sun Dancer, sired by Ch. Joanne-Chen's Maya Dancer, Ch. Maltes'a Martini, Ch. Maltes'a Miracle Maker, Ch. Maltes'a Only Angel, Am., Can. Ch. Maltes'a Radiant Desiree, and Ch. Maltes'a Martina.

Gayla

Gayla Maltese, bred by Mrs. Shirley Hrabak, were among the finest bred in Florida. Mrs. Hrabak began in the Chicago area and moved to Daytona, Florida, in 1972. Doubtless, she would still be breeding and exhibiting today, had she not lost her valiant fight against cancer on March 12, 1980.

Shirley faced the world with a smile and an air of calm—great assets at a dog show. She was honest and forthright; she loved her dogs, and was careful about how they were placed. She always managed to find the right home for the right dog. Those show quality dogs she could not place, she showed herself.

Shirley and Darlene Wilkinson formed a partnership. Many of the Gayla Maltese were co-owned between these two ladies. After Mrs. Hrabak's death, Darlene Wilkinson continued the Gayla bloodline.

Perhaps the most noteworthy of the dogs in the Gayla Kennels was the winner of the 9th AMA Specialty (1974)—Ch. Caramaya's Mister, bred by the Stewarts. Ch. Mister was the top stud dog at Gayla, having sired at least 20 champions, many of which belonged to Mrs. Hrabak herself.

One of the last dogs bred by Shirley Hrabak was 5¼ pound Ch. Gayla's Picolo Pete, co-owned by Pauline Dick and Carole Baldwin.

Others which were part of the Gayla breeding program are Ch. Gayla's Sunrise Serenade (Ch. Caramaya's Mister × Ch. Gayla's Some Sunday Morning II); Ch. Gayla's Strike Up the Band; littermates Ch. Gayla's Hold that Tiger and Ch. Gayla's Kerry Dancer, sired by Ch. Mister; Ch. Gayla's

Over the Rainbow (Ch. Caramaya's Mister × Gayla's Little Bit of Heaven); littermates sired by Ch. Mister, Ch. Gayla's Star Spangled Banner and Ch. Gayla's Beautiful Dreamer.

Bobbelee

After breeding and showing American Cockers for a number of years, Mrs. Roberta Harrison of the Bobbelee Kennels decided to become involved in a Toy breed. It was her contention that if one were to breed dogs, one should breed the most beautiful.

After studying several Toy breeds, Mrs. Harrison decided that the Maltese, though not too well known, nor popular at the time, was the gayest and most beautiful of all the Toys.

A bitch in whelp was purchased from Elvira Cox, Fairy Fay's Kennels. From this first litter came the Bobbelee foundation study, 3½ pound Ch. Bobbelee Marshmallow. His show career spanned the years of the early to mid 1960s. In his six years at stud he produced 11 champions of both sexes. They are Ch. Bobbelee Snow Sparkle, who was a Group placer; Ch. Bobbelee Tammy Too of Marcris, owned by Joyce Watkins; Am., Can. Ch. Bobbelee Frosty Knight; Ch. Bobbelee Beloved; Ch. Bobbelee Meringue; Ch. Bobbelee April Love; Ch. Bobbelee Enchanting; Ch. Duncan's Christopher; Duncan's Kimberly; Ch. Duncan's Bagpipe; and Ch. C & M's Our Dream.

Ch. Marshmallow's most famous daughter was Ch. Bobbelee April Love, a multiple BIS winner, owned by M. J. Chaisson. Ch. Marshmallow had numerous champion grandchildren and great grandchildren.

Lou-Win

Louise Winslow Carlsen had the Lou-Win Maltese in Miami, Florida. She began in 1959 with Quaker Girl of Gissing from Mrs. Hunter in England. Quaker Girl bred to Ch. Aennchen's Shikar Dancer produced Lou-Win's First champion, Ch. Dancing Princess of Lou-Win, born in June 1960.

Ch. Vicbritta Felicity was added as a brood bitch, and the third foundation. The second champion for Lou-Win, Am. Ch. Sylvester of Gissing, also came from England. The third brood bitch to arrive at Lou-Win was one of the last daughters of the famous Ch. Musi of Villa Malta, Love Pat of Lou-Win (our of Irvine's Mi-No-Angel).

Ch. Sylvester was bred three times to Fairy Fay's Queen Sita and produced three champions: Ch. Little Scotter of Lou-Win, Group placer; Ch. Lou-Win's Dixie Darling; and Ch. Lou-Win's Liberty Belle.

Other Lou-Win champions included Am. & Int. Ch. Villa Malta Carlito, bred by Dr. Calvaresi, Ch. Lou-Win Vicbritta Dottie (Mil-O-tie Prancer of Marcris × Lou-Win Suzie) and Ch. Lou-Win's Lover Infante, seventh champion at Lou-Win sired by Ch. Bobbelee Brag-A-Bout. Halia Taylor's Ch. Folklore True Blue Lou was sired by Louise Carlsen's Ch. Little Scotter.

Rand

Jean Rand of Miami, Florida, had Rand's Maltese for several years. Her foundation combined Aennchen, Jon Vir and Villa Malta bloodlines. Jean's top stud was Ch. Rand's Top Secret, sire of several champions. He finished undefeated at ten months. His get include the 1968 Westminster WB, Ch. Rand's White Magnolia.

Other Rand notables were two co-owned with Margaret Spilling Inmann, Ch. Rand's Top Hat of Shareen and Ch. Rand's Stormy Weather Shareen.

Aennchen's Dancers

As the saying goes, "save the best for last" and this certainly is the case here. If we were to chronologically place the names of those persons who have had the most influence on the history of the breed in this century, we would begin with Mrs. Agnes Rose Rossman, breeding the Arr bloodline in the 1920s. Dr. Vincenzo Calvaresi would hold the next place of distinction. His involvement, though lasting into the 1960s, had its greatest impact upon the breed from the late 1930s and into the 1940s and 1950s. During this same period, the abundant resources of Mrs. Virginia Leitch had tremendous impact upon the destiny of the Maltese in the United States. Beginning in the mid-1950s and lasting until the mid-1970s, one bloodline stood out far above any others of the time. The world-renowned Aennchen Maltese Dancers, owned, bred and shown by Mr. and Mrs. J. P. Antonelli of Waldwick, New Jersey, were the most sought-after of all Maltese.

Before beginning with Maltese, Aennchen taught ballet in her school of dance in Philadelphia, assisted by husband Tony. Tony Antonelli was artistically inclined, having studied the fine arts in Europe. Together, Aennchen and Tony created new dance forms. They were active and successful, being well-respected in the field of dance and well-received by American audiences.

When Aennchen suffered a tragic back injury, the doctors were not encouraging. They intimated she might never walk without assistance again. At that time, the Antonellis lived in New York City.

Tony, seeing the end of their "duet" as permanent, returned to school. At Columbia University he majored in art education and eventually earned a Master's degree. Only a thesis stood between him and his doctorate.

In the meantime, Aennchen grew despondent, thinking she would never be able to walk and function as before. Anyone who met or knew

Aennchen, with her great amount of energy and effervesence, can well understand why she might lose heart.

Tony passed by a pet store near Columbia University one day in 1953. In the window was a white ball of fluff, absolutely gorgeous! Hoping that Aennchen would be as entranced by the puppy's beauty as he, and thereby dedicated to its welfare, Tony purchased the little dog, unaware of the breed and without papers or pedigree. "Lover," as the Maltese bitch was known, became the catalyst for Aennchen's regaining locomotion. Aennchen slowly recovered from her disability in the process of loving and caring for her new pet.

The miracle was all due to the little white Maltese, and resulted in a great bond of love and devotion between the Antonellis and the Maltese breed.

The spark of interest in the breed had grown as well. The first dog show they attended was the 1954 Westminster show. They were so happy with the new experience, that the beginnings of the show careers of the Aennchen's Dancing Maltese had been sown. By 1955, the Antonellis were firmly involved in the fancy. They studied bloodlines and pedigrees, wrote to leading breeders and acquired a female and two males. They established their line upon the American Jon Vir, Villa Malta and Good Time bloodlines, as well as the Italian Electa bloodlines. Tony had seen photos of the Electa dogs and was completely enthralled by their type. He decided to breed Maltese which resembled the Electa's tiny size, as bred by the ancients and admired throughout the history of the breed in the United States. It must be understood that at the time the Antonellis began their breeding program, the official American Kennel Club Maltese Standard, which had been in effect since 1906, stated that the ideal Maltese weighed three pounds or under.

When they decided their apartment was no longer a proper home for their Maltese, the Antonellis moved to Moonachie, New Jersey, where they lived in a mobile home. Mr. Antonelli commenced a career in education. Mrs. Antonelli, now fully recovered, became involved once again in teaching and choreography of dance. The interest in the Maltese fancy grew and flourished, as well.

Of the two, Tony was the breeder and planned and executed the Aennchen's Dancers breeding program. Aennchen cared for and groomed the dogs. She trained them on the lead, and readied them for the show ring.

Their foundation stud dog was Am. & Bda. Ch. Aennchen's Raja Yoga MMA (Remo of Villa Malta × G. & H. Sweetness). Remo of Villa Malta (Ch. Electa Pampi × Ch. Electa Laila) was of pure Electa breeding. Ch. Raja Yoga was a potent force in the breed, the sire of 21 champions, and the grandsire of numerous others.

Ch. Raja Yoga had the distinction of being the first Bermudian champion Maltese. No other Maltese were in competition, however. There were three shows held on three consecutive days. Ch. Raja Yoga won three Toy Groups to earn his history-making title. The champions sired by Ch. Raja Yoga, earning him his Maltese Merit Award, are Ch. Aennchen's Puja Dancer, BIS Ch. Aennchen's Shikar Dancer, Ch. Aennchen's Singhalese Dancer, Ch. Aennchen's Shanta Dancer, Ch. Aennchen's Tala Dancer, Ch. Aennchen's Saci Dancer, Ch. Aennchen's Zen Dancer, Ch. Aennchen's Lakshmi Dancer, Ch. Aennchen's Miksha Dancer, Ch. Aennchen's Taza Dancer, Ch. Aennchen's Sahmba Dancer, Ch. Aennchen's Sikha Dancer, Ch. Aennchen's Tamil Dancer, Ch. Aennchen's Indra Dancer, Ch. Aennchen's Moghul Dancer, Ch. Aennchen's Siva Dancer, Ch. Aennchen's Yogini Dancer, Ch. Aennchen's Yama Dancer, Ch. Aennchen's Sita Dancer, Ch. Jo-Aennchen's Rajah Dancer and Ch. Caprice of Kismet.

The Antonellis became close friends of Virginia Leitch, of the Jon Vir Maltese, the great historian of the breed in America. The Antonellis came to share many ideas and ideals with Mrs. Leitch, from whom they received their first brood bitch, Aennchen's Jon Vir Royal Gopi (Ch. Jon Vir's Tiny Boy × Jon Vir's Dinah Mite). This daughter of the famous Ch. Jon Vir's Tiny Boy, produced the Antonelli's first top producing champion dam, Ch. Aennchen's Puja Dancer MMA. Ch. Puja was shown at Westminster in 1956, going BW at 11 months. She was named top-producing Maltese dam in 1961, producing a total of eight champion get. Ch. Puja was bred back to her father with superb results. Produced from this breeding were two of the most potent studs of the Aennchen bloodline, Am. & Bda. Ch. Aennchen's Siva Dancer MMA and his brother Ch. Aennchen's Shikar Dancer MMA.

The champion get out of Ch. Puja are Ch. Aennchen's Shikar Dancer, Ch. Aennchen's Tamil Dancer, Ch. Aennchen's Taza Dancer, Ch. Aennchen's Moghul Dancer, Ch. Aennchen's Siva Dancer, Ch. Aennchen's Lakshmi Dancer, Ch. Aennchen's Indra Dancer, and Ch. Aennchen's Yama Dancer.

The Antonellis never kenneled their Maltese. They were never put in cages, but rather allowed to run free. Soon a "bakers dozen" lived in their mobile home. There were newspaper articles written describing these two people and their beautiful dogs frolicking in a mobile home in New Jersey.

"The family kept growing," Tony once said. "Aennchen and I decided the family needed a new home." Waldwick, New Jersey became home and the dogs had more room, and a yard to play in. The home really was for the dogs, with the steps from the side of the house altered to facilitate easy exit and entry. They were kept in groups, each group having their own room. Most visitors to the Antonelli home visited outside, in the Maltese's fenced yard, or in the kitchen of the home. As in most Italian households, the kitchen was the center of life, where all family members met, when not off in their own private areas. It was a cheery, bright room, featuring murals

Ch. Aennchen's Lakshmi Dancer with Aennchen Antonelli.

Ch. Aennchen's Tasia Dancer.

The outstanding Ch. Aenn-chen's Smart Dancer. The only Maltese in the history of the breed to finish with two BIS and a Group 1st, all from the classes.

Courtesy AKC Library

Ch. Aennchen's Hindi Dancer, owned by the Roger Browns.

painted by Tony. These murals depicted all the major East Indian deities. The Antonellis had incorporated East Indian influences into their dancing. These carried over to their dogs, which were initially named for East Indian deities, cities, and so on. Their dogs were later named by combining parts of names of different dogs, and still later, many dogs received names which began with the letter "S," as such names had proven successful.

Guests were frequent at the Antonelli home. Eventually a visiting area was constructed, quite artfully, out of half of the garage building. There was room inside for the Maltese to run, gait and play, seating arrangements, a small desk and lots of Mr. Antonelli's artwork displayed. In addition, on one wall there was a gallery of photo portraits of all the top-winning Aennchen Maltese. It was a home and lifestyle geared to the Maltese that lived there, and the people who loved them.

Am. & Bda. Ch. Aennchen's Siva Dancer MMA was a most influential stud for Aennchen Maltese Dancers. He was the second Bermudian champion Maltese. Cobby and sound, with superb pigmentation and gorgeous coat, he passed on these qualities to his get, many of which became outstanding champions. Ch. Siva was not used at public stud. He was the sire of the outstanding Ch. Aennchen's Poona Dancer, as well as Ch. Aennchen's Mohini Dancer, Ch. Aennchen's Puri Dancer, Ch. Aennchen's Shah Dancer, Ch. Aennchen's Sisa Dancer, Ch. Bayhammond's Triplet Dancer, Ch. Alekai Hula Dancer, Ch. Aennchen's Pipal Dancer, Ch. Aennchen's Savar Dancer, Ch. Aennchen's Orissi Dancer, Ch. Aennchen's Siin Dancer, Ch. Bayhammond's Tomi Dancer, Ch. Aennchen's Imp of Gwenbrook, Ch. Aennchen's Rava Dancer, Ch. Aennchen's Timhi Dancer and Ch. Aennchen's Hindi Dancer.

Ch. Aennchen's Shikar Dancer MMA was the outstanding, universally admired full brother to Ch. Siva. Ch. Shikar was co-owned by Aennchen and Joanne Hesse. He finished his championship at nine months and replaced Ch. Clio of Arr as the American Kennel Club's breed model in *The Complete Dog Book*. He was BB at the 1963 Westminster show; he was a star of television, and much admired by all who saw him. Ch. Shikar was awarded five Bests in Show before his untimely death. At 3½ years of age he had sired six champions. By the time of his death, that number had grown considerably. His champion get, for which he was awarded a Maltese Merit Award, include Ch. Co-Ca-He's Aennchen's Raja Dancer, Ch. Mike-Mar's Shikar's Replica, Ch. Alekai Short Stop, Ch. Joanne-Chen's Dancing After Dark, Ch. Windrift Fantabulous, Ch. Bobbelee Touch of Frost, Ch. Co-Ca-He's Aennchen's Star Dancer, Ch. Aga-Lynn's Dancing Rajah, Ch. Co-Ca-He's Aennchen's Gay Dancer, Ch. Valley Views Mona Lisa, BIS Ch. Joanne-Chen's Sweet Shi Dancer, BIS Ch. Aennchen's Sari Dancer, Ch. Joanne-Chen's Sheeta Dancer, Ch. Joanne-Chen's Hadji Dancer, Ch. Joanne-Chen's Sweet He Dancer, Ch. The Sultan of Windrift, Ch. Aennchen's Mastyr Dancer, Ch. Joanne-Chen's Dancing Shiek, BIS

Ch. Joanne-Chen's Shieka Dancer, Ch. Bobbelee Brag-A-Bout, Ch. Joanne-Chen's Martin Dancer, Ch. Fiddle Dee Dee Igloo, BIS Ch. Co-Ca-He's Aennchen's Toy Dancer, Ch. Joanne-Chen's Aga-Lynn Dancer, Ch. Aennchen's Suci Dancer, Ch. Dancing Princess of Lou-Win and Ch. Cashmere's Maranna Dancer.

At the 1962 Westminster show, in a class of 11 specials, Winners Dog and Winners Bitch, a difficult decision was made by judge Mrs. Byron Hoffman. Best of Breed that year went to the WB, Aennchen's Smart Dancer. She had been sold by the Antonellis to Mrs. Henry J. Kaiser of the Alekai Kennels in Hawaii. Ch. Smart became a champion by going BIS from the classes, in 1962; her record for 1962 included seven BIS and 27 Group 1sts. She was #1 Maltese for that year, #32 all-breeds, and among the top ten Toys. Ch. Smarty had a BIS in Bermuda, and eventually tied the BIS record held by Mrs. Pendleton's Ch. Brittigan's Dark Eyes, when she was awarded her eighth Best. Soon after, she was retired from the ring and bred. Mrs. H. J. Kaiser also owned Ch. Alekai Aeenchen's Hula Dancer, who finished undefeated. She was an outstanding bitch of superb conformation and type. These dogs were shown for Mrs. Kaiser by the professional handler, Wendell Sammett.

Several dogs of Aennchen's breeding were purchased by Mr. Stimmler for his children, Anna Marie and Gene from Fairview Village, Pennsylvania. The first of these was Ch. Co Ca He's Aennchen Toy Dancer. Toy was shown to her many wins by the then 15-year-old Anna Marie.

In 1964, Ch. Toy made her debut at Westminster. She had a custom-made crate designed and built by Mr. Stimmler, an engineer. The crate was glass-enclosed on three sides, and had a golden lock and key. There was a panorama of dials and knobs, which controlled temperature, humidity, air filtering, lighting and ozone levels, to name a few. The controls were supplied with power provided by a huge battery, almost as large as the crate itself, which took up the entire benching space below the crate. The special crate was said to have cost $2,000.00 to construct, at the time.

Perhaps the crate was of assistance, for at the 1964 Westminster, Ch. Co Ca He's Aennchen Toy Dancer was the first Maltese in history to win the Toy Group at that show. Toy was a top-winning Maltese in 1964, taking the record for Bests in Show for a Maltese. Until then the record had been held by Anne Pendleton's Ch. Brittigan's Sweet William.

Toy won the first Specialty of the American Maltese Association under William L. Kendrick. Toy went on to win the Group that day at Columbiana (Ohio) KC, also under Mr. Kendrick.

BIS Ch. Aennchen's Sari Dancer was also purchased from the Antonellis and was shown by the Stimmlers when Ch. Toy was retired from the ring. In 1965, Ch. Sari was awarded two BIS and seven Group 1sts. She was one of the top ten Toy dogs in the United States in the first quarter of 1965. Ch. Sari was owned by Anna Marie and shown by her brother Gene.

Ch. Co-Ca-He's Aennchen Toy Dancer,
owned by Anna Marie Stimmler Burke.
Courtesy AKC Library

Ch. Aennchen's Taja Dancer,
multiple BIS winner, with
Aennchen. Her first BIS was
from the classes, on March
7, 1965.

Multiple BIS winner Ch. Aennchen's Sari Dancer.   *Courtesy AKC Library*

Other Maltese owned by the Stimmlers were gorgeous three pound Ch. Aennchen's Siin Dancer, who was WB at the 1966 Westminster show, and Ch. Aennchen's Orisi Dancer.

The Stimmlers did some limited breeding before they retired from Maltese. They produced Ch. Anna Marie's White Panther, who was Best of Breed at Westminster in 1971. Ch. Panther was owned and shown by Dr. Kenneth Knopf, of New York City. Dr. Knopf later acquired BIS Ch. Aennchen's Paris Dancer, a gift as a puppy from the Antonellis. Dr. Knopf has retired from the breed and now lives in Florida with a Ch. Paris daughter, Prima.

The Stimmlers eventually disposed of their Aennchen dogs, to the great dismay of the Antonellis. Several dogs went to Japan. The Antonellis never personally had sent any of their dogs to that country, since the Japanese wanted only the best of what the Aennchen line had to offer. Mr. and Mrs. Antonelli felt it much more important to have dogs of such quality here, available to be used by the fancy for the improvement of the breed. The Antonellis would have much preferred to purchase these dogs back, than lose them forever to Japan. They held nothing personal against the Japanese, despite the fact that the Antonellis never personally sent an Aennchen Dancer to Japan, when others did. The Aennchen Dancers became prominent forces in the development of the breed in Japan. The first Aennchen dog to arrive in Japan, Ch. Aennchen's Mastyr Dancer, was widely used at stud, siring many Japanese champions.

The Antonellis thought of their dogs, and the people who owned them, as "family." The many Aennchen champions and the people who owned them continued to breed champions, which were directly or indirectly related. Regardless of where you found them, they were a "family," and as in most large families, the bond was strong.

The Antonellis were proud of the fact that they had never sold an Aennchen Maltese for a four-figure price. Nor had they ever shipped a dog to its new owner. The dogs were always delivered in person or picked up by the new owners. Aennchen felt that it was important to meet prospective buyers personally, not merely to explain grooming techniques, but more importantly, to make contact, which ensured the continuation of the family relationship.

April 7, 1968 was a day which lasted forever in the memories of Aennchen, Tony and Frank Oberstar. On that day the great Am., Can. Ch. Aennchen's Poona Dancer won her 38th BIS and was retired from the show ring. Her overall record included 242 BB, 131 Group 1sts, 54 Group 2nds, 26 Group 3rds, 18 Group 4ths and two consecutive AMA Specialties, in 1967 in Los Angeles and 1968 in Pittsburgh. Ch. Poona won her first points the day Mr. Oberstar acquired her, at seven months.

Ch. Poona won the Toy Group at the 1966 Westminster show. On August 21, 1966, Ch. Poona broke the previous Best in Show record for a

Maltese, held jointly by Ch. Brittigan's Dark Eyes and Ch. Aennchen's Smart Dancer. This win was Ch. Poona's 11th BIS. She had accrued 37 BIS between 1965 and 1967. She was named outstanding Maltese and the top Toy dog by *Kennel Review* magazine, having won more Toy Groups in 1967 than any other Toy dog. She also broke all previous records for all Toy breeds by having won 61 Groups. Frank Oberstar and Ch. Poona are still the all-time record holders for the most Group 1sts for an owner-handled Maltese. In 1967, Ch. Poona was also awarded the Quaker Oats Award for top Toy dog. Ch. Poona was also named official mascot of the U.S.S. Lenawee.

All through Ch. Poona's career, and even after she was retired, the family contact was close. Aennchen said of Poona in January, 1972:

> I saw Ch. Poona only recently, and I actually believe that she does not feel "retired," but only resting in order that Frank may recover from the ordeal of too many auto accidents and too many shows. Frank allows that he would never go that hard with another one. However, I know Frank wouldn't trade a ribbon for the fun that he and Ch. Poona shared during the arduous days of campaigning.

Ch. Aennchen's Poona Dancer died in August of 1974.

Mrs. Joanne Hesse, of Indiana, played an important part in the Aennchen family. She co-owned Ch. Aennchen's Shikar Dancer, the highly regarded stud dog of the Antonellis' breeding. She bred from the Aennchen bloodline Ch. Toy Dancer, Ch. Maya Dancer and more recently Ch. Joanne-Chen's Mino Maya Dancer. Dogs bred by Mrs. Hesse used first the Co Ca He's Aennchen prefix. Later the prefix became Jo-Aennchen, until the present Joanne-Chen's Dancers prefix was developed.

Mrs. Harry Bounell of Louisville, Kentucky, owned and showed the impressive Ch. Aennchen's Puri Dancer. Ch. Puri was a wonderfully-coated bitch who finished with a Group 1st. Her outstanding record included four Groups at one and a half years.

Mr. and Mrs. Leonard Ellentuch joined the Aennchen family for a time, using the Mari-Aennchen prefix. Ch. Joanne-Chen's Shikar Dancer was bred in their home from their Aennchen's Asia Dancer. They also owned Aennchen's Manjatta Dancer, dam of the lovely dog Aennchen's Sabre Dancer by Ch. Aennchen's Savar Dancer. They bred Mari-Aennchen's Siin Dancer, of pure Aennchen breeding. Siin produced the Group winner from the classes, Ch. Yogi Nimble Vic, sired by Group winning Ch. Aennchen's Soomi Dancer.

Ch. Aennchen's Midas Touch Dancer was owned and shown by the Ovingtons, originally from Maryland, now residing in Florida.

For a brief time, the Wegmanns, Agnes and Linda, of Glen Cove, Long Island, were associated with the Aennchen bloodline. They purchased Ch. Aennchen's Timhi Dancer, Ch. Aennchen's Shana Dancer and Ch.

BIS winning Ch. Aennchen's Paris Dancer, shown with his owner, handler, Dr. Kenneth Knopf.

Group winning Ch. Anna Marie's White Panther.

Ch. Aennchen's Savar Dancer, shown as a champion at seven months of age.

Ch. Aennchen's Mastyr Dancer.
Courtesy AKC Library

Ch. Aennchen's Love of Aga Lynn.

Aennchen's Love of Aga-Lynn, a Group winner. Following a parting of the minds, the Wegmanns severed their family ties, and in a short time were no longer active in the show ring, or the fancy.

Jeanne Oddy was the member of the Aennchen family who showed the public that Aennchen Dancers were not only top drawer in the conformation ring, but could also shine in the obedience ring. Ch. Shikar's litter brother, Aennchen's Moghul Dancer, CDX, did the family proud.

Aennchen herself continued to enjoy immense success in the show ring. Ch. Aennchen's Taja Dancer represented the fifth generation of champions for the Antonellis. In 1965, Ch. Aennchen's Taja Dancer, or T.J. as she was affectionately known to all who loved her, was the 14th Aennchen Toy Group winner and also won a BIS. The Aennchen Dancers had a fantastic January to October that year, winning 102 Group placements, 30 of which were 1sts. Ch. Yogi sired his 27th champion, and Ch. Shikar his 18th. Another Aennchen Dancer who was a star in the ring in 1965 was the beautiful Ch. Aennchen's Taza Dancer, also a BIS winner.

Perhaps one of the most beautiful bitches ever bred by the Antonellis was the stylish, compact and lovely Ch. Aennchen's Sitar Dancer. She was, indeed, so beautiful it was hard to believe she was real. This gorgeous 3½ pound bitch became a champion at 15 months, the same way her famous mother, Ch. Smart Dancer, by winning the Toy Group and Best in Show from the classes. Ch. Sitar's sire, Aennchen's Manushya Dancer, was a litter brother to Ch. Poona Dancer. In 1968, Ch. Sitar won five Group 1sts and a BIS.

Equally beautiful, though in a more masculine way, being cobby, typey and sound, was Ch. Sitar's litter brother, Ch. Aennchen's Taran Dancer. Ch. Taran finished with a BB over specials, enroute to Toy Group 2nd.

Considered by the Antonellis to be the epitome of their breeding program was Ch. Aennchen's Savar Dancer, perhaps the youngest Maltese champion on record. Ch. Savar completed his title at the Eastern Dog Club show in Boston, at age seven months, weighing just three pounds. He was the culmination of the dream that had begun in 1953. He represented the ideal that Aennchen and Tony had strived to achieve, the Maltese dog, as held in high regard by the ancients, and by every lover of the Maltese dog down through the ages. Ch. Savar exhibited all the superb qualities of both his parents, Ch. Aennchen's Siva Dancer and Ch. Aennchen's Sitar Dancer, in a compact, sound, tiny package. His career was prematurely halted due to the grave illnesses which beset Mrs. Antonelli. Throughout her dreadful ordeals, first with open heart surgery, and then cancer, Ch. Savar was kept in full show coat! Aennchen never gave in, nor would she accept defeat. She was certain she and Ch. Savar would someday stand beside the BIS sign somewhere.

While Ch. Savar never did win a BIS, he did get to show his prowess as a potent stud. In the last litter bred by Aennchen and Tony Antonelli, there were three males by Ch. Savar out of Aennchen's Sharika Dancer. All finished and two became Group winners. One is Group winning Ch. Aennchen's Suni Dancer, owned and shown to his title by Dr. Roger and Nancy Brown. Ch. Suni won three consecutive four-point majors, a Group 4th and six BBs enroute to his championship. Ch. Suni is now king of the roost at the Browns' home in Omaha, Nebraska. Another is Ch. Aennchen's Sadana Dancer, owned and shown by Mr. and Mrs. E. Kannee. Max, as he is affectionately called, is the sprightly, spirited master of his territory, with the pigmentation of a yearling. He lives in Sun City West, Arizona. Group winning Ch. Aennchen's Soomi Dancer MMA, owned and shown by Nick Cutillo and residing at his parents' home in Lodi, New Jersey, is the last of this trio. Ch. Soomi finished on the Florida circuit in 1974. He was top-winning class dog on that circuit taking two five-point majors, four four-point majors, three BB, and a Group 3rd enroute to his title. Ch. Soomi is bright, alert, and sound. He has passed on his superb qualities to his many champion offspring.

Other Aennchen champions of note include Ch. Aennchen's Manipuri Dancer, Ch. Aennchen's Sisa Dancer, Ch. Aennchen's Pooki Dancer, owned by Messrs. Oberstar and Ward, Ch. Aennchen's Shree Dancer, Ch. Aennchen's Sisa Dancer, Ch. Aennchen's Surah Dancer, Ch. Aennchen's Moltini Dancer, Ch. Aennchen's Rava Dancer, Ch. Aennchen's Shah Dancer and Ch. Aennchen's Shambu Dancer.

In addition to the great contributions made to the Maltese breed, in breeding dogs awarded the highest honors, Aennchen and Tony Antonelli also contributed to the foundations of the Maltese fancy as it is today.

In 1957, Aennchen representing the Eastern United States, Eloise Craig the Midwest, and Helen Poggi (then Shiveley) the West, started a movement to consolidate all American Maltese breeders of note into a national Maltese club under the name of the *Maltese Dog Fanciers of America (MDFA)*. Fifty-three names made up the charter membership. Meetings were held East and West. A constitution and by-laws were drawn up. Regional matches were held and new applicants sought membership. The AKC files were overflowing with official papers, pictures, new bulletins, club papers (*The Maltese Gazette*). Everything that could help to gain AKC recognition was done.

On June 10, 1958, Aennchen, loaded with documents required for recognition, boarded a bus in the driving rain for AKC headquarters. On her arrival, she had to pass through many doors, delayed for hours, but would not give up until she could meet the right person, Mr. Brownell. Their meeting made history for the Maltese. Mr. Brownell was greatly impressed with her credentials and very interested in the Club's efforts so far, but it would take a minimum of five years to complete the requirements. Elated, Aennchen returned home to report by Western

Union: *"To Maltese Dog Fanciers of America, Inc.: Message—Mr. Brownell very impressed with data. Looks encouraging. Love, Aennchen."*

In 1960, Aennchen went to San Francisco for the Golden Gate show. She brought with her Ch. Lakshmi Dancer who topped the breed. But her real reason for going was to meet with members of the Maltese Dog Fanciers Association to discuss a plan for merger of the two existing clubs, MDFA and AMA. This was the AKC's wish in order to establish a "parent club" that would eventually gain AKC recognition. It was a difficult decision, for it meant the end to a very active, strong breeder-exhibitor club. Thanks to Aennchen, the group was convinced it was the only thing to do and a unanimous "yes" vote resulted in favor of an attempt to establish a parent Maltese club through merger of the two existing groups.

On April 4, 1961, Aennchen with her committee, met with Mr. Alfred Dick, AKC executive secretary. Facts and figures previously polled by Tony Antonelli were received with surprise and satisfaction. Finally, after subsequent meetings on July 25 and October 1, at a meeting in New York, the American Maltese Association was born on December 3, 1961. Five anxious years of hard work had accomplished a consolidation of Maltese owners into ONE organization.

Immediately the Antonellis launched the campaign for AKC recognition. They piloted the new organization through financial difficulties, and the many required matches. Finally, eight years later, on June 10, 1969, the American Maltese Association became an AKC member Club with a membership of nearly 400. Aennchen's dream had come true.

Tony, of course, had been very much involved in this effort, as well. Tony, it may be said, was the master planner of this talented and motivated duo. As he planned out and executed the Aennchen Dancers' breeding program, with his great artistic touch and flair, so too did he formulate all else with which he and Aennchen were to become involved.

As mentioned earlier, Tony was an educator in the fine arts. He was responsible for the imaginative ads, which told the world about the Aennchen Maltese Dancers.

Indeed, the world did hear about and see the Aennchen Maltese. They were seen on numerous television programs, in fashion shows, and in commercial ads. In the April issues of *American Home, Good Housekeeping, Better Homes and Gardens* and *McCall's* magazines, Ch. Raja Yoga and Aennchen's Lord Krishna modeled in an ad for Johnson's Wax. Additional dogs were used in Revlon ads, as well, appearing in such magazines as *Vogue* and *Mademoiselle.*

Tony designed original stationery, cards and notes for Aennchen's correspondence. Every year he designed and executed their novel Christmas cards. He did a series of head studies, unique in themselves, depicting the many facial expressions of the Maltese. To say they are superb is to understate.

Ch. Aennchen's
Suni Dancer.

The perfect balance and elegant beauty of 3½ pound Ch. Aennchen's Sitar Dancer are readily apparent in this photo portrait.

Ch. Aennchen's Sitar Dancer (left) and her litter brother, Ch. Aennchen's Tarzan Dancer, graced the cover of *Pure-Bred Dogs— American Kennel Gazette.*
Courtesy of the AKC

Tony with the last litter bred by the Antonellis.

Aennchen family portrait, Ch. Aennchen's Siva Dancer (center), Ch. Aennchen's Taja Dancer (right), and Ch. Aennchen's Tasia Dancer (left).

The Antonellis were nominated for *Kennel Review's* "Breeder of the Year" award, in both 1969 and 1970. Anna Katherine Nicholas, in her review of Toys for 1967, wrote in *Popular Dogs* magazine,

> If the Toy fancy awarded a citation to an outstanding breeder, certainly it would go to Aennchen Antonelli, for the fantastic record she has attained in producing Best in Show Maltese. Just think of Poona, Toy, Sari and T. J., among those either bred by Aennchen or from her stock. Recall the quality of the competition in which they win, and send along that basket of dogwood or an orchid to this extremely talented breeder.

Aennchen was one of those bubbling personalities one seldom meets. Her enthusiasm was contagious. Her indomitable spirit, in the face of great pain resulting from major surgery, and her will to live were a true inspiration to all who knew her.

Aennchen lost her long, painful battle to cancer on February 2, 1975, but lives on in the memory of many, not only as a true pillar of the Maltese, but as the kind of friend one is privileged to have.

Aennchen was a vice president of the AMA, the Progressive Dog Club and the Dog Fanciers' Club in New York City. She was past president of the Maltese Dog Fanciers of America.

The Aennchen family, in addition to breeders and exhibitors, also included members of royalty, and the political and theatrical worlds. In spite of their very active lives, the Antonellis always found the time to encourage newcomers, and to share family experiences and reminiscences about their wonderful years in the Maltese fancy.

Near the time Aennchen died, most of the younger dogs were given to friends. The author got two of the last males of their breeding, Ch. Soomi, mentioned earlier, and Ch. Aennchen's Shiko Dancer MMA, both by Ch. Savar out of different bitches. He also got Ch. Aennchen's Tasia Dancer, a Ch. T. J. daughter sired by Ch. Siva, and Ch. Aennchen's Pompi Dancer MMA, a half-sister to Ch. Soomi, through their dam, and sired by Ch. Taran Dancer, Ch. Sitar's litter brother. He was also given a 2 lb., 9 oz. bitch bred by Jerline Brooker, Ch. Jerline's Libra Dancer, which he showed and finished for Aennchen. Ch. Libra finished with two five-point majors.

Following Aennchen's death, Tony Antonelli retired from teaching. He sold the house in Waldwick, New Jersey, and moved to Florida, with the few dogs he had left, including Ch. Savar. He occasionally will make an appearance at a local show, as a spectator only.

Other Important Breeders

Several other breeders worthy of note in this period would include Liz Walker, of Lizara Maltese, who showed the multiple Best in Show Am., Can. Ch. Lizara's Karousel, co-owned with John Stoecker.

Ch. Aennchen's Soomi Dancer MMA.

Another Ch. Aennchen's Savar Dancer son, Ch. Aennchen's Shiko Dancer.

Roma Pikarsky, Casa Remmo Maltese of Florida, based her line on a Ch. Shikar Dancer son, Ch. Windrift's Fantabulous.

Marjorie and Norman Nelson, Conquest Maltese of New Mexico, are noted for Ch. Conquest's Mr. Chips, who finished in three shows and BIS winner, Ch. San Su Kee Ringleader Too.

William and Ida Mae Marsland of Youngstown, Ohio, owners of BIS Ch. Maltacello's Issa of Buckeye, shown by Dorothy White.

Mrs. Fran Duncan of Duncan Maltese, noted for Ch. Duncan's Nicholas, in 1972 won a BIS from the classes.

Sally Thrall Campbell of Salteer Maltese in Florida was most noted for multiple BIS Am., Can. Ch. Salteer Glory Seeker, owned by Irene Reasons, and later Mr. and Mrs. D. Passe.

Of note is Rose Infante, also of Florida, whose Infante Maltese, a combination of Aennchen, Bobbelee and Marcris bloodlines, produced the sire of multiple BIS Ch. Oak Ridge Country Charmer, namely, Ch. Infante's Mystic Caper.

Other noteworthy breeders and kennels include: Dorothy Hochrein, Mil-Ottie Maltese; Lucille Carter, Cal-Mar Maltese; Margaret Spilling Inmann, Shareen Maltese; Loretta Zuckman, Ha-Lo Maltese; Bonnie Bounell, Midas Touch Kennels; Ruth Eckes, Eckes' Maltese; Kitten Haven; Pat Connelly and Charlcee Burns, Pachar's Maltese, Houston, Texas; Helen Johnson, Le Grand Maltese; Norma and George Kantellis, Villa Norma Maltese; Marcia Keith, Markeith's Maltese; Betty J. O'Donnell, Midhill Maltese; Virginia Pantaloni, Pantaloni Maltese; Margaret Shieves, Schmar's Maltese; Joyce Steen, Malsteen Maltese; Pat Clark, Cla-Mal Maltese; Dorothy Faust, Wynfield Maltese; Carol Fellows, LaLace Maltese; Claudette LeMay, Sugartown Kennels; Juanita Lewis; A. Piper; Marcia Richardson, Sabrina's Maltese; Mary Taylor, Margese Maltese; Alfredo Tollis, Alfredo Maltese; Verna Reed; Mrs. and Miss Irvine, Irvine's Maltese; and Arline Grady, D'Arlene's Maltese, among numerous others.

3

The American Maltese
Fancy Into the 1980s

THE AUTHOR was first introduced to the beauty and charm of the Maltese in 1961 by his high school art instructor, Tony Antonelli. Tony brought news articles and press clippings into class about Aennchen's Poona Dancer and Anna Marie Stimmler's Ch. Aennchen's Toy Dancer. Mr. Cutillo later visited at the Antonelli home, where Aennchen personally introduced him to several of their charming beauties. He was enchanted by both the Maltese dogs, and Aennchen. He decided he would, upon finishing school, acquire a Maltese of his own. Meanwhile, his association with Tony Antonelli grew very close. They developed a strong friendship, with great respect and admiration for one another.

Aennchen's Dancers (with Nick Cutillo)

After graduating high school, Mr. Cutillo studied fashion design in New York City as a scholarship student. Upon graduation, he moved to New York City, got his first position as a designer, and felt it was the proper time to have his own Maltese. He went to Aennchen, who had no show prospect herself then available.

Mr. Cutillo was directed to Aga-Lynn Kennels on Long Island. He acquired his first Maltese in 1968, Aennchen's Yuki of Aga-Lynn (Ch. Aennchen's Timhi Dancer × Joanne-Chen's Fan Dancer), an eight-month-old bitch, with pleasant head and lovely coat. Mr. Cutillo learned upon this bitch the rigors of coat care. She was always the bridesmaid, never the bride in the show ring with 32 reserve wins.

Mr. Cutillo remained staunch in his dedication to Yuki, though she never won a point. His dedication and perseverance were rewarded when Aennchen and Tony presented him with Ch. Aennchen's Tasia Dancer, a half sister of the great Ch. Poona Dancer. Ch. Tasia shared the same sire as Ch. Poona, the great Ch. Aennchen's Siva Dancer. Ch. Tasia's dam was the lovely and acclaimed BIS Ch. Aennchen's Taja Dancer.

Ch. Tasia finished her championship at the 1972 AMA Specialty, held with the International KC show in Chicago, Illinois. She was awarded a five-point major there, taking WB, BW and BOS over specials, to Ch. Joanne-Chen's Maya Dancer, winner of the Specialty that year. Ch. Maya went on to win BIS at that show. Ch. Tasia was a consistent winner in the breed ring, placing in the Toy Group on numerous occasions.

While showing Yuki and Ch. Tasia, Mr. Cutillo became a very close friend to Aennchen. Ch. Savar Dancer was being shown at the time, so Aennchen and Nick drove together to many dog shows. It was during those countless hours on the road that Aennchen exchanged ideas and thoughts about the breed with Nick. At the shows, Nick would help Aennchen, and she would instruct Nick on the proper way to prepare a Maltese for the show ring.

Ch. Aennchen's Pompi Dancer MMA (Ch. Aennchen's Taran Dancer × Aennchen's Sharika Dancer) was next to arrive at the Cutillo household. Ch. Pompi proved herself a worthy dam, producing three litters of one puppy each. Each finished and became champion producers.

While Ch. Pompi was being shown, Aennchen suffered several physical setbacks. "The family" came to her aid, helping to keep all the Aennchen Dancers in condition.

At one time, all of the Aennchen Dancers, including those being shown and those retired from the ring, were kept in full, show coats. The Antonellis never oiled nor wrapped their Maltese, as dogs kept in that way were esthetically displeasing to them. A handful of Aennchen's closest friends would appear at her home once or twice a week to share grooming chores, keep her company and help lift her spirits.

During this time Ch. Aennchen's Savar Dancer, the last dog Aennchen showed, was used at very limited stud. One of his litters was out of Aennchen's Sharika Dancer, a Ch. Siva and Ch. Taza granddaughter, whelped July 17, 1972.

It was a litter of three outstanding males. Two were placed—one to Dr. Roger and Nancy Brown, to become Group winning Ch. Aennchen's Suni Dancer; the second to Gene and Anne Kannee, to become Ch. Aennchen's Sadana Dancer.

The third brother remained with the Antonellis. They came to call him "Sexi," for obvious reasons. He was given to Nick as a birthday present, after he had cared for and come to know little "Sexi" very well over several months at the Antonellis' home. Renamed Aennchen's Soomi Dancer, he became the third champion in this all champion litter, that was to be the last bred by the Antonellis. Ch. Soomi was BB from the classes at his very first show. The next time out he was awarded a four-point major and BB over several champions. He finished the day placing Toy Group 3rd. Ch. Soomi then took a short trip to Florida in 1974, where he became the top-winning class dog on the Florida Circuit that year, taking WD in four out of the six shows, and gaining two four-point and two five-point majors. Ch. Soomi had a very limited specials career. Shown just 19 times, he won 18 BBs, one BOS, one Group 1st, one Group 2nd, two Group 3rds and two Group 4ths.

Ch. Soomi has had a limited but worthwhile career as a stud, being awarded a Maltese Merit Award (MMA) for siring five champions: Yogi Nimble Vic, Rolynda D'Aennchen, Aennchen's Stela Dancer, Ethanbet's Miss Lacey Love and Aennchen's Cari Krana Dancer.

Ch. Yogi Nimble Vic, out of Mari-Aennchen's Siin Dancer, finished with a Group 1st and three Group 2nds from the classes. He was BB over three specials and a Group 2nd at his very first show.

Ch. Aennchen's Stela Dancer, out of Aennchen's Kara Dancer, finished in five shows, undefeated, with several Group placements. She, like her half-brother Ch. Yogi, excelled in head type and coat.

Ch. Aennchen's Cari Krsna Dancer was the result of breeding Ch. Soomi to Cari Joanne-Chen's Munchkin, owned by Jean Carioli, Cari's Maltesc. Ch. Krsna was a mother twice before beginning her successful show career. She finished at four years and has been much admired by other breeders for her superb type.

Mr. and Mrs. Antonelli had acquired a very tiny, beautiful bitch bred by Mrs. Jerline Brooker of Jerline's Maltese dancers. She was Ch. Jerline's Libra Dancer (Ch. Joanne-Chen's Mini Man Dancer × Benjerbo's Juliette DiNeve). This two pound, nine ounce bitch was sheer perfection in the eyes of the Antonellis. Since Aennchen was unable to enter the ring with Ch. Libra, or "Shorty," she was turned over to the author and finished in record time, with two five-point majors.

The noted Italian journalist, Chiara Pisani, of New York City, owned Aennchen's Kara Dancer. Bred to Ch. Savar, Kara Dancer produced Ch. Aennchen's Shiko Dancer. Shiko, a 3¼ pound dog, was of superb type, being very square, with a dead level topline, gorgous head with expressive eyes, held high on a swanlike, arched neck. His superb conformation was covered by a mantle of correct, flowing, silky hair. His coat was one of the easiest to care for, never matting, and growing at a great rate. This puppy was in specials coat before he was a year old. Ch. Shiko was given as a present to the author on Mrs. Antonelli's birthday. His show career was short, as he swiftly completed his championship, undefeated, with all majors. Ch. Aennchen's Shiko Dancer MMA never took on the rigors of a specials career, but was shown sparingly. He proved a superb stud, siring eight champions in extremely limited breeding. His champion get include

Ch. Aennchen's Soomi Dancer MMA, weighing in at 3¾ pounds, was a Group winner. He was from an all-champion litter, the last litter produced by the Antonellis.

Ch. Aennchen's Shiko Dancer MMA finished his championship undefeated with all majors. Ch. Shiko proved to be an outstanding stud, siring eight champions. He was top producing stud, 1982. Owned and shown by the author.

Aennchen's Cari Apollo Dancer and Aennchen's Cari Jyoti Dancer, littermates; Aennchen Indra Dancer, Le Shiek Dancer DuBarrie, Aennchen's Jnani Dancer, Aennchen's Ananda Dancer and Aennchen's Soada Dancer.

Ch. Shiko died August 4, 1982.

Ch. Aennchen's Soada Dancer, out of Ch. Pompi, finished at ten months in seven shows with two five-point majors and two three-point majors. He took a back seat as a stud, until recently, giving way to his father and uncle, Ch. Soomi. He is currently being used at stud with gratifying results.

Ch. Aennchen's Cari Jyoti Dancer, out of Cari Joanne-Chen's Star Dancer, in one month of shows as a special, won two Group 2nds, two Group 3rds, and one Group 4th. Thereafter, she was retired and bred. Ch. Jyoti's litter brother, Am. & Jap. Ch. Apollo, enjoyed a brief, successful show career here. He was then sold to Japan by his breeder-owner, Mrs. Jean Carioli. Ch. Apollo became a strong stud dog in Japan, siring many champions.

Ch. Aennchen's Jnani Dancer, out of Ch. Pompi, had a brief, successful ring career, garnering three four-point majors. Ch. Jnani is of pure Aennchen breeding, and is a potent stud. After completing his title, Ch. Jnani was given to Mrs. Betty M. Charpie, where he enjoys retirement from the shows and duties as a stud.

The lovely, three and a half pound Ch. Aennchen's Indra Dancer, out of Aennchen's Padu Dancer, was bred by the author and finished in six shows with two five-point majors. At an AMA-supported entry show, Ch. Indra went WB over 16 bitches, for five-points, and then BOS over a large class of specials.

Ch. Aennchen's Ananda Dancer, out of Ch. Pompi, is one of the last bitches of pure Aennchen breeding, having both parents bred by Aennchen and Tony.

Another outstanding dog is Ch. Aennchen Ethanbet Snow Dance, out of Ch. Ethanbet Miss Lacey Love, a Ch. Soomi daughter. This extraordinary dog finished in two weekends at five shows, with three four-point majors. He finished with a BB over specials, at 11 months of age.

Ch. Snow was shown as a special five times and was BB each time. He is now retired and is siring lovely puppies.

As mentioned earlier, the author received his original stock from Mr. and Mrs. Antonelli in the late 1960s and early 1970s. Because his breeding program was based on the Aennchen bloodline, it was Mrs. Antonelli's wish that Mr. Cutillo continue to use the Aennchen prefix.

In the late 1970s, the author introduced several new bitches into his breeding program. He acquired a bitch descended from the Good Time line of Maltese, which had been based upon Jon Vir and Villa Malta breeding. These had been the original foundation bloodlines of the Aennchen line.

Ch. Aennchen's Jnani Dancer, a Ch. Shiko Dancer son of pure Aennchen breeding, bred by the author and co-owned with Betty Charpie.

Ch. Aennchen's Soada Dancer (Ch. Shiko × Ch. Pompi), finished his championship at ten months of age in seven shows. Owned and shown by the author.

Multiple Group-winning Ch. Aennchen's Ruari Dancer had a Group 1st and Group placings from the classes. Bred by the author, owned by Barry Giske.

102

The get from the bitch include Ch. Aennchen's Indra Dancer and her litter sister, Aennchen's Siimi Dancer, co-owned with Mrs. Betty M. Charpie. Siimi has proven herself an outstanding brood bitch. In her first litter, she produced Ch. Aennchen's Ruari Dancer. Ruari had a Group 1st and two Group 2nds from the classes, enroute to his championship. Siimi Dancer has produced eight champion get. Six became champions in 1983, making her top producing bitch that year.

Mr. Cutillo bred his Ch. Soomi Dancer to a bitch of pure Villa Malta breeding. From this he obtained a pick of litter bitch, Ch. Rolynda D'Aennchen. Rosie, at nine months, won a five-point major and BOS, and the following weekend was awarded a three-point major and a BB over specials, on the way to her title. One of the newer champions for the Aennchen Dancers is Ch. Aennchen's Arjuna Dancer, a much-admired bitch, possessing a lovely head and superb coat. Ch. Arjuna, who was BW every time she was WB, has produced a litter of two bitches by Ch. Snow Dance. Both have produced champions themselves.

One of the only sons of Ch. Aennchen's Soomi Dancer, Aennchen's Soomi3un Dancer, has been well received in the ring. He is owned by Shirley Patterson.

Others of Mr. Cutillo's noteworthy Aennchen Dancers include Ch. Vijar, Saida, Gita, Jiva, Nabu, Maurya, Isvara, litter sister to Ch. Ruari, and Abdu, owned by AKC judge Dolores Woods. Miss Woods is training Abdu for both the conformation and obedience rings.

Nicholas Cutillo maintains a close relationship with Mrs. Betty M. Charpie, Char Mar Maltese, of Cleveland Heights, Ohio. Mrs. Charpie is devoted to the well-being of her dogs, striving constantly for the betterment of the breed.

The author co-owns several dogs with her, including Aennchen's Mancka Dancer, Aennchen's Sidhu Dancer and Aennchen's Shadra Dancer as well as Char Mar's Julia, Char Mar's Magnolia, Char Mar's Alexandra and Char Mar's Melissa. These Char Mar dogs are basically of Aennchen, Joanne-Chen breeding.

The author is an active member of the dog fancy. He was president and AKC delegate of the AMA. He also served on the board of directors of the parent club. He was president of the Metropolitan Area Maltese Association, a member club of the AMA, for many years. He is a current member of the Maltese Club of Greater Houston, and former member of the California Maltese Club.

Mr. Cutillo has been guest speaker at numerous organizations, speaking on the Maltese. These included a presentation for the Dog Judges' Association symposium in New York City; the Progressive Dog Club; the Manhattan Savings Bank's Annual Dog presentation, on several occasions.

He has also made many contributions to publications dealing with the Maltese, including the official AMA news magazine, the *Maltese Rx*. He has been a contributing author for *Pure-bred Dogs—American Kennel Gazette.*

Nicholas Cutillo continues in his endeavors to keep within the Maltese fancy those ideas and ideals which were so strongly instilled in him by the late, great, Aennchen, and her wonderful husband, Tony Antonelli.

Cari

Mrs. Jean Carioli established her Cari Maltese in Huntington, New York, based on Joanne-Chen, Aennchen and Villa Malta bloodlines. Her kennel was always kept small, and puppies were reared in the home. With her limited stock, Jean produced some outstanding winners.

Some of her foundation bitches included Joanne-Chen's Jeweled Dancer, Lyndale's Miss America and Ch. Joanne-Chen's Sniffles Dancer.

Noteworthy dogs bred here include Ch. Joanne Chen's Mini Man Dancer by Ch. Joanne-Chen's Maya Dancer. Ch. Mini Man took his first major from the puppy class and finished at one year in less than two months of showing. Handled by Jane Forsyth and Wendy Carioli, he had two BBs over specials. He proved to be an outstanding stud, and was later sold to Japan.

Ch. Cari Joanne-Chen's White Radar, CDX, is owned by Dolores Woods. Am. & Can. Ch. Cari Joanne-Chen's Charisma was co-owned by Sharmion Aune Foucault and Mrs. Carioli. Ch. Joanne-Chen's Carime Dancer was bred by Mrs. Carioli and owned by Joanne Hesse.

Mrs. Carioli bred to both Ch. Savar Dancer sons owned by the author. Breeding Cari Joanne-Chen's Munchkin Dancer to Ch. Soomi Dancer, Ch. Aennchen's Cari Krsna Dancer was produced. Breeding Cari Joanne-Chen's Star Dancer to Ch. Aennchen's Shiko Dancer produced a two champion litter, Ch. Aennchen's Cari Jyoti Dancer owned by the author and Ch. Cari Aennchen's Apollo Dancer, sold to Japan after finishing.

Brown's Dancers

Dr. Roger and Nancy Brown of Omaha, Nebraska, have bred and shown Maltese in both the conformation and obedience since 1963. Their breeding is based upon the Joanne-Chen and Aennchen bloodlines. They are strong believers in line breeding.

The Browns originally lived near Washington, D.C. Dr. Brown, a veterinarian, specialized in cataract and other eye surgery for dogs. Working with a research colleague, he had access to equipment which uses ultrasound methods to remove cataracts. He and his compatriot were the only veterinarians in the United States to have pioneered, and to have had the opportunity to use and do research with this apparatus.

Nancy Brown wrote the "Health and Education" column for the AMA newsletter, *The Maltese Rx,* for several years and she and Roger co-

104

Ch. Curi Joanne-Chen's White Radar, CDX, one of the few Maltese to attain both a championship and a CDX title. Owned by Dolores Woods.

Multiple Group-winning Ch. Aennchen's Hindi Dancer, a Ch. Aennchen's Siva Dancer daughter, owned by Dr. Roger and Nancy Brown.

Ch. Kaga of Khandese, owned by Dr. Roger and Nancy Brown.

Group-winning Ch. Sun Canyon California Kid, bred and owned by Miriam Thompson.

Ch. Cari Joanne-Chen's Bar Bar, owned by Mrs. Jean Carioli.

authored the Maltese column in *Popular Dogs* after Aennchen's retirement. Nancy helped found the Potomac Maltese Fanciers Club.

The Browns began in Maltese with Walker's Smart Angel. From Angel they bred Ch. Kaga of Khandese (by Cla-Mal Sir Jumbie), the first of their breeding using the Khandese prefix.

The Browns were attracted to the type and qualities of the Aennchen Maltese. They were directed to Mrs. Joanne Hesse, from whom they purchased Joanne-Chen's Meiya Dancer, Ch. Joanne-Chen's Dancing Shiek, Ch. Joanne-Chen's Theri Dancer, which they co-owned with Mrs. Hesse for a time, and the lovely Ch. Joanne-Chen's Sheeta Dancer, WB and BW at the 1968 Pittsburgh Specialty.

Aennchen presented the Browns with the lovely Aennchen's Hindi Dancer (by Ch. Sim Dancer). They showed her to her championship and an impressive show record. She won a number of Group placements enroute to her championship and went on to become a multiple Group winner.

From the last litter of three male champions bred by Aennchen and Tony Antonelli, the Browns received Group winning Ch. Aennchen's Suni Dancer mentioned earlier.

The Browns dropped their original Khandese suffix, and adopted Brown's Dancers in naming their dogs.

Mrs. Shirley Derhamner of Crofton, Maryland, owns a litter sister to Ch. Joni Dancer, Ch. Brown's Saci Dancer. Mrs. Derhamner also owned and showed Ch. Sakhi of Khandese (Ch. Mike Mar's Joanne-Chen Dancer × Martin's Smart Angel), bred by the Browns. Ch. Sakhi was WB and BW for a five-point major at the 1971 Westminster show.

As mentioned earlier, the Browns were active in obedience as well as conformation. Two of their titled dogs were Brown's Dandi Dancer, CDX, and Joanne-Chen's Gay Dancer, CD.

The Browns are not now active in the ring, but their dedication to the breed remains strong. Dr. Brown spoke on the Maltese before the Dog Judges Association in New York City, sitting on a panel which included the author and Frank Oberstar.

Kannee

Mrs. Anne Kannee and her husband Gene have been involved in the Maltese fancy since the early 1960s when Mrs. Kannee saw a pet Maltese, and became determined to own one. She acquired their Kannee's Jungle Gem (Tarzan) over the objections of Mr. Kannee. The misgivings evaporated quickly as the Kannee household became firmly dedicated to the breed. Within time, a second Maltese, Duncan's Kannee Jane, a bitch, complemented their home. The Kannees now had their own Tarzan and Jane!

Mrs. Kannee met Aennchen Antonelli, and the two soon became friends. Seeking a show quality bitch, Mrs. Kannee was directed by Aennchen to the Aga-Lynn Kennels, from which she purchased her first show bitch, Ch. Aga-Lynn's Boona Cheemer, a lovely headed and coated bitch, sired by Ch. Aennchen Timhi Dancer. Ch. Boona Cheema won two five-point majors and was BB over specials, enroute to her championship. Mrs. Kannee also got one of the last dogs bred by Mr. and Mrs. Antonelli, Ch. Aennchen's Sadana Dancer, mentioned earlier.

Killarney

Hazel Hamm has bred Maltese for almost three decades. She purchased her first, a bitch named Jambon Rosie O'Grady, from Ray Eckes. Her kennel name is Killarney and her foundation bloodline is Villa Malta. Hazel has provided many newcomers with good breeding stock and sound advice.

Mrs. Hamm sometimes uses outcross breeding; she believes, generally, that line breeding is better. Her closest breeding was father to daughter, and produced very good results.

Valley High

Peggy Lloyd, of Sugar Land, Texas, has been breeding and exhibiting Maltese since 1968. She has been very involved in all aspects of the fancy. Her foundation bloodlines are Aennchen and Villa Malta.

She began with Ann Morris, breeding the Valley High Maltese. Their top-winning bitch, which was among the top ten Maltese in the country when being shown, was Am., Can. Ch. Valley High Sugar Cookie. Another bitch of note bearing the Valley High prefix is Valley High's Misty Pebbles MMA, dam of four champions. Ch. Valley High's Wish Me Love was co-owned with Richard Reid. Two champions by Ch. Diavolino of Villa Malta at Valley High were Ch. Valley High First Mate and Ch. Valley High's Rockin' Robin.

Miss Lloyd's major stud is the Group winner, Am., Mex., Int. Ch. Mac's Apache Joray of Everon, bred by Evelyn Schaefer. To date, Ch. Mac is the sire of seven champions.

Pegden

Miss Lloyd's association with Miss Morris was concluded, and the Pegden Kennels were formed in association with the professional handler, Denny Mounce. Miss Lloyd, herself, became a professional handler.

Noted Pegden Maltese are Ch. Pegden's Foolish Pleasure, 3½ pound bitch which finished at 11 months; Ch. Pegden's Top O' the Morning; Ch.

Am., Mex. & Int. Ch. Mac's Apache Joray of Everon, Group winner, owned and shown by Peggy Lloyd.

BIS-winning Ch. Russ Ann a Touch of Class, bred by Anna Mae Hardy, owned by Maurice Melvin.

Pegden's Majic Touch; Ch. Pegden's Wishful Thinking and Ch. Pegden's Luck O' the Irish (Ch. Rebecca's Desert Valentineo × Al Mar's Magic Genie).

Miss Lloyd is a charter member and past president of the Maltese Club of Greater Houston, and served on the board of the AMA several times.

Tical

Another Texas fancier, Maurice Melvin and her Tical Kennel, is located in Dallas.

Her first Maltese, Ma Key's Sea Mist of Fisa, produced only two litters, both by BIS Ch. San Su Kee Star Edition. Three became champions: Ch. Tical's Sundae Mist, Ch. Tical's That's Class and Ch. Tical's Delta Dawn, who finished as a puppy. Tical also owns BIS Ch. Russ Ann a Touch of Class, Ch. Joanne-Chen Aennchen Tiny Tim and Ch. Al. Mar's Friendly Ghost.

Joanne-Chen

Mrs. Joanne Hesse, of New Haven, Indiana, has an important place in Maltese history. Mrs. Hesse, originally from Long Island, New York, was, in the late 1950s and early 1960s, a close associate of the Antonellis.

Her foundation dogs were of the Aennchen bloodline. Her early breeding was shown with the Co Ca He's Aennchen prefix. Notable among these are BIS Ch. Co Ca He's Aennchen Toy Dancer, owned by the Stimmlers, and her own BIS Ch. Co Ca He's Aennchen Raja Dancer.

Many of Mrs. Hesse's early winners were by Ch. Aennchen's Shikar Dancer. Bred by the Antonellis, Ch. Shikar was shown by Mrs. Hesse and became a champion in 1959, at nine months.

Mrs. Hesse bred eight BIS dogs, and over half a dozen Group winners and multiple Group winners. The list of the champions bred by her is long and impressive. For a time her prefix became Jo-Aennchen. Ultimately, the Joanne-Chen prefix was developed and used on many of her top-winning dogs.

All her stud dogs have been of either the Aennchen or the Joanne-Chen bloodline. One exception was Ch. Cla-Mal Sir Jumbie, which she introduced into her breeding program about ten years ago. There were many rumors as to why an outside dog was introduced into the highly successful Joanne-Chen line, most were negative. However, Mrs. Hesse simply liked the dog.

Noteworthy of her BIS dogs is Ch. Joanne-Chen's Maya Dancer, owned by Joe and Mamie Gregory. Ch. Maya was shown by professional handler Peggy Hogg to all his wins. He died at Mrs. Hogg's kennel in 1980. Ch. Maya, the top-winning BIS Maltese to date, had an impressive show career. In 1972, at the AMA national Specialty, he went on to win Group 1st at International which included the Specialty, and then BIS over 3,975

Ch. Joanne-Chen's
Mino Maya Dancer,
number one Maltese
and top Toy dog
in 1980, bred by
Joanne Hesse.

Multiple Group-
winning Ch. San Su
Kee Joanne-Chen
Rocket, bred by
Joanne Hesse and
owned by Dorothy
Palmersten, San Su
Kee Maltese.

Multiple BIS winner
Ch. Joanne-Chen's Sweet Shi
Dancer, bred and owned by
Joanne Hesse.

dogs. Ch. Maya was BB at Westminster in 1972 and 1973. His final record was 43 BIS and 134 Group 1sts. In 1972, Maya was awarded the Quaker Oats award for top Toy dog (he was number two Toy dog, all breeds) and the Kennel Review award for top Toy, as well. His handler, Mrs. Hogg was honored as well for being the best limited handler.

Another "great" bred by Mrs. Hesse is Ch. Joanne-Chen's Mino Maya Dancer, owned by Mrs. B. Tenerowicz. Ch. Mino's record placed him as #1 Maltese and #1 Toy in 1980. He was the top Group winning Maltese in 1980, with 50 1sts and won the Quaker Oats award for top Toy dog. Ch. Mino's final record included 29 BIS, 150 Group 1sts, two AMA Specialty BBs, including one from the Veteran Class.

Multiple BIS Ch. Joanne-Chen's Sweet She Dancer MMA, sired by Ch. Mike Mar's Joanne-Chen Dancer, was a top show dog and a top producer. Her champion get includes Ch. Joanne-Chen's Sweet He Dancer, top stud dog and #2 Maltese in the United States in 1968. Ch. Sweet He was sired by Ch. Joanne-Chen's Shikar Dancer. Ch. Sweet He was a consistent winner in the ring in 1969, taking BB 25 of the 26 times he was shown.

Other American breeders having added Joanne-Chen stock to their kennels are Mrs. DiGiacomo, Kathan Maltese, Carol Klotz, Joanne Dinsmore, Anne Marie Wright, and the Browns.

In Canada, Mrs. Glenna Fierleller acquired one of the last Ch. Aennchen's Shikar Dancer children, Am., Can. Ch. Joanne-Chen's Shieka Dancer. This lovely, four-pound bitch was most successful in the U.S.A., and Canada, as well.

Bar None

Mrs. Michel Roberson Perlmutter has been breeding Maltese since 1963 but had been in dogs since childhood. She originally approached Mrs. Antonelli to acquire a Maltese. The breed struck her fancy, and she greatly admired the Aennchen Dancers, in particular. Unable to supply her with a dog, Aennchen referred Michel to Joanne Hesse.

From this introduction, a close friendship developed between these two ladies. In addition to their dog dealings, Mrs. Hesse was an inspiration for Mrs. Perlmutter, in striving for her goals.

The Bar None bloodline is based upon a Ch. Aennchen's Shikar Dancer son and daughter. Her first dog, Ch. Joanne-Chen's Dancing Shiek, was affectionately known as Chief. Her first bitch, Ch. Joanne-Chen's Baby Doll Dancer, was bred to Chief. From this breeding came the prolific Ch. Bar None Scribble, in 1967. Ch. Scribble did not complete her championship until she was seven and a half years old. Her show record, despite her age, is impressive as she finished undefeated, going BB over specials. She produced three litters before finishing. Eight puppies came from these litters; seven finished. Two of Ch. Scribble's champions were Group winners. In addition, Ch. Scribble is granddam of two BIS dogs.

As mentioned earlier, the Bar None bloodline was based solely upon Ch. Aennchen's Shikar Dancer. Later, additional dogs were acquired from Joanne Hesse, as well as one Sun Canyon dog, Ch. Sun Canyon Fancy Free.

Mrs. Perlmutter bred and owned multiple Group-winning Ch. Bar None Popeye. Ch. Popeye began his show career in the East, where he won several Groups. He went to professional handler Tim Brazier in California, where he was a consistent Toy Group winner.

Mrs. Perlmutter began using the services of professional handler Dee Shepherd with her Group winning Ch. Bar None Buckaneer. Ch. Bucky won the Toy Group at the Trenton Kennel Club show in strong competition.

The year 1980 was very good for the Bar None Maltese at the AMA national Specialty. Ch. Bar None Sally May was WB and BW while Ch. Bar None Electric Lady was BOS to Ch. Joanne-Chen's Mino Maya Dancer. Later that evening, Mrs. Perlmutter was named AMA breeder of the year.

Recently, Mrs. Perlmutter has finished Ch. Bar None Joanne-Chen Jama Boy. She also has just completed a specials career for her Best in Show Ch. Bar None Big Man On Campus, handled by Dee Shepherd.

Windrift

Vivian Horney Edwards has, for many years, been breeding the Windrift Maltese, in Florida. She purchased her first bitch, Fairy Fay's Nick Nack, from Elvira Cox.

As Mrs. Edwards became more familiar with the breed, she came to admire the quality and type of the Aennchen Maltese. She was especially impressed by the universally acclaimed Ch. Aennchen's Shikar Dancer. Breeding Ch. Shikar to his daughter, Sultan of Windrift, resulted in her prolific foundation stud, Ch. Windrift's Fantabulous. Also produced was Ch. Windrift's Dreamspun. This was an immensely successful father to daughter inbreeding. For many years, lasting into the early 1970s, Ch. Windrift's Fantabulous remained the top stud at Windrift, producing numerous champions, both for Mrs. Edwards and others.

Especially noteworthy of the Windrift dogs are Ch. Inge of Windrift MMA, producer of five champion get and 3½ pound Ch. Oak Hills Dancer of Windrift (Ch. Windrift's Fantabulous × Ch. Julie Ann of Windrift).

Arline Grady of D'Arlene's Maltese bred to Ch. Windrift's Sharazad, producing Chs. D'Arlene's Sasu, Dark Eyes, Taboo and Kiu Kiu. Ch. D'Arlene's Kiu Kiu was the 10th champion for Ch. Sharazad, finishing at 11 months of age.

114

Ch. Bar None Tom Terrific, owned and bred by Michelle
Perlmutter.

Multiple Group-winning
Ch. Bar None Popeye,
bred and owned by
Michelle Perlmutter.

Multiple Group-winning Ch. Joanne-Chen's Teddy Bear
Dancer, bred by Joanne Hesse and owned by Marcia
Hostetler.

The noted stud, Ch. Infante Mystic Caper was acquired from Rose Infante in 1968. Mrs. Edwards later sold Mystic Caper to Alan and Sharon Rhoades of Miami, Florida, in 1969. Upon the Rhoades' divorce, Mystic Caper was sold to Mr. and Mrs. T. Neth of the Oak Ridge Kennels in 1970. Mystic Caper became the Neth's foundation stud dog.

Gayla (with Darlene Wilkinson)

Darlene Wilkinson began in Maltese as a professional handler. Initially she showed Ch. Caramaya's Mister for Shirley Hrabak of Gayla Maltese. Eventually, she and Mrs. Hrabak co-owned several dogs including Ch. Gayla's Hold That Tiger, Ch. Matelase's Nefetari, Ch. Gayla's O Suzannah and Ch. Gayla's Sunrise Serenade.

After the death of Mrs. Hrabak, Mrs. Wilkinson continued using the Gayla prefix in her own breeding program. Later, there was an association between the Gayla Maltese and the Tampier Maltese owned and bred by Sue Kuecher. Noted of the Tampier-Gayla association is Ch. Tampier's-Gayla Pretty Polly.

In 1980, Mrs. Wilkinson announced that Gayla Maltese were forming an association with Joanne Hesse and her new prefix would be Gayla-Joanne-Chen.

Mrs. Wilkinson's daughter Karen was seen in the show ring as a junior handler. She bred, owned and showed her own dogs.

March'en

Marcia Hostetler has had Maltese for 20 years. In 1967, she bought a male and female of the Joanne-Chen bloodlines. Joanne-Chen's Teddy Bear Dancer had a short, successful career. He was specialed only three times and won the Toy Group twice. Sadly, Teddy died at an early age. The bitch was Joanne-Chen's Sheeba Dancer, littermate to BIS Ch. Joanne-Chen's Maya Dancer. Sheeba was a lovely Maltese who was not shown, but was a good producer.

In 1970, Mrs. Hostetler purchased Joanne-Chen's Mini Maid Dancer, who had two litters, consisting of two females and a male who were all finished. One of the females, Ch. March'en Bali Dancer, had three litters with a total of four puppies. Three of them have finished.

Throughout the years, Mrs. Hostetler's only desire has been to produce a few top quality Maltese retaining the honesty of their bloodline. Some of the early March'en Maltese carried the Joanne-Chen prefix. The beautiful Am., Can. Ch. Joanne-Chen Wakham Dancer was one of these.

Due to time limitation, with always one or two in full coat, Mrs. Hostetler has not specialed any of her dogs. All but two of her champions have had Group placements from the classes. Several have had BB wins over BIS specials. All but one of the March'en Maltese have been owner-handled.

Twice Mrs. Hostetler attempted out-cross breedings and was not happy with the results. Her program of line breeding and occasionally inbreeding has consistently given her good results with type, soundness and size. Several March'en Maltese have been issued Dam or Sire of Merit certificates by the American Maltese Association, and several more are eligible.

Mrs. Hostetler's favorite stud dog is Am, Can. Ch. March'en Top Hat Dancer, a son of Ch. Joanne-Chen's Square Dancer and Ch. March'en Bali Dancer. Topper has sired seven litters and five champions with others pointed.

Al Dor

One of the leading forces in the Maltese fancy since 1958 is Mrs. Dorothy Tinker of Las Vegas, Nevada. Mrs. Tinker's Al Dor bloodline is based upon Mrs. Elvira Cox's Fairy Fay bloodline, from whom she received her first important stud dog.

Mrs. Tinker, who owned a pet shop in Las Vegas, was introduced to the breed through a woman who, being on the verge of a nervous breakdown, brought her pet Maltese bitch to Mrs. Tinker, hoping that Mrs. Tinker could help in placing the dog in a good home.

Mrs. Tinker brought the bitch home for a few days. In those few days, her admiration for the breed was established. She bought the bitch, and began the search for a quality stud dog.

Until this time the Tinkers, including Mrs. Tinker's daughter Nancy, were involved in Shetland Sheepdogs. Nancy, a professional handler, has also been closely associated with Maltese. She has judged Puppy Sweepstakes at AMA national Specialties, as well as having been invited to judge Maltese in England.

Mrs. Tinker was a member of the Maltese Dog Fanciers Association, and was helpful in 1962, with its disbanding to form the AMA, in which she and Nancy hold charter memberships. Mrs. Tinker has been active in the California Maltese Club, as well as being founder of the Las Vegas Maltese Fanciers. She has served on the board of the AMA. Several very successful Maltese national Specialties have been held under the superb tutelage of Mrs. Tinker.

The Tinkers' efforts to procure a quality stud resulted in the acquisition of Fairy Fay's Figaro (Ch. Tulio of Villa Malta × Fairy Fay's Rosita), whelped September 24, 1959. Ch. Figaro was shown 12 times, losing only once. He finished with 17 points, ten BBs and four Group placings at one year of age. Eventually, Figaro would also earn championship titles in Bermuda and Mexico. He became foundation stud of the Al Dor line. Figaro was shown in a brace with another early bitch owned by

Mrs. Tinker, Am. & Mex. Ch. Fairy Fay's Kapu. Ch. Figgy, as he was known, became a star on television, as well as in the dog show ring and was one of the most noted Maltese in the West. His final record included five Group 1sts, 25 Group placements and 50 BBs.

The first brood bitch acquired by Mrs. Tinker was Fairy Fay's Staretta, also bred by Mrs. Cox. Staretta lived an active, productive life at Al Dor. She was over 14 years of age at her death. In her first litter, bred to Ch. Figaro, she produced three puppies; all finished. They were, Int. Ch. Al Dor Jollo of Vegas. Ch. Jollo had one Group 1st, 18 placements and 34 BBs. His littermates were Ch. Al Dor Nicy of Vegas and Ch. Al Dor Little Fella of Vegas. Staretta was also the dam of Ch. Al Dor High Hopes of Vegas and Int. Ch. Al Dor Nina of Vegas, by Ch. Figaro. Am. Ch. Nina was sent to England, where she became a multi-national champion.

Mrs. Tinker imported several English dogs, from Margaret White, Vicbritta Maltese. The results were of benefit to the Al Dor line. Her first English import was Ch. Vicbrita As Always MMA. This bitch was by Eng. Ch. Vicbrita Fidelity, who sired a breed winner at Crufts. Ch. As Always was considered to be one of the best bitches out of England at that time. She became a top-producing dam in 1969, producing seven champions, earning her the Maltese Merit Award.

Am. & Mex. Ch. Al Dor Pzazz and his litter sister, Ch. Al Dor Liza Lu (Ch. Fairy Fay's Figaro × Ch. Vicbrita As Always), were bred by Mrs. Tinker, owned by Mrs. Grace Hendrickson Anderson of California, and shown by Nancy Tinker. Ch. Al Dor Pzazz became a multiple Group winner, and was rated in the top ten Maltese at the time. His sister, Ch. Liza Lu was BOS to Dr. Knopf's Ch. Anna Maries White Panther, at the 1971 Westminster show. Mrs. Anderson also owned Ch. Al Dor Pure Magic, out of Ch. Vicbrita As Always. Ch. Vicbrita As Always was also the dam of Ch. Al Dor Esquire.

Three other English imports at Al Dor were Vicbrita Paper Lace, by Eng. Ch. Sebastian, then top Maltese and top Toy in England. Am. & Eng. Ch. Vicbrita Tobias was also at Al Dor. Ch. Tobias was bred to Fairy Fay's Pitti Sing II, producing Ch. Al Dor Kissimee and Ch. Al Dor Rogue. Last of the English imports was Am. & Eng. Ch. Vicbrita Tranquility.

Al Dor Maltese have also been important to several other breeders. Al Dor Kristi, owned by Ann Glenn, produced Ch. Al Dor Randy, CD (by Ch. Maltacello's Romeo). Ch. Randy sired the Group placing Ch. Al Dor's Cherrys Jubilee (out of Fairy Fay's Pitti Sing II). Ch. Cherrys Jubilee was owned and shown by Don Rodgers.

Ch. Al Dor Little Rascal, bred by Mrs. Tinker and owned by Mrs. Agnes Cotterell, sired 13 champions. Ch. Rascal won the Veterans' class at the 1979 AMA national Specialty. Group-winning Ch. Al Dor Zeke of Cotterell was also a product of Mrs. Tinker's association with Mrs. Cotterell.

Dorothy Tinker with Ch. Fairy Fay's Figaro.

Ch. Al-Dor Liza Lu, daughter of Ch. Figaro, was bred by Dorothy Tinker, owned by Grace Anderson and shown by Nancy Tinker.

Multiple Group-winning Ch. Al-Dor Pzazz, son of Ch. Figaro, was bred by Dorothy Tinker, owned by Grace Anderson and shown by Nancy Tinker.

119

Ch. Fairy Fay's Kapu, a half sister to Figaro, is shown here winning a strong Toy Group at Santa Barbara KC, handled by Evonne Chashoudian.

Foundation stock at Rolling Glenn, Ch. Al-Dor Kristi and son, Ch. Rolling Glenn's Dresden, owned by Anne Glenn.

Living in Las Vegas, Mrs. Tinker has had close association with several show business personalities. Ch. Al Dor's High Hopes, dam of a litter of three champions, was retired at the home of veteran actress Shirley Booth.

Grace H. Anderson

Grace Hendrickson Anderson has been a Maltese fancier for many years. Her first was Ch. Issa of Publius, CD.

Mrs. Anderson was introduced to Mrs. Tinker, and several top-winning Al Dors went to her in California. They included Ch. Al Dor Liza Lu, Ch. Al Dor Pzazz and Ch. Al Dor Pure Magic.

For many years Grace edited and published the noteworthy *California Maltese Club Reporter. The Reporter* was the official voice of the California Maltese Club. It was a respected, successful publication, which Mrs. Anderson published free of charge, but for postage. Those in the fancy who were lucky enough to own subscriptions to this excellent newsletter, today own fine collector's items. *The Reporter,* though small in size, was large in quality, information and photographs.

Rolling Glenn

Mrs. Ann Glenn has been in the Maltese fancy since 1969. Originally, she and her Maltese lived on Rolling Glenn farm in Milton, Vermont. While there, she placed a CD degree upon her first Maltese, Rolling Glenn's Aschenia, CDX.

In 1970, the Glenns' home was destroyed by fire. Mrs. D. Tinker, on hearing of the Glenns' tragedy, presented them with Am. & Mex. Ch. Fairy Fay's Peter Pan. Their gratitude for this generous kindness was great.

The Glenns relocated their Rolling Glenn farm first to Williston, Vermont, and finally to Clarkston, Michigan, where they currently reside.

They acquired Ch. Al Dor Kristi and the Rolling Glenn Maltese were established.

By breeding their Ch. Kristi to Mrs. Tinker's Ch. Vicbrita Tobias, litter brothers Ch. Rolling Glenn's Dresden and Ch. Rolling Glen's Westminster resulted.

The entire Glenn family shares in the joy brought to them by their Maltese dogs. Ann's daughters, Heather, Shelley and Lisa have each been at the end of a lead in the show ring.

Alma

Alma Smithson has been an avid Maltese fancier for many years. A breeder and professional handler, Alma judged Puppy Sweepstakes at the 1976 AMA Specialty, in Las Vegas, Nevada.

Ms. Smithson's Alma's Maltese are based on Villa Malta and Vicbrita bloodlines.

Wil-Lan

Lance (Bud) and Willamina (Willie) Howe are from Newark, California. In the fall of 1968, they began to seek the ideal companion dog.

The Maltese was selected as the breed, after reading information available on the Toys. The Howes visited several Maltese kennels, never finding what they wanted close to home.

A year later, on a vacation to Mexico, they visited all the breeders they could locate between their home and Phoenix, Arizona. In Phoenix, they met Alma Smithson, who had a six-week-old male she planned to keep. However, she welcomed the Howes to her home to see the puppy and his parents, and answer any questions they might have about the breed.

A rapport between the Howes and the puppy was formed. The roots of the puppy's quality became apparent when the Howes saw his dam and sire, Al Dor Snow Bunny and Fairy Fay's Peter Pan.

Arrangements were made to have the puppy shipped to California. He was to become Wil-Lan's Mr. Chipper.

The Wil-Lan kennel was named at the suggestion of Dorothy Tinker. Nancy Tinker became Mr. Chipper's handler. In 1970, Nancy showed Mr. Chipper at Westminster, where he placed in his class. That was the beginning.

The Howes then added Reed's De De, Al Dor Snow Bunny, and the famous Wil-Lan's Billy Full O' Fire from Alma Smithson. Billy was an outstanding force in the breed, especially in Northern California. At 4½ pounds, he improved coats, passed on big beautiful eyes, and reduced the size of puppies out of large bitches. Seven of his offspring went into the show ring. One of the more noted was Ch. Gordon's Fire N' Ice, bred by Pauline Dick. These two dogs became their foundation stud dog and bitch.

Together, these two Maltese produced many lovely puppies including Ch. Wil-Lan's Lady Divinity. Ch. Divinity was their first homebred champion. She was shown by both Mrs. Howe and Nancy Tinker.

Billy, bred to Ms. Smithson's Al Dor Lisa, sired a bitch, Ch. Alma's Cameo O' Wil-Lans. Ch. Cameo and Billy became top breeding stock, producing lovely puppies.

On December 30, 1982, Billy Full O' Fire died, followed three weeks later by Ch. Divinity.

The breeding stock at Wil-Lan was nil, as the Howes had sold all of their breeding, due to the demand by the fancy. They purchased new stock, and continue in the show ring as well as their breeding program. The new dogs bring back to Wil-Lan's the same bloodlines behind Bill Full O' Fire, namely Villa Malta and Vicbrita.

122

Ch. Wil-Lan's Billy Full O' Fire, bred by Alma Smithson and owned by the Howes.

Ch. Wil-Lan's Lady Divinity, daughter of Ch. Billy Full O' Fire, owned by the Howes.

Mr. and Mrs. Howe are avid fanciers. They maintain memberships in the AMA. Mrs. Howe is past president of the California Maltese Club, later known as the Bay Area Maltese Club.

Brenda's Fancy

Brenda Morris, of Las Vegas, Nevada, owns Brenda's Fancy Maltese, begun in 1976.

Her first champion, Am. & Mex. Ch. Brenda's Fancy Faye (Ch. Al Dor Randy × Morris' Juliette) was bred and is owned by Ms. Morris. She was shown by Nancy Tinker.

Ms. Morris was elected first president of the Las Vegas Maltese Fanciers (originally called the Southwest Maltese Fanciers), organized in 1976.

Other Maltese at Brenda's Fancy include: Ch. Al Dor Jamboree, co-owned with Dorothy Tinker; Ch. Brenda's Fancy Annie O' Glenn, bred by Ann Glenn; Am. & Mex. Ch. Brenda's Fancy Mande, a daughter of Ch. Fancy Faye; and Ch. Brenda's Fancy Maxim.

Reveille

Dr. Helen Schively Poggi, a chiropractic doctor from California, has been a motivating force and avid fancier of the Maltese dog for many years.

She founded her Reveille Kennel upon her first stud dog, and her first Maltese, Lester's Morning Reveille, in 1957. Morning Reveille was purchased from Mrs. Alfreda Lester, whose dogs descended from Jon Vir's Sensation and Jon Vir's Penelope.

In 1958, at the Santa Clara show, Revie was BB from the classes. Before being claimed by cancer at two years of age, Revie had won 15 BBs and two Group placements, an outstanding record for a Maltese on the West coast at the time. At his death he had sired four champions including Ch. Douglas' Gamina, owned by Margaret Douglas.

In 1958, Dr. Poggi acquired a daughter of Ch. Invicta Nicker, Greer's Sappho, who became the foundation bitch of the Reveille bloodline.

Ch. Wee Holiday Snowman, a son of Ch. Morning Reveille, had a short trip to his championship in 1960. He was BB and Group 1st from the classes at the Two Cities show. The following day he repeated the win at the Sacramento show. He also placed second and third in the Toy group from the classes, with a total of 15 points in four shows.

Maltese champions bearing the Reveille suffix include, Aurora Mimi, Sir Soni Rava, CDX, Sir Jim Jiminy Soni, Robin Rava, owned by Agness Cotterell, Issa Merry Mary, and Lady Saphronia Reveille MMA, dam of three champion get to carry the first Maltese Merit Award.

Six Reveille Maltese champions also earned CD degrees. Some

Reveille dogs bearing CD titles include Ch. Sir Jiminy Rava Reveille, CD, Sir Buddy Soni Reveille, CD, and Sir Joel Morning Reveille, CD.

As of 1980, when Dr. Poggi kept about 20 Maltese, she noted that she owed everything to good, healthy brood bitches.

Dr. Poggi was originally a member of the Maltese Dog Fanciers Association. When the prospect of a national club was proposed, she became very influential in what was to become the AMA, working with Aennchen Antonelli and Eloise Craig. Dr. Poggi became a charter member of the AMA, as well as serving as an officer and on its board of directors.

She has also been active in the California Maltese Club, now the Bay Area Maltese Club. She edited and published that club's newsletter, the *Bay Area Maltese Club Reporter,* for one year before its demise, and helped organize club sanctioned matches.

Perhaps Dr. Poggi will be most remembered by the fancy for her dedicated effort culminating in the publishing of *The American Maltese Heritage,* which she compiled with the help of Pauline Dick. These books were to be the American Maltese family tree from 1888 to 1980. Three installments were planned; two were actually published.

Mrs. V. Leitch, in her book, *The Maltese Dog,* had recorded every Maltese registered by the AKC from 1888 to 1952. In 1952, the AKC established the official stud register. Since then it has recorded only sires and dams producing litters.

Eloise Craig, in the *Maltese Rx,* the official AMA publication, picked up registrations from 1952, and published those from that time through 1963. Errors were common in the early AKC registrations, as well as in other Maltese publications. An attempt was made to correct these errors in *The American Maltese Heritage.*

The first installment begins with the first Maltese registered in the United States in 1888, #9178, Snips, a bitch. It continues through to the "I" registrations.

The second volume was released in 1978. It included those Maltese with certificate registration numbers beginning with "TA," which appeared in the stud register. It also contained a limited amount of information with tips on breeding from a few breeders. The third volume, which was planned but never completed, was to have contained all the "TB" registrations.

Primrose

Marge Stuber has bred her Primrose Maltese in Lima, Ohio, since 1958. She began with an English foundation matron, Ch. Vicbrita Rozeta, showing her to her championship, owner-handled. Ch. Rozeta produced eight puppies in four litters; four finished.

Mrs. Stuber usually followed line breeding, but eventually decided that too close relationships are not desirable, regardless of the excellence of

Ch. Wee Holiday Snowman, Group winner, owned by Dr. Poggi.

Group-winning Ch. Primrose Little Toot of Al-Mar, owned by Marge Stuber.

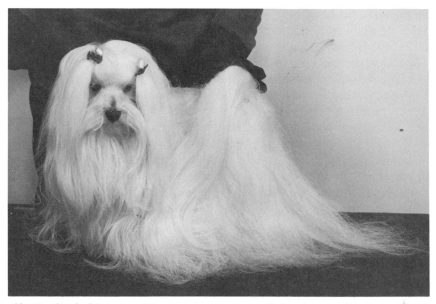

Ch. Gaylord of Primrose Place had a coat seven inches longer than he was tall. Bred by Marge Stuber and owned by Lillian Harrington.

the breeding stock. Breeding on a very limited scale, Marge finished some 45 Primrose champions. She rarely had more than three bitches at one time. Mrs. Stuber does not kennel her dogs. The Primrose Maltese are allowed to run free in her home and enjoy a fenced yard, in which they play.

Marge both breeds and acquires puppies. She has sent her Primrose Maltese to handlers to be shown, as well as successfully showing some herself. The Primrose name appears today in the pedigrees of many of the top-winning Maltese in the United States.

Mrs. Stuber's Group-winning Am., Can. Ch. Beland's Little Smarty was a four pound double grandson of Musi of Villa Malta. This dog, as well as Group-winning Ch. Andrena of Primrose Place, was shown for Mrs. Stuber by then professional handler, Edna Voyles.

Am., Can. Ch. Primrose Little Toot of Al Mar was a 3½ pound Group winner from the classes.

Ch. Primrose Amanda produced Ch. Trina of Primrose, CD, who finished with four majors, breeder-owner handled. A champion niece of Trina was the lovely Primrose Pica-Dilly.

The first CD dog to be bred by Marge was Primrose Bonnie Petite, CD. Mrs. Stuber has been as active and interested in obedience as in conformation.

Mrs. Stuber has enjoyed associations with several other breeders of note. Included among these are Mrs. Trudie Dillon of Tutees Toysome Acres Kennels. A number of important dogs resulted from this association.

Ch. Primrose Winget of the West, which was bred by Marge, out of Vicbrita's Serena Primrose, is owned by Dr. and Mrs. J. R. West of Leighton, Utah. Mrs. West, an artist, created a sculpture of a Maltese based upon their dogs. It was called *Maltese in Motion* and was offered as a prize at an AMA Specialty.

Marge Stuber is a charter member of the American Maltese Association, and served as its corresponding secretary for about 20 years. When the Mid West Maltese Club was formed, Mrs. stuber was elected its first president.

Mrs. Stuber wrote the breed column for *Dog World* magazine for many years, and many articles on the Maltese for several other publications, as well. Marge was also a constant contributor and regular columnist for the *Maltese Rx.*

Mrs. Stuber has written two books on the breed. Her first, *I Love Maltese,* was written from a breeder, exhibitor, owner-handler's point of view. *Breeding Toy Dogs, Especially Maltese,* was her second book.

The first outstanding member of the year award, presented by the AMA, was awarded to Mrs. Stuber in 1980.

Marge Stuber has been noted for her artistic abilities in representing the Maltese. For years she had tried to collect Maltese-related memorabilia. Such items were near impossible to find, so she decided to create some of her own. She enrolled in a sculpture class at the Lima Art Association. Having never attempted anything of the sort before, it took her some time to become adept at producing an acceptable Maltese representation.

The results of her efforts were admirable. She has created Maltese figurines in all poses, and in varied sizes and a variety of ceramic jewelry.

Rebecca's Desert Maltese

Mrs. Freda Tinsley has been breeding her Rebecca's Desert Maltese since 1967, in Arizona. Along with her husband, Ted, and her daughter, Rebecca, she has bred and shown many champions.

Mrs. Tinsley's first Maltese was a pet bitch, Susie of Scottsdale, acquired in 1967. Her bloodlines are Villa Malta, Aennchen, Boreas and Primrose. She prefers outcross breeding and has inbred with good results.

The Tinsleys maintain about 20 Maltese in a custom-built room in their home.

Mrs. Tinsley said in 1972 that if love of the breed has anything to do with success, she would eventually have top winners. Her credo held true for she owned two AMA national Specialty winners, in 1976 and 1982. The latter dog became top winning Maltese in 1982, as well as a top winning Toy dog in America.

Rebecca Tinsley, for whom the Tinsley's Maltese are named, has been active and successful in the show ring. She began as a child showing their Maltese. At 16 years of age, she guided one dog to BB at a national Specialty.

Early winners at Rebecca's Desert Maltese were Ch. Rebecca's Desert Angel, a Ch. Boreas Fancy So Free daughter, and Ch. Primrose Peppe of Scottsdale, bred by Marge Stuber. Both dogs were shown in 1970.

Breeding Ch. Peppe to Ch. Angel produced Ch. Rebecca's Desert Love and Ch. Rebecca's Desert So Big. Both finished their championships on the same day!

Ch. So Big's Desert Delight (Ch. Rebecca's Desert So Big × Codere's D. D. Delight) was bred by Donna and Donald Codere, and owned by the Tinsleys. "Missy" was BB at the 1976 Las Vegas Specialty, with 16-year-old Rebecca at the other end of the lead. Ch. Desert Delight went on to win the Toy Group at the Silver State show the next day, also with Rebecca at the helm.

Ch. Desert Delight's son, Ch. Rebecca's Desert Valentino, bred by the Tinsleys, began his show career in August, 1979. Ch. Valentino was shown at Westminster in 1981. The entry that year was one of the largest in the history of the breed at Westminster. Ch. Valentino was BB in an entry of 43.

Ch. Valentino was BIS at the Beverly Hills show and went on to

Ch. So Big's Desert Delight, BB at the 1976 AMA national Specialty. She was shown by Rebecca Tinsley and owned by the Tinsleys.

Multiple BIS-winning Ch. Rebecca's Desert Valentino, the number one Maltese dog in the nation in 1982, owned and bred by the Tinsleys.

become a multiple BIS winner, as well as top Maltese dog in the nation in 1982.

Titanic

George and Barbara Searle reside in Salt Lake City, Utah. Their kennel prefix is Titanic. Barbara's involvement in Maltese commenced with a small female, purchased in Denver, Colorado, by Ray Ecke's Ch. Ecke's Top Hat and Tails.

Thereafter, with the assistance of Lynn Weir in Canada, numerous champions have been produced. Foremost of these has been Titanic's Am., Can. Ch. Moppet's Bolero of Normalta. In 1982, at the Maltese Club of Greater Houston Specialty, a Ch. Bolero grandson, Ch. Titanic's Omega Toy of Adonis, was WD to finish. He is known as "Killer." Although only four pounds, he has been accused of killing one St. Bernard and two Great Danes, when they choked on him! Ch. Omega's crate is graced by a sign reading, "Beware—Don't put fingers in my crate—I don't bite, but my owner Barb does."

Titanic is home to 26 Maltese, many are champions. The Titanic Kennel is beautiful and unique. The entire roof of the large home was removed, and a second story was designed to accommodate all the dogs. Attached to the "rooftop" kennel, erected on metal poles, is a greenhouse, used as a protected run. The greenhouse is used to exercise the Maltese, as well as being a place for them to soak up sun.

The kennel is cooled in summer by a swamp water cooler, that gives the humidity needed in the arid desert climate of Utah. The winters are cold, but the greenhouse keeps the dogs dry and comfortable, as well as keeping coats from becoming tangled and snarled in inclement weather.

So that the kennel is always clean, there are individual runs, as well as large areas where the dogs may run. Small rag type throw rugs are laid out on the floor. The dogs exercise on these. The rugs are washed daily so that hygiene is always maintained.

The kennel floors are covered in seamless linoleum, which climbs a foot up the walls from the floor to facilitate cleaning, especially with males about.

Cotterell

Agnes Cotterell has been in the Maltese fancy since 1968, although she purchased her first, Sugar, from Marjorie Lynch of Richaland, Washington, in 1966. She uses the Cotterell prefix in her breeding program, which is based upon Villa Malta, Al Dor and Fairy Fay bloodlines.

After Sugar, Mrs. Cotterell purchased a bitch from the Villa Malta Kennels. She acquired a stud dog from Dorothy Tinker, Al Dor's Little Rascal, who was then two years old. Mrs. Tinker had advised that this little male could never be shown, due to his being terribly spoiled. Mrs. Cotterell persevered, working with him in preparation for the show ring. He was exhibited by both Mrs. Cotterell and professional handler, Knox Buchanan, and eventually finished. She line bred him to her Villa Malta bitch, with superb results. Ch. Rascal produced 13 champions, and was last shown at the AMA Specialty show in 1979, winning the Veterans class as the age of 13 years. Ch. Rascal died at age 16 in January, 1982.

After a time, though producing lovely stock, Mrs. Cotterell decided that she was inbreeding too much. She acquired Sir Buddy Soni Reveille, CD, from Dr. Helen Poggi, as a total outcross. Mrs. Cotterell attributes the success of her line to Ch. Rascal, Sir Buddy and her Villa Malta bitch.

Mrs. Cotterell has been fortunate in having bred two outstanding Maltese. These were the multiple Group winning Ch. Cotterells Rascal's Tid Bit, and Am., Can. Ch. Couer-de-Lion, known as Rex, a BIS dog who sired 20 champions, owned by Trudie Dillon.

Noted dogs of Mrs. Cotterell's breeding include, Am., Can. Ch. Cotterell's Cally of Rascal and his half brother, Am., Can. Ch. Regan of Rascal, a Best in Show dog in Canada. Both of these dogs were sired by Ch. Rascal. Ch. Cotterell's Love of Tenessa MMA, owned and shown by Anette Feldblum. This bitch has produced seven champion get, earning her the Maltese Merit Award. Ch. Love's litter mate was Ch. Cotterell's Kippi Kai O'Rascal.

Tutee's

Trudie Dillon has bred Maltese at Tutee's Toysome Acres, located in Graham, Washington, since the 1960s. She is a long-time member of the AMA, and has enjoyed association with several other notable Maltese fanciers.

Her first Maltese was Little Enticer of Hick Manor. Her first champion was Si Tika of Toysome Acres, followed by Ch. Tutee's Tuffi's McDuffie.

Mrs. Dillon and Anita Arnstead had close ties, being from the same area of the country. Mrs. Dillon finished several dogs for Mrs. Arnstead, including Ch. Anita's Snowhite Tammie J and Anita's Tutees Rex Anthony.

Mrs. Dillon's major stud dog, BIS winner Am., Can. Coeur-De-Lion, was acquired from Agnes Cotterell, in Boise, Idaho. Ch. Lion proved to be an amazing little stud dog. Within an 11-month period, this potent little dog sired ten American champions. Seven others were pointed and near their championship, five of his get earned Canadian championships. In addition, one dog earned an American and Canadian CD degree, another an American CDX.

Ch. Coeur-de-Lion was awarded the 1974 *Kennel Review* top

producer award for siring 11 champions, five of which were also Canadian champions.

The champion get of Ch. Coeur-de-Lion include: Ch. Holli Ro Famous Fama O' Midhill, owned by the O'Donnells; Am., Can. Ch. Myi Tutees Prester John, owned by the Passes; Ch. Golden Glow Buzz Buzz; Am., Can. Ch. Moppet's Starshine, CD, owned by Lynn Weir; Am., Can. Ch. Tutees Repeat O' Rex; Am., Can. Ch. Tutees Fun and Frolic; Ch. Shokase Tutee's Bel Air Tessa, owned by the Passes; Am., Can. Ch. Myi'Krystal's Hare Krishna, owned by the Passes; Ch. None Such of Midhill, Faith Noble owner; Ch. Primrose Chip O'Dillon, CDX, Marcia Folley owner; Ch. Sno Shoos of Midhill, owned by Mrs. O'Donnell; Ch. Tutees Tiny Carri Rachel, owned by Mrs. Dilon; Ch. Tutee's Bel Air Merry Melissa, also owned by Mrs. Dillon; Ch. Myi's Richard the Lion Hearted, owned by the Passes; Ch. Tutee Primrose Sparky, co-owned by Mrs. Dillon and Mrs. Stuber; and Ch. Tutees Mark Anthony and Ch. Myi's Bit Of Glory, owned by the Passes.

Ch. Tutee's Stan Bar Delores and Ch. Tutee's Bit of Glory were sired by Mrs. Beverly Passe's Ch. Stan Bar's Spark of Glory.

Mrs. Dillon has enjoyed a close relationship with Mrs. Marge Stuber, and her Primrose Maltese. Through this association, several Maltese have either been co-owned, co-bred or exhibited between these two kennels. Am., Can. Ch. Primrose Little Toot of Al Mar is a good example of this association. Ch. Toot was bred by Marge Lewis. He was owned by Marge Stuber, and was kept at Tutee's Toysome Acres for a time, garnering his Canadian title. He was used at stud by Mrs. Dillon before returning to Mrs. Stuber.

Dil-Dal

Mrs. Rita Dahl is a newcomer to the Maltese. She was introduced into the fancy by Mrs. Dillon, and also has an association with Mrs. Arnstead. She uses the Dil-Dal prefix.

Several of her dogs include Dil Dal's Tutees White Fancy, Tutees Primrose L'Esperance, Ch. Tutees Chutzpah, Tutees Primrose Picca-Dilly, and the Group winner, Ch. Dil Dal's White Lite'n of Anitas.

Anita's Snowhite Maltese

Anita Arnstead of Anita's Boston Kennel in Tacoma, Washington, was one of the pioneers of the Maltese breed in the Pacific North West. Her Anita's Snowhite Maltese are well known in that area of the country. Her first dog, Lester's Bill Murphy, was acquired from Alfreda Lester. She then acquired Neva Wee Melita and imported Invicta Sampson from Mrs. White in England. There have been numerous Anita's Snowhite Maltese

BIS-winning Ch. Couer-De-Lion, bred by Agnes Cotterell and owned by Trudie Dillon.

Multiple BIS-winning Ch. Talia of Villa Malta, bred by Dr. Calvaresi and owned by Margaret Rozik.

champions produced over the years. Her dogs have been the foundations for many other Maltese breeding programs.

Some of Anita's Snowhite Maltese include: Ch. Anita's Snowhite Wee Tuffy; Ch. Anita's Snowhite Tammie, owned by Trudie Dillon; Ch. Dil Dal's White Lite'n of Anita; Ch. Anita's Snowhite Camilla; and Ch. Anita's Snowhite Chuck O' Luck.

Villa Malta (with Margaret Rozik)

Mrs. Margaret Rozik began with Maltese in 1950, assisting Dr. Calvaresi at Villa Malta. She was at the other end of the lead with many of Dr. Calvaresi's top winners.

When Dr. Calvaresi retired, Marge kept a number of the Villa Malta dogs, and continued to use the Villa Malta prefix. Mrs. Rozik continues to actively breed the Villa Malta bloodline at her home in Belle Vernon, Pennsylvania.

While Mrs. Rozik has retired from the show ring herself, dogs of her breeding are well represented there. Stock from her breeding program have gone to other Maltese kennels all over this country, as well as to foreign lands.

Of the Villa Malta dogs which came from Dr. Calvaresi, several attained remarkable ages. Ch. Preciosa of Villa Malta, whelped June 8, 1958, died at 23 years of age. Ch. Preciosa was by the outstanding BIS dog Ch. Musi of Villa Malta, her dam was Hulpa's Bonita. Ch. Talena of Villa Malta, whelped February 19, 1959, died at 22½ years of age. Ch. Talena's sire was the famous Ch. Ricco of Villa Malta, her dam was Tana of Villa Malta. At this writing Marge still has Ch. Tentina of Villa Malta, whelped June 26, 1964. Ch. Tentina was sired by Ch. Stellino of Villa Malta, out of Missida of Villa Malta.

Those who based their breeding upon Mrs. Rozik's Villa Malta bloodlines include:

Mrs. Lillian Harrington of Lyndale Kennels acquired and finished Ch. Villa Malta Tai of Lyndale, Ch. Villa Malta Roxy of Lyndale, Ch. Villa Malta's Miss Stacey, Ch. Villa Malta Heide of Lyndale and Ch. Villa Malta Tai of Lyndale.

Mr. and Mrs. E. Woodard, of Gresham, Oregon, founded their Jessigo Bear Kennels upon Mrs. Rozik's breeding. Included in their champions of the Villa Malta bloodline are Ch. Villa Malta's Woogidee Bear, Ch. Villa Malta's Jessigo Bear and Ch. Villa Malta's Sukawin Bear.

Other breeders using Mrs. Rozik's stock include Mr. and Mrs. Berquist, who acquired Su Le's Oriole and Ch. Su Le's Snow Bird; Mr. and Mrs. W. Monahan, who acquired Ch. Mac Monte's Benny Button and Ch. Villa Malta's Mr. Silks; Frances Wright, who acquired Villa Malta Mitchel and Ch. Villa Malta Wilhemina; Madona Garber, who acquired Ch. Villa

Malta Little Heather and Ch. Marcan's Majestic Colonel; Jennie Malone, who acquired Ch. Villa Malta Olivia, Ch. Villa Malta Jen-C Sable and Ch. Malone's Chris-Ter-Fer of Villa Malta.

Other dogs include: Ch. Villa Malta Chiffon to Linda Pyatt; Am., Can. Ch. Villa Malta Kimba to Marcia Richardson; Ch. Lou Wan's Ounce of Gold to Mr. and Mrs. L. Gee; Sugar Baby of Villa Malta to Mr. and Mrs. James Kollins; Ch. Villa Malta's Maestro of Lin-Lee to Linda and Lee Coleman; Villa Malta Aries DeTetrault, owned by Miss V. Davey; Villa Malta's Kotie (Ch. Villa Malta Arumus × Villa Malta Spring Song), owned by Sue and Dale Padgette; Am., Can. & Mex. Ch. Encore Le Ore, owned by Bill Bissell; Ch. Villa Malta's Happy Talk to Nancy Shapland, which was later sold to Japan; Ch. Villa Malta's Timothy to Doris Wexler.

Mrs. Rozik was voted AMA member of the year in 1980, and remains quite active. Mrs. Rozik plans to continue on with the breed that has brought her many friends, happiness and success.

Pen Sans Maltese

Gloria Busselman, founder of the Pen Sans Maltese Kennel in Richland, Washington, has been active in the fancy since the late 1960s. Her first champion was from Miriam Thompson, of the Sun Canyon Kennels, Ch. Sun Canyon Prelude.

The first Maltese to bear her Pen Sans prefix was Ch. Pen Sans Cassandra. These two dogs were shown as a brace after both completed their championships. Mrs. Busselman was active in the obedience ring with Malsteen Pirate of Pen San.

A professional handler for many years, Mrs. Busselman is now approved to judge several Toy breeds.

Of the Pen Sans Maltese, the best known was the multiple BIS dog, Ch. Pen Sans Moonshine. Ch. Moonshine sired several champions, including Ch. Le Grand's Little Moonbeam.

One of the largest Maltese litters ever reported was whelped at the Pen Sans Kennels. On June 4, 1969, Mrs. Busselman was presented with a litter of nine puppies, six of which survived.

Jo Ann's Maltese

Jo Ann Dinsmore of Arlington Heights, Illinois, breeds the Jo Ann line of Maltese.

She purchased her first Maltese in 1964. Her first champion was Stentaway Sonny Boy, finished in both the United States and Canada, bred by Mary Hechinger. She subsequently purchased Joanne-Chen's Maja Dancer. Maja finished with five majors and two Group placings. She also acquired Joanne-Chen's Melodee Dancer from Joanne Hesse. They became the foundation of her small kennel.

BIS-winning Ch. Joanne-Chen's Maja Dancer, bred by Joanne Hess and owned by Joanne Dinsmore.

Multiple Group-winning Ch. Jo Ann's Merrylane Match-maker, breeder, owner, handled by Joanne Dinsmore.

Ch. To The Victor of Eng, sire of over 60 champions, owned by Bob and Barb Bergquist.

Ch. Maja, specialed only four times, won one BIS and was retired for maternal duties. Ch. Jo Ann's Majestic Minstrel Man was Mrs. Dinsmore's first homebred champion. The lovely Ch. Jo Ann's Merrylane Matchmaker has won (through 1982) 70 BBs, eight Group 1sts, 12 Group 2nds, eight Group 3rds, and 12 Group 4ths.

She is also the breeder of the top obedience Maltese for 1980-1982, Ch. Ginger Jake, UD, Canadian CDX. He was trained and owned by Faith Ann Maciejewski of West Allis, Wisconsin. Matchmaker's first breeding produced three males; all finished. He also has a number of other champions to his credit.

In association with Anne Marie Wright, Mrs. Dinsmore co-owned Ch. Maree's Kandi Man. Also co-owned and co-bred by Mrs. Dinsmore and Anne Marie Wright is Ch. Jo Ann's Shady Lady Dancer. Ch. Joanne's Majestic Maree Dancer is another dog produced in this association.

Eng

Anna Engstrom of Grand Rapids, Michigan, has bred the Eng Maltese for many years, based upon the Aennchen, Fairy Fay and Villa Malta bloodlines.

Mrs. Engstrom is a quiet force within the fancy. However, she has bred several champions which have formed the nucleus of a number of kennels. Most notably, the Su Le Kennels of Robert and Barbara Berquist, which is based upon three Eng Maltese, the super stud Ch. To The Victor of Eng, and two BIS bitches, Ch. Su Le's Robin of Eng and Ch. Su Le's Wren of Eng.

Ch. Merry Miss Lilivic of Eng, sired by Ch. To The Victor of Eng, is co-owned with Mrs. Heckerman.

Fleecy

Mr. and Mrs. Ron Graham (Jean), originally from Canada, have been active in the Maltese fancy for a number of years. Their dogs have won in both Canada and the States.

The Grahams presently reside in Phoenix, Arizona. One room in their home is devoted to the Maltese. There is a trap door from the master bedroom which opens out into a fenced yard. Mr. and Mrs. Graham enjoy the company of their dogs, and several sleep with them each evening.

Their foundation dogs are of the Eng bloodline. Their first bitch, Am., Can. Ch. Fleecy's Taskadero of Eng (Ch. Su-Le's Road Runner × Merry Miss Marquis of Eng) was a Group dog in Canada before earning her American championship.

The Graham's kennel name is Fleecy Maltese. Am., Can. Ch. Fleecy's Mr. Kite of Eng (Ch. Su Le's Road Runner × Merry Miss Marquisa of Eng) has continued to bring honor to this new kennel. The newest addition at

Fleecy is Ch. Manorinn's Ebony Eyes (Ch. Bar None Tom Terrific ×
Maltes'a Marci of Manorinn). Ch. King-don's Satin Doll also calls the
Fleecy Kennels home.

Su-Le

Barbara and Robert Berquist have Su Le Maltese in New Boston,
Michigan. Mrs. Berquist purchased their first Maltese from Anna Engstrom
on Christmas eve, 1968. Their foundation stock also includes Joanne-
Chen, Primrose and Villa Malta breeding.

That first bitch, Group-winning Am., Can. Ch. Su Le's Robin of Eng
MMA, weighed four pounds and produced four champion get. Among
them: Ch. Su Le's Sandpiper (Ch. Irco's Diamond Marquis × Robin) and
littermates, Group-winning Ch. Su Le's Road Runner and Ch. Su Le's
Starling, by Ch. Victor of Eng. Ch. Victor has sired 64 American and seven
Canadian champion get to date, and is the main reason for the success
enjoyed at Su Le. Also acquired from Mrs. Engstrom was BIS Am. & Bda.
Ch. Su Le's Wren of Eng as the second foundation bitch for Su Le.

Ch. Primrose Di Di of Su Le, bred by Mrs. Marge Stuber, was an
important part of the Su Le foundation. From Mrs. Joanne Hesse Su Le
acquired Joanne-Chen's Saltana Dancer. They also showed and finished
Ch. Joanne-Chen's Sweet Man Dancer in 1976.

Ch. Primrose Di Di produced a Group winner from the classes, Ch. Su
Le's Martin (by Ch. Victor of Eng). Ch. Martin's litter brother became
Am., Can. Ch. Su Le's Sparrow. From Joanne-Chen's Saltana Dancer
came Ch. Su Le's Blue Jay, a Ch. Aennchen's Shikar Dancer grandson. He
finished in 1977. Sired by Ch. Blue Jay was Ch. Su Le's Meadowlark (out of
Joanne-Chen's Saltana Dancer), a grandson of Ch. Joanne-Chen's Siva
Dancer. Ch. Meadowlark was bred and shown by Barbara, then sold to
Jean Dempsey Wallace. One of the Su Le's top-producing bitches, Ch. Su
Le's Jacana MMA, dam of 15 champions, was also by Ch. Blue Jay out of
Saltana Dancer. She is the top producing bitch in the history of the breed.
Su Le introduced Villa Malta breeding into the bloodline through Ch. Su
Le's Snow Bird, bred by Marge Rozik, and several others.

The foundation stock and breeding programs of several kennels both
here and in Canada, trace to Su Le. Among these are the Kathan Maltese
bred by Mr. and Mrs. Anthony DiGiacomo of New Jersey. Kathy
combined Aennchen, Joanne-Chen bred dogs with the Su Le dogs to form
her bloodline. Mrs. DiGiacomo has finished and shown many Su Le
champions in the East.

Notable at Su Le is multiple BIS Ch. Su Le's Jonina, who was BB at
the 1978 AMA Specialty. Other Su Le champions of note are the Group-
winning Ch. Su Le's Bunting, a Ch. Joanne-Chen's Maya Dancer
daughter; Ch. Su Le's Kea (Ch. Victor × Ch. Dove); litter sisters Ch. Su Le

138

Sanderling; Ch. Scarlet Macaw and Ch. Surf Scooter; Ch. Su Le's Jerita, sired by Ch. Victor out of Pacan.

Group-winning Ch. Su Le's Screech Owl was co-owned by Mrs. DiGiacomo, Mrs. Berquist and Mrs. Jerri Walters of Saddle River, New Jersey. Mrs. Madonna Garber of Richelieu Maltese acquired Ch. Su Le's Junco.

Both Mr. and Mrs. Berquist are active within the fancy, both serving as AMA officers. Mr. Berquist is an AMA past president. The Berquists have bred over 100 champions.

Lin-Lee

Lin-Lee's Maltese, owned by Linda and Lee Coleman, located in Finleyville, Pennsylvania, started with Oak Ridge Melissa (Ch. Infante Mystic Caper × Bali Hai's Misty Pebbles) in 1973. She finished in November 1974, after just 23 shows, to become their first champion—novice, owner-handled by Lee.

Their next Maltese, Su Le's Teal (Ch. To the Victor of Eng × Su Le's Oriole) began her show career, while Ch. Oak Ridge Melissa was being specialed. Ch. Su Le's Teal finished owner-handled at the York show.

Ch. Oak Ridge Melissa continued to be shown as a special, owner-handled, and also shown by professional handler, Barbara Alderman. She won two all-breed BIS, 11 Toy Groups, and numerous Group placements.

The Colemans then commenced their breeding program. After searching for a stud and show dog, they acquired Villa Malta's Maestro of Lin-Lee. Maestro was owner-handled to his championship in five shows with all major wins. Subsequently he went to Mrs. Chieko Toda of Japan.

Ch. Maestro was bred to Ch. Melissa's half-sister, Shasta, siring Lin-Lee's Melodie and Lin-Lee's Melanie. Both went on to finish their championships.

The success of this breeding prompted the breeding of Ch. Maestro to Ch. Oak Ridge Melissa. This mating produced Lin-Lee's Marquis and Lin-Lee's Magnum.

In July 1978, Lin-Lee's Marquis won the puppy Toy Group in his first three Canadian shows. Both finished their Canadian champions owner-handled.

Lin-Lee's Marquis received four BBs and three Group 1sts from the classes in nine shows, enroute to his American championship, owner-handled by Lee. Am., Can. Ch. Marquis was bred to Lin-Lee's Oriana, which produced Lin-Lee's Maverick. Marquis went south in October 1979 with Barbara Alderman, and won the Toy Group in Macon, Georgia, the first weekend out. Lin-Lee's Maverick went to Barbara Alderman for the 1980 Florida circuit. He finished in eight shows with five majors from the puppy class. After Maverick finished, Ch. Marquis returned south in

BIS-winning Ch. Su Le's Jonina, bred and owned by the Bergquists. *Courtesy AKC Library*

Multiple BIS-winning Ch. Oak Ridge Melissa, bred by Carol Neth, owned by Linda and Lee Coleman and handled by Barbara Alderman.

BIS-winning Ch. Lin-Lee's Marquis, show with handler Barbara Alderman, bred a owned by the Colemans.

February. On his first weekend back in Florida with Barbara, Marquis became the first Maltese in 1980 to obtain an all-breed BIS.

Sun Canyon

Miriam Thompson is the breeder of the outstanding Sun Canyon Maltese, located in Sun Valley, California. She acquired her first Maltese, Sun Canyon Co-Star, in 1959. The bitch was bred by Gladys Cecial and sold to her by Mrs. Alfreda Lester. Co-Star was of pure Jon Vir breeding, and finished handily.

Ch. Co-Star was bred only three times. Her first litter, of two bitches, sired by Marge Lewis' Ch. Al-Mar Patrick of Villa Malta, was whelped in 1962. One of those, Ch. Sun Canyon Starlet, was awarded an all-breed BIS at age nine months! She finished soon afterward. Her litter sister, Ch. Sun Canyon Patricia, finished two months later.

Ch. Co-Star was bred a second time to Ch. Patrick, producing two males. The Standard at the time called for a Maltese dog to be three pounds or under, the smaller, the better. Mrs. Thompson sold one puppy, and kept the other. He became Ch. Maestro of Sun Canyon.

Mrs. Thompson then acquired Idnar's King Midas, a carefully linebred male of the Jon Vir bloodline. An outcross for Sun Canyon, he quickly earned his championship title.

Ch. Midas was bred to Ch. Co-Star. The resulting puppies were Ch. Sun Canyon Limelight and Ch. Sun Canyon Matinee Idol II. Ch. Matinee Idol was sold to Mrs. Dorothy Palmersten, of the San Su Kee Kennels in Minneapolis, Minnesota. At San Su Kee, he became a top-producing foundation stud.

Mrs. Thompson had succeeded in establishing a linebred Jon Vir bloodline. Ch. Co-Star's dam, Lester's Lilly Lady Cecil, was of the Jon Vir bloodline and had the coat for which Jon Vir dogs are most noted. It was long, straight and white with no trace of curl or cotton.

Mrs. Thompson acquired two more females of identical breeding as her Ch. Co-Star from Mrs. Cecil. One of the bitches, Cecil's Donna Cami Isle D'Malta, was a brood quality bitch. Ch. Cecil's Donna Cari Isle D'Malta was a show quality female of proper size for breeding. Ch. Cari, bred to Ch. Patrick, produced Sun Canyon Rena, Little Me, Temptation and Ch. Sun Canyon the Actress. Ch. Actress won the second "B" match held by the then fledgling American Maltese Association, from the 4-6 month puppy class.

Sun Canyon Rena whelped seven puppies in four litters, all by Ch. Midas. One of these, Ch. Sun Canyon Drummer Boy, was acquired by Mary Hechinger. He became the foundation stud at Mrs. Hechinger's Stentaway Kennels, and himself sired six champions.

Sun Canyon Little Me of Encore whelped four champions between

Ch. Sun Canyon Starlet, shown winning a BIS at nine months of age, owned by Miriam Thompson.

At Orange Empire on January 26, 1969, Best Team in Show went to the Maltese, Ch. Sun Canyon Aztec Idol, Ch. Sun Canyon Inca Idol, Ch. Sun Canyon The Bandit and Ch. Sun Canyon Tiger Rag, owner-handled by Miriam Thompson.

Multiple BIS-winning Ch. Sun Canyon
Reach for the Stars, number one Maltese
in 1976, bred and owned by Miriam
Thompson, handled by Madeline Thornton.

Multiple BIS-winning Ch. Sun Canyon The
Heartbreak Kid, number one Maltese in
1977, bred by Miriam Thompson, owned
by Jacklyn Hungerland, handled by
Madeline Thornton.

Group-winning Ch. Sun
Canyon Inca Idol, bred and
owned by Miriam Thompson.

Ch. Sun Canyon Matinee Idol II, bred by
Miriam Thompson and owned by Dorothy
Palmersten.

1966 and 1970. Three were by Ch. Matinee Idol, including Ch. Aztec, Mayan and Group winning Inca Idol. Ch. Inca went on to sire Ch. Sun Canyon Reach for the Stars, a BIS dog with multiple Group wins.

Mrs. Thompson decided she needed to strengthen the Villa Malta influence in her line. One of the champion get produced by Little Me, Ch. Sun Canyon Double-O-Seven, was sired by Ch. Al Mar Patrick of Villa Malta. Ch. Double-O-Seven went on to sire five champions.

Sun Canyon Temptation produced five champions from 1960 to 1970. Three were by Ch. Midas. The others were by Ch. Midas' sons, Ch. Sun Canyon Top Gun and Ch. Sun Canyon Aztec Idol.

Setting records was not the foremost thought in Mrs. Thompson's mind, but rather the betterment of the breed, and improvement in the quality of her breeding stock. Ch. Midas could easily have produced 50 champions, counting all his get which were pointed and those which were never shown. He had to settle with siring 27 champions. His sons, daughters and grandchildren carry on for him at Sun Canyon.

In 1971, Mrs. Thompson acquired Ch. Ha-Los Mini Mite Dancer, bred by Loretta Zuckerman. Ch. Mini Mite's sire was of pure Aennchen bloodlines. His dam was a Ch. Midas daughter.

Bred to Sun Canyon Sweet Marie, a Ch. Midas granddaughter, Ch. Mini Mite sired five champions in two years. Of these, three were top winners, including Ch. Gabriel and Jenelle. Ch. Jenelle was a multiple BIS winner in 1973. Ch. Mini Mite sired 13 champions in three years.

Mrs. Thompson feels that her best dogs resulted from a combination of the Jon Vir, Villa Malta and Aennchen bloodlines. Ch. Sun Canyon Reach for the Stars was top-winning Maltese in 1975.

Ch. Sun Canyon the Heartbreak Kid was a blend of Aennchen and Jon Vir bloodlines. He was the top winning Maltese in 1976 and sire of 12 champions. Ch. Sun Canyon Heartbreak Kid's grandmother, Sun Canyon Carmen, was a top producing Sun Canyon brood bitch. She produced eight champions in four litters—five from the Ch. Midas grandson, Aztec. Ch. Sun Canyon Mell-O-Dee of Love MMA produced three champion offspring as well, at the San Su Kee Kennel of Mrs. Palmersten, in Minneapolis.

Ch. Heartbreak Kid's litter sister, Sun Canyon Devilla, produced seven champions, including the noted stud, Ch. Sun Canyon Prince Charming II. She also produced litter brothers, Ch. Sun Canyon Jazz Singer and Ch. Sun Canyon Casanova.

The best results at Sun Canyon seemed to come from doubling up on the grandsire. Mrs. Thompson has never bred daughter to sire, or son to mother. The methods she followed were successful, for Sun Canyon Kennels have produced 118 champions, an amazing number for any breed.

Mrs. Thompson is still breeding and active within the fancy, though in a somewhat more limited scope. She is a charter member of, and has served on the board of the AMA, attending the 1982 AMA Specialty in Las Vegas, Nevada. She had four champions entered in the Best of Breed class.

Mrs. Thompson's granddaughter, Linda Orland Graham, a professional handler, has been showing Mrs. Thompson's Maltese for several years. Mrs. Graham's first winner of note was the multiple Group winner, Ch. Susan's Black Eyed Brandy (Ch. Ha-Lo's Mini Mite Dancer × Sun Canyon's Sweet Marie). She is seen often in the ring with other Maltese of her grandmother's breeding.

San Su Kee

Mrs. Dorothy Palmersten has been breeding Maltese since 1965, using the San Su Kee prefix. She received her first dog, a finished champion, Ch. Sun Canyon Matinee Idol II (Ch. Idnar's King Midas × Ch. Sun Canyon Co-Star), from Miriam Thompson's Sun Canyon Kennels. Mrs. Palmersten also acquired two Sun Canyon bitches, Ch. Sun Canyon Mell-O-Dee of Love and Ch. Sun Canyon Doll Face, which she finished. These dogs were of Jon Vir line breeding. Mrs. Palmersten's mother, Mrs. Ruth M. Small, also a Maltese breeder, became the owner of Ch. Sun Canyon Doll Face. Ch. Matinee Idol was specialed in a limited way, shown by Mrs. Palmersten and Mrs. Doris Kitten. Ch. Idol was the foundation of her breeding program.

Ch. Sun Canyon Mell-O-Dee of Love produced two champions by Ch. Matinee Idol—Ch. San Su Kee Sunrise Serenade and Ch. San Su Kee Wendy of Course, which finished with five majors at 14 months. Ch. Wendy was shown by professional handler Mrs. Peggy Hogg. Also produced by Ch. Mell-O-Dee was Ch. San Su Kee Melody Too, sired by Ch. Mike Mar's Ringleader II.

Prior to this, Mrs. Palmersten had been successful in obedience. However, due to illness, she was kept from the obedience ring, and began to use the services of Peggy Hogg, who finished dogs for her.

Mrs. Palmersten bred Int., Am. & Can. Ch. San Su Kee Little Bit of Idol, who was a BIS winner in Canada. He was owned by Mary and Douglas Olver, of Canada. Ch. Idol became the top-winning Maltese in Canada in 1970.

In 1970, Mrs. Palmersten acquired Mike Mar's Ring Leader II. Ringo, as he was known, finished undefeated in six shows, with Group placements enroute. Ch. Ringo became a Group winner, with Mrs. Hogg on the lead, and earned a Maltese Merit Award for having sired numerous champions.

A dog of note of Mrs. Palmersten's breeding was BIS Ch. San Su Kee Ring Leader Too, sired by Ch. Ringo. This top-winning dog, the first bred by Mrs. Palmersten, was owned by Mr. and Mrs. Norman Nelson. Another outstanding dog bred by Mrs. Palmersten was multiple BIS Ch. San Su Kee Star Edition MMA (Ch. Mike Mar's Ring Leader II × Revlo's Star of

145

Ch. Mike-Mar Ringleader II, Group winner, owned by Dorothy Palmersten.

Ch. San Su Kee Ringleader Too, bred by Dorothy Palmersten, owned by Mr. and Mrs. Norman Nelson.

Ch. San Su Kee Star Edition, multiple BIS winner, bred and owned by Dorothy Palmersten.

Midway), which she co-owned with Mr. Richard Reid. Ch. Star Edition won his first Toy Group and BIS at one year and one day of age. Ch. Star Edition was BB at the 1975 Westminster show and went on to place third in the Toy Group. His final record included four BIS, ten Group 1sts, 47 Group placements and 73 BBs.

Another Group placer was Ch. San Su Kee Show Stopper. Ch. San Su Kee Starshine was WB at the 1976 Westminster show, and repeated the win at the 1976 AMA national Specialty in Las Vegas. After finishing, Ch. Starshine was awarded five Group 1sts. Ch. Starshine was one of three champions produced by Ch. Mike Mar's Ringleader II and Revlo's Star of Midway. This combination produced two multiple BIS dogs, Ch. San Su Kee Star Edition and Ch. Revlo's Ringo Star, as well as the multiple Group winner Ch. San Su Kee Starshine.

Ch. San Su Kee Show Off (Mike Mar's Ringleader II × Mike Mars Promises Promises) was pointed from the puppy classes. He is owned by Joyce Watkins. Show Off sired Ch. Marcris Sweet Talk, and an offspring of this same bloodline is Ch. Marcris Marshmallow, Best Puppy in Sweepstakes at the 1982 AMA Specialty in Las Vegas. Ch. Show Off sired three champions in 1979.

Ch. San Su Kee Joanne-Chen Rocket, bred by Joanne Hesse, was the first champion sired by Ch. Joanne-Chen's Mino Maya Dancer. He won two Group 1sts.

Myi

Beverly and Dean Passe own the house of Myi Maltese, located in Gig Harbor, Washington. The Passes' connection with the breed stems mainly from the initial interest of Mrs. Passe.

In the 1920s, Maltese were briefly popular in the Pacific North West. Mrs. Passe's grandmother owned and posed with a Maltese for many glamorous parlor pictures, which as a child, Mrs. Passe looked at on many occasions.

The first Myi Maltese was purchased from Janet Pender of Tacoma, Washington, in 1965. Janet Pender had produced many Maltese by blending Invicta breeding with the Jon Vir line. Since the AMA Standard had just been changed from *under three pounds ideal* to the present, *under seven, four to six pounds preferred,* this bitch, Ch. Janet's Krystal Mist of Torgy, reflected the new Standard. She was six pounds and was larger than many of her contemporaries. Krystal finished with several BBs and Group placements from the open class.

During this period, Mrs. Passe made friends with many other Maltese fanciers. She became a charter member of the now defunct North West Maltese Fanciers, and joined the AMA. Her husband Dean is a member as well.

Ch. Krystal is important to Myi Maltese because of the two key bitches she produced, Ch. Myi's Krystal Dance of Glory and Ch. Myi Krystal's Hare Kryshna, who were retained and bred to lay the foundation for the Maltese to follow.

Since the Passes consider themselves fanciers rather than breeders, few litters were born during the period, 1965-1978. After the acquisition of multiple BIS Am., Can. Ch. Salteer Glory Seeker (1971-1975), Dean and Bev became interested in breeding Maltese on a small scale. Ch. Glory Seeker accumulated five all-breed BIS, 35 Group 1sts, 33 other Group placements in the United States and Canada. He was #1 Maltese in Canada and #2 Maltese in the United States in 1975.

From a handful of litters Glory Seeker, who was inbred on Ch. Aennchen's Shikar Dancer line, produced ten champions, two BIS winners, and several top producers, as well as BIS and Group winning grandchildren.

The Myi breeding program inched its way through the 1960s and 1970s where the best bitch from each generation was retained, shown, then bred. With Krystal and Glory Seeker as key dogs, the best was inbred or linebred, doubling and redoubling on a genetic pool. Close to 100 champions have sprung from this combination of genes, but Mrs. Passe has never kept a count as she has always felt quality, not quantity to be the ultimate measuring stick.

Noted among the Maltese at the house of Myi are BIS Am., Can. Ch. Myi's Glory Seer, and her littermate, Ch. Myi's Ode to Glory, which are both Ch. Glory Seeker daughters. They have produced 11 champions between them. Ch. Seer has produced five champions to date, including the #2 bitch in the United States in 1980, Ch. Myi's Seeker of Glory.

An outstanding stud dog at the house of Myi is the multiple Best in Show winning Am., Can. Ch. Stan-Bar's Spark of Glory, a Ch. Glory Seeker son. Ch. Sparky has proved himself a star both in the show ring, and at stud. He has sired 19 champions, and won the Stud Dog class at the 1979 AMA Specialty. In October 1982, in Las Vegas, he was named Best Veteran. Another Toy Group win he made at nine years of age was a first for the breed in America.

Am., Can. Ch. Myi's Sun Seeker is by Ch. Sparky and a grandson of Ch. Glory Seeker. Ch. Sun Seeker is owned by Mr. Akira Shinohara of the A. S. Gloria's Maltese in Osaka, Japan. He was shown to his wins in this country by Dean Passe, his breeder. Ch. Sun Seeker's record includes seven BIS and 58 Group 1sts in the United States and Canada. When being shown, Ch. Sun Seeker was the #3 Maltese in the United States and #2 in Canada. He left six champion progeny here in the United States, out of six bitches, before going to Japan. There he has produced several BIS winners.

Maltese of the house of Myi may be found in the breeding programs and kennels of several fanciers across the nation. Included among them are

Multiple BIS-winning Am. & Can. Ch. Myi's Glory Seer, bred and owned by Dean and Beverly Passe, handled by Dean Passe.

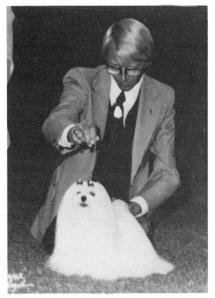

Multiple BIS-winning Am. & Can. Ch. Myi's Sun Seeker, owned by Akiro Shinohara, handled by Dean Passe.

Multiple BIS-winning Am. & Can. Ch. Stan-Bar's Spark of Glory, owned by Dean and Beverly Passe.

Ch. Myi's Morning Glory, a multiple Group-winning bitch, owned and shown by Mr. Lenard Reppond. Ch. Myi's Dream Again was shown to her title by Dean, and is owned by Claudia Strickland. Ch. Myi's Asia Minor, also shown by Dean, is owned by Dr. and Mrs. Kusten Jones. Ch. Myi's Style Seeker, who was WB at the Houston Specialty for five points, lives with the Searles and their Titanic Maltese in Salt Lake City, Utah. Ch. Myi's Super Seeker was shown to his championship by Miss Alma Jones of Al Jon's Maltese, located in Short Hills, New Jersey.

Fantasyland

Fantasyland Maltese are bred by Mrs. Carole M. Baldwin in Novato, California. Mrs. Baldwin acquired her first Maltese, Ch. Markeith's Wee Waif, in 1966. Shortly after acquiring Waif, she purchased a second Maltese bitch, Markeith's What's New Pussycat. Pussycat and Waif were her foundation bitches. Waif's lines were mostly the old Villa Malta, with a little Jon Vir, Good Time and Invicta. Pussycat had a little of each of the same lines, but was heavier in Good Time, Jon Vir and Invicta.

Since the late Ch. Bobbelee Brag-A-Bout seemed to have desirable qualities, her bitches were bred to his sons. In doing this she brought in the Aennchen and Fairy Fay bloodlines on their dams' sides of the pedigree, and more of the Jon Vir dogs, as well.

The puppies resulting from the breeding of these dogs were then interbred. Ch. Fantasyland Bugalewy MMA is an example of the result of these breedings. His double granddam is Ch. Markeith's Wee Waif. His sire is a great grandson of Ch. Bobbelee Brag-A-Bout and on the other side of his pedigree, his grandsire is a son of Ch. Bobbelee Brag-A-Bout. Half brother-sister is the favorite type breeding done at Fantasyland.

Although the Baldwins do not keep many dogs for their breeding program, they have bred and owned many champions. Their goal is to breed show quality dogs which can produce or surpass their own quality. They feel a champion that cannot produce is of no use. The Baldwins feel that there have been many BIS dogs which have never produced a single champion offspring. Since the Baldwins have a breeding kennel, it is important to them that their dogs produce champion quality pups. They strive for top producers that produce top producers.

Some Fantasyland dogs of note are Fantasyland Juliette MMA, the dam of several champions; Ch. Fantasyland Billy Jo MMA, daughter of Juliette and also the dam of champions; Ch. Fantasyland Pete R Wabbit, son of Billy Jo who had multiple BBs from the classes over Group and BIS dogs, while still under ten months. He finished going WD and BW at the 1981 AMA Specialty. He was specialed in seven shows, taking five more breeds in strong competition.

Marcris

Joyce Watkins has been breeding Marcris Maltese in Miami, Florida, since 1959. Her Marcris prefix is derived from the names of her two children, Mark and Christe. She bought her first Maltese in 1959, an English import, Vicbrita Felicity, and sold her to Louise Carlsen of Lou-Win Maltese, who finished her.

Since Mrs. Watkins lives in a residential area, she does not keep a large number of Maltese at any one time. She kennels her adult dogs, only keeping puppies, pregnant bitches and show dogs in the house. Her foundation bloodlines were Jon Vir, Villa Malta and Aennchen.

One of her first, and most successful studs was Marcris Winsome Lad MMA. This dog accrued 11 points toward his championship, and had sired eight champions before his untimely death.

Mrs. Watkins began the movement for, and received final acceptance of the Maltese Merit Award (MMA), awarded by the AMA. This was done in memory of her stud, Winsome Lad. She felt that successful producers should be recognized. Therefore, she petitioned to have this award initiated by the AMA in recognition of bitches which have whelped three champions or more, and dogs having sired five or more champion get. The award system was approved by the AKC. Maltese whose owners or breeders have applied to the AMA for this award of recognition for accomplishment are permitted to place the letters MMA after the names of their dogs only after they have received their MMA certificates from the AMA.

The other stud dog at Marcris at the same time Winsome Lad was active was 4½ pound Marcris Love and Kisses, who later finished. The early bitches at Marcris were Marcris Happy Holly, owned by Mrs. Watkins' son Mark, and a lovely bitch, Marcris Cherish Infante, bred by Rose Infante and sired by Winsome Lad.

A friend for many years, Anna Mae Hardy, also used the Marcris prefix for a time. She showed and bred the first Marcris champions, Ch. Gidget of Marcris, followed by Ch. Tammy of Marcris.

Two Marcris Maltese were acquired by Dorothy Hochrein of the Mil Ottie Maltese. These littermates were Ch. Mil Ottie Pixie of Marcris and Ch. Mil Ottie Prancer of Marcris, which were shown to their championships by Bennie Dennard.

Mrs. Watkins' Winsome Lad sired Rose Infante's Ch. Infante's Mystic Caper and Ch. Infante's White Cameo. Ch. Mystic Caper would eventually go to Mrs. Carol Neth, to become her foundation stud, producing the famous multiple Best in Show winning Ch. Oak Ridge Country Charmer. Mrs. Infante also owned Marcris Ba-Ba-Lu-Lu, which was the dam of Ch. Marcris Love and Kisses.

The Marcris Kennels enjoyed a close association over many years with the C & M Kennels of Carol Thomas. Some of the dogs resulting from this

Ch. Fantasyland Baby of Moderna, bred by Jari Bobbilot, owned by Carole Baldwin.

Ch. Fantasyland Pete R Wabbit, shown here with breeder, owner, handler, Carole Baldwin.

Ch. Myi's Masterpiece of Marcris, bred and owned by Joyce Watkins.

Ch. Marcris Marshmallow, bred and owned by Joyce Watkins.

association include Marcris Love of C & M and Ch. Marcris Ruff Stuff of C & M, bred by Carol Thomas and owned by Joyce Watkins. This dog was the eighth champion sired by Ch. Valentino of Midhill MMA. Ch. C & M's Felina of Marcris was bred by Mrs. Watkins, and owned by Mrs. Thomas.

Mrs. Watkins has been active in the fancy over many years. She was founder and charter member of the Florida Maltese Club, later known as the Maltese Club of Greater Miami, which was very active for several years. She has been an officer of the AMA.

Russ Ann

Anna Mae Hardy was introduced to the breed by her neighbor, Joyce Watkins, in 1964. Mrs. Hardy was fascinated by Mrs. Watkins' Maltese, and was determined to own one. Mrs. Watkins offered to lease Hansen's Silka of Marcris to Mrs. Hardy.

The produce of the first litter whelped by Hansen's Silka was given to Mrs. Watkins. In her second litter two females were produced. Having no kennel name of her own, Mrs. Watkins gave Mrs. Hardy permission to use the Marcris prefix in registering these puppies. One female was sold to Mrs. Carole Thomas. Mrs. Thomas' dog was shown in the obedience ring, and became Tiki of Marcris, CD. The other bitch remained in the Hardy household, and became Ch. Gidget of Marcris.

While showing Ch. Gidget to her championship from the Bred By Exhibitor class, Silka was bred to Ch. Bobbelee Marshmallow. One bitch puppy resulted, which became Ch. Bobbelee Tammy Tu of Marcris, shown by Bennie Dennard.

In the early years of her involvement, Mrs. Hardy was guided by Mrs. Watkins, Mrs. Roberta Harrison of the Bobbelee Kennels and Louise Carlsen of the Lou-Win Kennels. She began to use the Russ Ann prefix. The first dog bearing the Russ Ann prefix was Group winner, Ch. Russ Ann Honey of Marcris.

The multiple BIS bitch, Ch. Russ Ann Petite Charmer MMA, sired by Ch. Marcris Love and Kisses, was a top dog, nationwide. Ch. Charm, as she was known, was handled by the professional handler, John Thyssen. She accrued an impressive record, including three BIS, ten Group 1sts, 13 Group 2nds, nine Group 3rds, three Group 4ths and 147 BBs.

At the end of her specials career, Ch. Charm was bred several times, producing seven champions, and earning the Maltese Merit Award. Among her get are Ch. Russ Ann Bonus Baby, sired by Ch. C & M's Valentino of Midhill, bred by Anna Mae. Ch. Charm also whelped Best in Show Ch. Russ Ann A Touch of Class, which is now owned by Mrs. Maurice Melvin. Ch. Johnny, as this dog is known, received his Best in Show while still in the possession of Mrs. Hardy.

BIS-winning **Ch. Russ Ann A Touch of Class, bred by Anna Mae Hardy, owned by** Maurice Melvin.

Ch. C & M's Valentino of Midhill, multiple Grou winner, co-owned by Carole Thomas and Mary Day

Ch. C & M's Pride of Moderna, owned by Carole Thomas.

Mrs. Hardy became a member of the AMA in 1964. She was a director and vice president before serving as president for two terms, 1975 and 1976.

C & M Maltese

Carole Thomas, of Miami, Florida, has enjoyed great success with her C & M Maltese. She was first introduced to the breed in 1962. Her first Maltese came from Anna Mae Hardy, Ti Ki of Marcris. Tiki was a wonderful pet, and a success in the obedience ring, where she earned her CD title.

Success led to an increased interest in breeding and exhibiting, and Mrs. Thomas acquired Fairy Fay's Tina from Elvira Cox. The Bobbelee dogs owned by Mrs. Harrison were admired by Mrs. Thomas. So Tina was bred to the famous Ch. Bobbelee's Marshmallow. From this breeding came the first champion at C & M Kennels, Ch. C & M's Our Dream. Another bitch, Fairy Fay's Minissa, also from Mrs. Cox, was shown to her championship and had several Group placements.

From Margaret Rozik's Villa Malta Kennels, came Ch. C & M's Camero of Villa Malta, co-owned by Mary Day. Many C & M dogs were co-owned or co-bred by Mrs. Thomas in conjunction with Mrs. Day.

Another early champion at C & M was Tiny Moonglow, as well as Ch. C & M's Serina of Mil Ottic, bred by Dorothy Hochrein.

The first winner of note at C & M was the homebred, owner-handled Group winner, Ch. C & M's Torrino of Camero, owned by Mrs. Day and Mrs. Thomas.

Ch. C & M's Tiny Moonglow, a bitch, and her litter brother, multiple Group winning Ch. C & M's Valentino of Midhill, were bred by Mrs. Thomas and co-owned by Mrs. Day. Ch. Valentino was BB at Westminster, 1976, over 19 specials.

Ch. Valentino of Midhill MMA sired a total of eight champions. His eighth champion get was Ch. Marcris Ruff Stuff of C & M, owned by Joyce Watkins. Ch. C & M's Felina of Marcris (Ch. Marcan's Majestic Colonel × Ch. Marcris Melody of Love) was bred by Mrs. Watkins and called the C & M kennels home.

Noble Faith

Faith Noble from Fort Lauderdale, Florida, began her Noble Faith's Maltese line in 1970. The foundation was based upon the C & M dogs of Mrs. Thomas and Mrs. Day. Her first bitch, and first champion, was Ch. C & M's Noble Faith MMA (C & M's Camero of Villa Malta × Patrick Twinkle Little Star). Ch. Noble Faith produced three champions, including littermates Ch. Noble Faith's Whisper of Gigolo, a Group placer, and Ch. Noble Faith's Wee Bit of Majic. Their sire was Ch. None Such of Midhill

Ch. C & M's Noble Faith, winner of the veteran class at the 1979 AMA national Specialty, owned by Faith Knoble.

Multiple BIS-winning Am. Bda. Ch. Noble Faith's White Tornado, winner of the 1983 AMA national Specialty, bred and owned by Faith Knoble, handled by Barbara Alderman.

(Ch. Coeur de Lion × Bunny Boop of Midhill). A repeat breeding produced Ch. Noble Faith's Phoebe Finale, winner of five Group 1sts, in a limited specials career. Ch. Phoebe was bred to Ch. Oak Ridge Country Charmer, resulting in Ch. Noble Faith's Charmin Fellow, and his litter sister, multiple BIS Ch. Noble Faith's White Tornado. Ch. Torrie was the #1 Maltese and #5 Toy dog in 1984. She was shown to her wins by professional handler Barbara Alderman.

An English import came to Noble Faith's Maltese and it became Am., Can. Ch. Ellwin's Marianna.

Oak Ridge

Mr. and Mrs. Tom Neth of McMurray, Pennsylvania, began their Oak Ridge Maltese in 1964, after purchasing Koukla Lady of Rhodes, bred by Gini Sunner. Koukla was a combination of Good Time, Invicta and Aennchen bloodlines. She later became the foundation of Carol's breeding stock. At this time, the Neths used the prefix of Bali Hai. Koukla was bred to Ch. Duncan's Kimberly, producing Bali Hai's Misty Pebbles.

In 1969, the Neths acquired a stud of their own, Ch. Infante Mystic Caper, from Mr. and Mrs. Alan Rhodes, bred by Rose Infante. He complemented their Bali Hai's Misty Pebbles, producing their first homebred BIS winner, Ch. Oak Ridge Melissa, owned by the Colemans of Lin Lee Maltese. Later he produced BIS Am., Can. & Bda. Ch. Oak Ridge Country Charmer, and many other champions. He was still producing until his death in 1980. His last get were Ch. Oak Ridge Country N' Lace and Oak Ridge Country Caper, born after Cappy's death.

In 1970, Carol had Evelyn Schaeffer show her dogs for her. Mrs. Schaeffer also taught Carol about Maltese and finished Ch. Oak Ridge Puffnstuff at nine and a half months, with four majors and two BBs. Ch. Puff became one of Mrs. Neth's best producers, with many champions to his credit. One of these, Ch. Oak Ridge Pippin Fresh, is out of a Charmer sister, Oak Ridge Sand Pebble. Both he and his mother are Maltese Merit Award producers.

Mrs. Schaeffer later purchased a bitch, Ch. Eve-Ron's Jendi from Oak Ridge, which she finished. After Mrs. Schaeffer's death in 1981, Ch. Jendi was returned to Oak Ridge, along with her daughter and granddaughter.

February 27, 1975 saw the birth of Oak Ridge Country Charmer. He finished with BBs and Group placings from the classes. Later, his litter sister, Oak Ridge Country Luv, was shown to her championship.

The Neths attended the 12th AMA Specialty in Elizabeth, New Jersey, in 1977 where breeder, judge Mr. Frank E. Oberstar officiated in the regular classes and Joanne Hesse judged Puppy Sweepstakes. At that show Oak Ridge Sweet Alyssum was Best in Sweepstakes and Best of Winners in the regular classes. Ch. Country Charmer was Best of Breed and Ch. Oak

Ridge Melissa, owned by Lin Lee Maltese, and handled by William Cunningham, was BOS—a great year for the Oak Ridge Maltese.

After his first Specialty win, Ch. Charmer was shown briefly by Barbara Alderman, who placed the first Bests in Show on him. After returning to Oak Ridge, he was handled exclusively by his breeder-owner, Mrs. Neth.

Carol, with her husband Tom and daughter Wendy, travelled to dog shows all over the country. Ch. Charmer became a winner in the United States and Canada as well. The Neths particularly enjoyed the beautiful show of shows, a Canadian show which one may enter by invitation only. At this prestigious International show, held in Montreal, Ch. Charmer was BIS under both Canadian and American judges. They made the trip to Canada quite often and finished several dogs there, including Ch. Oak Ridge Portrait of Puff.

This was the same year Ch. Charmer did his owners proud at Westminster, where he was again BB under Mr. Oberstar.

By now, Ch. Charmer was proving himself an excellent stud. One of his first get, Ch. Oak Ridge Justa Charm, was exhibited at the 13th AMA Specialty (1978) in San Mateo, California, and was Best Junior Puppy and RD in a class of 27. A short time later, he finished from the puppy classes. Ch. Charmer, at this specialty, was judge Mr. Merrill Cohen's choice for BB over a large entry.

The following day he was Group 1st at the Sir Francis Drake show. This second Specialty win made Ch. Charmer one of the few males to win the AMA Specialty twice.

That November, Carol and Tom flew to Bermuda where Ch. Charmer started off by going BIS the first day under Mr. Stanley Dangerfield of England. The following three shows also resulted in three Group 1sts, making him #2 on this circuit and earning his Bermudian title in three shows.

In December 1980, at Western Reserve in Cleveland, Ohio, Ch. Charmer won his final Group 1st, and has since been retired. His total record included 237 BBs, 23 BIS, 92 Group 1sts, 43 Group 2nds, 36 Group 3rds and 21 Group 4ths.

Ch. Charmer has sired a total of 15 champions at the close of 1982, with Group winners and a multiple BIS daughter, Am. & Bda. Ch. Noble Faith's White Tornado, owned by Faith Noble of Miami, Florida. Mrs. Noble is also the owner of a Ch. Charmer son, Ch. Noble Faith's Charmin Fella.

In 1981, along with finishing Ch. Oak Ridge Poppin' Fresh on the Florida Circuit, Mrs. Neth also took Mystique's Country Charmin to her championship for owners, Donna and David Perrett of Pensacola, Florida. This breeding was later repeated, which produced Ch. Oak Ridge Dust Buster.

158

BIS-winning Ch. Oak Ridge Country Charmer, owned by Carol Neth, is shown winning BB at the 1979 AMA national Specialty, with his daughter, Ch. Noble Faith's Pheobe's Finale BOS, handled by Glynette Cass and owned by Faith Knoble.

Ch. Oak Ridge Justa Charm, bred and owned by the Neths.

159

A Ch. Charmer daughter, Oak Ridge Illusive Dream, started her career by going BB over specials. Another Ch. Charmer daughter of note is Ch. Oak Ridge Free Spirit, owned by Mrs. Elsie Westrope of Canada. Ch. Oak Ridge Winn Dixie finished her championship as a tribute to her father, Ch. Oak Ridge Puffnstuff, and was his last champion daughter. Another bitch worthy of mention is Ch. Oak Ridge Country Heather, who is the daughter of Ch. Oak Ridge Justa Charm and Ch. Oak Ridge Sweet Alyssum. Heather is owned by Pat Brown, of Venice, Florida.

By 1982, Ch. Oak Ridge Poppin Fresh had produced Ch. Oak Ridge Sugar Pop and Ch. Oak Ridge Crispy Critter. Both were bred and shown by Mrs. Neth. Crispy was sold to Japan the day he finished and Sugar resides at Oak Ridge.

Carol and Tom have another champion at their house, their daughter Wendy. Wendy began showing dogs at age six, and at age 14, had gone on to become the Top Maltese Junior Handler for 1980, 1981 and 1982. Although Wendy can't brag of a particular dog she has handled exclusively, she alternates dogs and breeds. She helps her mother with Maltese, and has finished several Beagles for her father. In 1982 she was the #2 all breed national junior handler, alternating between several Maltese youngsters and her Beagle, Ch. Oak Ridge Double Trouble.

Crown Jewell

Mrs. Dorothy White got into the Maltese fancy in the late 1960s. She received her foundation stud, Ch. Maltacello's El Cid, from Mrs. Ginni Evans Sunner. Ch. El Cid, a 3½ pound dog, finished his championship in three shows. Ch. El Cid won the Puppy Sweepstakes at the Detroit AMA Specialty and became a Group winner.

The first show dog owned by Mrs. White came to her from Mrs. Ann Pendleton, Am., Can. Ch. Pendleton's Jewell. Ch. Jewell was the Top Toy Dog by *Kennel Review* for 1969 and 1970. She was the #4 dog in the nation, all breeds in 1969, and was #2 in the nation, all breeds, in 1970. Ch. Jewell had the distinction of being the only Maltese in history to be named Best of Breed at three consecutive AMA Specialties. Ch. Jewell won the parent Specialty in Chicago, in 1969, held in conjunction with the International show. She went on to Group 2nd at that show. Ch. Jewell was also BB at Westminster in 1970, and went on to place second in that strong Toy Group.

In Canada, Ch. Jewell enjoyed the same success she had in the United States. She won her Canadian title in just three shows, earning three Group 1sts and two BIS along the way.

Ch. Jewell also has the great distinction of being the first Maltese in history to win at the KC of Philadelphia, that very old, prestigious fixture.

Her final record included 29 BIS, in addition to her three consecutive Specialty wins.

Owner-handled at all times, Jewell was an outstanding specimen of the breed. Even at age ten, she was BOS at the AMA Specialty in Detroit.

Mrs. White has several anecdotes about Ch. Jewell's show career. In one, she recalls a summer show in Missouri, where the weather was very hot. Mr. Haskell Shuffman pointed to Jewell for BIS while Mrs. White was kneeling with Jewell in front of her. Mrs. White did not have the lead in hand. Upon being pointed out as Best, Jewell took off like a jet. She ran up the ramp to the BIS spot, and wagging her tail, looked at Mrs. White, who was still kneeling in the spot where several seconds earlier they both had been. "This is the stuff great show dogs are made of," adds Mrs. White, "With tons of love between the handler and the dog."

Mrs. White also recalls the time she and Jewell were waiting ringside to go in for BIS, with Jewell groomed to perfection. Suddenly, disaster—a little boy spilled a cup full of Coke all over Jewell. All Mrs. White could say was "Oh!"

Mrs. White got the noteworthy Ch. Maltacello's Issa of Buckeye from Mrs. Ginni Evans Sunner, as well. She subsequently sold this bitch to William and Ida Marsland, and showed her throughout her career. Ch. Issa finished before one year of age. She went on to become a BIS winner with Mrs. White at the helm.

Ch. Issa was bred just once by the Marslands. Bred to Mrs. White's Ch. Maltacello's El Cid, she produced three champions. All finished before a year of age—Ch. Issa's Suni Morn of Buckeye, Ch. Issa's September Dawn of Buckeye and Ch. Issa's Morning Dove of Buckeye.

In 1981, Mrs. White began to use the Crown Jewel prefix. The first of her champions to bear this prefix was Ch. Crown Jewel's Liebestraum (Ch. Maltacello's El Cid × Ch. Issa's Morning Dove of Buckeye), who became a Group winner.

Non-Vel

The Non-Vel Maltese, bred by Helen Hood of Lubbock, Texas, had their beginning in 1959 with a male pet from the Gissing Kennel of Mrs. C. M. Hunter in England. Nonpareil of Gissing was later joined by Haljean's Velveteen of Jon Vir and Skytop breeding from the kennels of Mrs. Jeanette Whistler. Both dogs were shown in obedience.

The first champion and foundation bitch came from Ms. Barbara Bender Florimbio. She was Ch. Marletta D'Lacy, sired by Diavolino of Villa Malta MMA out of Ch. Dimity of Villa Malta. Dimity was the daughter of Ch. Lacy of Villa Malta, BIS bitch of Mrs. Alma Statum. Her foundation sire, Ch. Non-Vel's Weejun of Carno MMA, also was sired by Diavolino of Villa Malta MMA out of Floriana Weissertraum Diane.

Ch. Maltecello's Issa of Buckeye, owned by Mr. and Mrs. William Marsland, handled by Dorothy White.

Ch. Non-Vel's Weejun, bred by Helen Hood, owned by Candace Mathes, was BB at the 1985 AMA Specialty.

While not the breeder of record on Ch. Weejun, he was bred at Non-Vel. His dam at the time was on loan from Dennis Carno. Both dogs went on to do well in the show ring, and as producers.

Ch. Non-Vel's Karenina D'Lacy was a daughter of the top-producer of 1970, Ch. Windrift's Sharazade, out of Marletta D'Lacy. Ch. Non-Vel's Psyche was sired by Ch. Weejun out of Ch. Karenina D'Lacy. Another Non-Vel dog of note is Ch. Non-Vel's Demitasse D'Lacy.

In 1982, all of the Non-Vel breeding stock were in a direct line from either Ch. Weejun of Carno or Weissertraum Diane or both. Ch. Non-Vel's Mariel and Ch. Non-Vel's Weejun in 1982 were both ranked among the top show Maltese in the United States.

Mrs. Hood is exceptionally talented with the camera. For years she has been known for her portraits of the Maltese.

Richelieu

Madonna Garber began her line of Richelieu Maltese in Southgate, Michigan, in 1970. She acquired her first, an adult female of Invicta, Jon Vir and Villa Malta bloodlines. This bitch, Anush Candy Kane, called Candy, was to be her foundation bitch.

Candy produced Ch. Dazzlyn Dove. She is a granddam of Ch. La Bianca's Fabrizo. Ch. Fabrizo, bred to Richelieu's Cute as a Button, sired the litter sisters, Ch. Richelieu's Sassy Lizette, owned by Elsie Burke, and Group placing Am., Can. Ch. Richelieu's Fabrienne, owned by Les Aires Kennels of Candace Mathes and Mary Senkowski. Ch. Fabrizio's litter sister is Group placing Ch. La Bianca's Carita. Also descended from Candy are Ch. Misty Morning Breeze, Ch. La Bianca's Tatiana and Ch. Dazzlyn Dicking. Candy was bred to Ch. Victor of Eng and produced a bitch, Richelieu's Martonique.

The second foundation bitch at Richelieu Maltese was acquired from Jeanne Underwood's Dazzlyn Kennels, in Howell, Michigan. Dazzlyn Display was bred to Ch. Su Le's Roadrunner and produced two litter brothers of note, Group placing Ch. Richelieu's Christmas Dream and Group placing Ch. Richelieu's Christmas Classic, known as Ch. Sharm.

Ch. Sharm sired a Group placing dog, in both the United States and Canada, Am., Can. Ch. Richelieu's Dennae. Ch. Dennae was out of Villa Malta Little Heather. Ch. Sharm also sired Group-winning Ch. Gulfstream Radiant Rhapsody, Ch. Le Aries Tasmanian Devil, owned by Candace Mathes and Mary Senkowski, and Fantasyland Richelieu Charm, owned by Carol Baldwin. Ch. Sharm is grandsire to Ch. Gulfstream Melody and noted Group winner in the United States and Canada, Am., Can. Ch. Louan's Cherokee Sunshine, owned by Elsie Burke. Ch. Sharm's pointed get includes Le Aries Flambeau Fantasia T. T.

Ch. Richelieu's Odessa, breeder, owner, handled by Madonna Garber.

Am. & Can. Ch. Richelieu's Fabrianne, bred by Madonna Garber, owned by Candace Mathes.

Ch. Richelieu's Sassy Lizette, bred by Madonna Garber and owner-handled by Elsie Burke.

164

The third brood bitch acquired by Richelieu was Doll House. This bitch of Villa Malta and Al Mar bloodlines is known as Toot. Bred to Ch. Richelieu's Christmas Classic, Toot produced Richelieu's Cute as a Button MMA. Buttons is the dam of Ch. Richelieu's Odessa, Ch. Richelieu's Sassy Lizette and Group placing Am., Can. Ch. Richelieu's Fabrianne. Buttons is the granddam of the noted Ch. Louan's Apache Dancer, owned by Elsie Burke.

An outstanding addition to the Richelieu stud force is the multiple Group placing dog, both here and in Canada, Am., Can. Ch. Marcan's Majestic Colonel (Ch. Tamborino of Villa Malta × Villa Malta Vanessa). He was bred by Marge Rozik. Ch. Colonel gained his Canadian title in just three shows, undefeated, and sired Ch. Cariel Easy Lovin, C & M's Moticka of Richelieu, Richelieu's Midnight Drifter, out of Kinos Moonflower.

Louan

A relative newcomer to the fancy is Elsie Burke of Louan's Maltese, located in Farmington, Michigan. She acquired her first Maltese in 1976, two bitches from Madonna Garber's Richelieu Maltese. They were her first show dogs—Ch. Richelieu's Sassy Lizette (Ch. La Bianca's Fabrizo × Richelieu's Cute as a Button) which she handled to its championship. The second bitch, also owner-handled to its championship, was Am., Can. Ch. Louan's Cherokee Sunshine, which became a Group winner in Canada, and a Group placer in the States. From the Su Le Kennels, Mrs. Burke has acquired Ch. Su Le's Pica Pica, a male.

Le Aries

Le Aries Maltese, located in Allen Park, Michigan, is relatively new on the Maltese scene, co-owned by Mary H. Senkowski and her daughter, Candace Mathes. Originally Mrs. Mathes was alone in this venture. However, with the purchase of Richelieu's Spirit of C & M, Mrs. Mathes was joined by her mother as co-owner in Le Aries.

They acquired their first in 1978, from Madonna Garber's Richelieu Maltese. As complete newcomers to both Maltese and the show ring, they were fortunate to have the assistance of Mrs. Garber in their first attempt at campaigning a dog to its championship. Am., Can. Ch. Richelieu's Fabrianne, known as Ch. Bria, first completed her Canadian title, undefeated in five shows. She won her American title 15 months later, in July 1980, with a Group 4th, and three majors, including a five-point win. Ch. Bria is a combination of the Su Le and Dazzlyn lines.

A brood bitch was acquired of the Villa Malta bloodlines who produced Ch. Le Aries Tasmanian Devil. Ch. Devil, shown by professional handler William Cunningham, is the first homebred champion for Le Aries, finishing at one year.

In addition, several dogs have been acquired outside of the bloodlines now represented at Le aries. These dogs are very closely linebred within their respective families. They were acquired with the ultimate expansion of the Le Aries breeding program in mind and include Ch. Fantasyland Dream Baby, bred by Carole Baldwin; Ch. Richelieu's Spirit of C & M, a Group winner, also shown by Mr. Cunningham, who finished in two weeks at seven shows; Ch. Myi's Flame of Glory, a winner of two five-point majors; Ch. Su Le's Mot Mot, from the Su Le Kennels, BB over specials enroute to the title and Ch. Su Le's Purple Martin, a champion with five majors. He was briefly specialed, shown six times. He was awarded four BBs, a Group 1st and Group 2nd. The most recent acquisition at Le Aries is Group-winning Ch. Non-Vel's Weejun, bred by Helen Hood.

Martin-Cid

Marjorie Martin and her Maltese reside in Columbus, Ohio. She uses the Martin's prefix in conjunction with the -Cid suffix, in naming her dogs. She acquired her first Maltese in 1972.

Her aim had been for better quality Maltese. She did not enjoy much luck, however, until her Alkay's Rose Bud was bred to Ch. Maltacello's El Cid, producing Ch. Martin's Michael-Cid. She then bred two granddaughters of Ch. Maltacello's El Cid, Sugar and Cookie. These broods have produced many Michael babies including Ch. Martin's Foxwell-Cid, Ch. Martin's Maxwel-Cid, Ch. Martin's Rachel-Cid and Ch. Martin's Annabel-Cid.

Ms. Martin is quite adept with the camera. The photos of her dogs exhibited are examples of her talents.

Rancho Villa

Norma Hughes breeds her Rancho Villa Maltese in Saginaw, Michigan. One of her early stud dogs was Playboy of Gallo, a dog of Villa Malta and Vicbrita bloodlines. An early bitch was Ch. Hughes Missy. Playboy bred to Ch. Missy produced the first homebred champion at Rancho Villa, Ch. Issa Dora of Rancho Villa. She attained her championship by garnering four major wins.

Acquired from Mrs. Dorothy Tinker was Al Dor Amron of Rancho Villa. Another champion at Rancho Villa, acquired from the Berquists, is Ch. Su Le's Nightengale.

Al-Mar

Mrs. Marjorie Lewis founded her Al-Mar kennels in the late 1950s at

166

Ch. Martin's Michael-Cid, bred and owned by Marjorie Martin.

BIS-winning Ch. Nicholas of Al-Mar, a top winner bred at Al-Mar.

Multiple BIS-winning Ch. Al-Mar's Mary Poppins, daughter of Ch. Button's 'N' Bows of Al-Mar, breeder, owner, handled by Marjorie Lewis.

Independence, Missouri. Her foundation stock was Villa Malta. However, Mrs. Lewis is a firm believer in outcross breeding, and thus has had and used several of the finest dogs and bloodlines in her breeding program. Mrs. Lewis is a professional all-breed handler. She has specialized in Maltese, Lhasa Apso and Shih Tzu. To date, Mrs. Lewis has put championship titles on more than 75 Maltese.

The first important hombred winner at Al-Mar was Am., Can. Ch. Patrick Al-Mar of Villa Malta (Ch. Ricco of Villa Malta × Ch. Tanella of Villa Malta). This dog was much noted in Mrs. Lewis' area of the country before he was exchanged for a time with Halia Scott Taylor of the Folklore Maltese in California. In return, Mrs. Lewis received Ch. Mimino of Villa Malta from Mrs. Taylor. While in California, Ch. Patrick was a consistent show winner, and sired a number of champions. Eventually, Ch. Patrick was returned to Mrs. Lewis, and Ch. Mimino went home to California.

One of Ch. Patrick's champions was Kenny's Majic Madge of Al-Mar, which was out of Hulta's Cuddles. Whelped in 1961, this Maltese was owned by Sallie Sajonce and produced ten champions.

Mrs. Lewis also bred Group-winning Am., Can. Ch. Primrose Little Toot of Al-Mar, owned by Marge Stuber of Primrose Maltese in Ohio. He was kept for Mrs. Stuber by Trudie Dillon, Tutees Maltese.

Also of note at Al-Mar was Ch. Charlie Brown of Al-Mar (Eng. Ch. Twintop the Snowman × Ch. Tiny Tiana of Al-Mar). This typey little male attained his championship at eight months of age.

Mrs. Lewis has bred a number of BIS Maltese. Among them are Ch. Nicholas of Al-Mar, shown by Dee Sheperd and Ch. Al-Mar's Mary Poppins (Ch. Pegden's Magic Touch of Al-Mar × Ch. Buttons N' Bows of Al-Mar). This lovely bitch won five BIS and ten Group 1sts in limited showing.

Mrs. Lewis had the great pleasure and honor of being voted to judge the Puppy Sweepstakes at the 1982 AMA Specialty. The winner of her choice was very popular with the fancy—Ch. Marcris Marshmallow, bred and owned by Joyce Watkins of the Marcris Kennels.

Dazzlyn

Dazzlyn Maltese are bred by Jeanne Underwood in Howell, Michigan. Commencing in 1969 with a blend of the Aennchen and Villa Malta bloodlines, Dazzlyn Maltese have a history of good class wins at AMA Specialties. The tradition began with Dazzlyn's first champion, Ch. Gay Acres Sherry Sir Sparkle, BW at the 1969 national Specialty.

Ch. Sir Sparkle sired Ch. Dazzlyn Sir Twinkle. Ch. Sir Twinkle was WD at the 1970 Specialty.

In 1971, Ch. Dazzlyn Dinah-Mite, also by Ch. Sir Sparkle, was WB and BW at the 1971 Specialty.

Ch. Dazzlyn Dinah's Dress-up was WB at the 1975 Specialty. Ch. Dress-up was by Ch. Dazzlyn Dartana out of Ch. Dinah-Mite.

In 1977, Ch. Dazzlyn Dictator took WD at the Specialty.

Royal'tese

Until her death in 1983, Mrs. Ila Vargas was a dedicated Maltese breeder and fancier in Anaheim, California. Her kennel name was Royal'tese.

She began with Star Bright's Mr. De Marco, a dog, from the Joanne-Chen line. Several bitches were acquired, among them Ch. Joanne-Chen's Rhapsody Dancer, Joanne-Chen's Sweet Mana Dancer and Ch. Joanne-Chen's Sweety Pie Dancer.

A noted dog at Royal'tese, Ch. Maya Li'l Design of Royal'tese, resulted when Mrs. Vargas bred Ch. Joanne-Chen's Sweetie Pie to Ch. Aennchen's Maya Dancer. Another stud at Royal'tese was Maya's Keepsake of Royal'tese. Keepsake was bred to Ch. Joanne-Chen's Rhapsody Dancer, producing Ch. Zip a Dee Do Da.

Royal'tese was the home of Ch. Wee Mal Rocki Dew. Ch. Rocky was WD at the 1976 AMA Specialty. Sired by Ch. Maltacello's Romeo out of Midhill Trend of Moderna, this four pound beauty was owner-handled to his fine record.

Gemmery

Naomi Erickson has Gemmery Maltese in St. Paul, Minnesota, and has had Maltese since 1977. She first acquired Ch. San Su Kee Tiara Star of Stars, litter sister to Group-winning Ch. San Su Kee Angel Face, bred by Mrs. Palmersten.

Her next acquisition was Am., Can. Ch. Maltes'a Radiant Desiree', whelped December 24, 1974. This bitch became a top producer for Mrs. Erickson, with five champions in three litters. Bred to Ch. Joanne-Chen's Mino Maya Dancer, she produced champion littermates Ch. Gemmery's Ruby Tiara and Ch. Gemmery's Opal Tiara, whelped July 4, 1978. Bred to Ch. Oak Ridge Country Charmer, she produced Ch. Gemmery's Amethyst Charm, whelped January 14, 1979. Bred to Ch. Martin's Sweet Bean Puff, she produced littermates Ch. Gemmery's Turquoise Bean and Ch. Gemmery's Citine Bean, whelped November 19, 1980.

Ch. Turquoise Bean won two Group 1sts, handled by Mr. Tim Lehman. Ch. Citrine Bean became a multiple BIS winner.

Marsh Maltese

Muriel Marsh Bittle breeds the Marsh Maltese in Prior Lake, Minnesota. She purchased her first Maltese in 1976 from the late Richard

Reid and finished her a year later. Ch. Morning Song's Minuette was a delight to show, winning a Group 3rd her fourth time in the ring, from the puppy class. She has since produced several champions.

She was bred to Ch. Joanne-Chen's Mino Maya Dancer, producing Am., Can. Ch. Marsh's Disco Dancer. He finished in the United States with four majors and, in Canada, he finished in four shows, with a Group 1st and 2nd. He is now the sire of a Group winner and grandsire of a multiple BIS winner.

Minuette, bred to Ch. Myi's Sun Seeker, produced Ch. Marsh's Morning Seeker. He placed in the Group from the classes. Also finished in that litter is Ch. Marsh's Morning Sky, owned by Dixie Lee Krasky. He also placed in the Group from the classes, and was finished by Mr. Tim Lehman.

Mrs. Bittle's breeding program is built around Ch. Gemmery's Turquoise Bean, a multiple Group winner, purchased from Naomi Erickson. He sired WD at Westminster in 1983, Ch. Gemmery's Alexandrite-Tee.

Ch. Ronalta April Marsh was purchased from Veronica Landreville of Edmonton, Alberta, Canada. She is linebred on Beverly and Dean Passe's highly successful Myi bloodline.

Simone

Mrs. Simone Smith has been breeding her Simone's Maltese in Sayville, New York, since 1974.

Her first Maltese, and foundation stud was acquired from Carol Fellows of LaLace's Lorac Maltese, also in Sayville. Ch. LaLace's Lorac Dream Dancer was six months old when she acquired him. His bloodline was Aennchen, Joanne-Chen with some of the Villa Malta and Alpond bloodlines, as well. He matured into a three-pound dog and at one year of age was shown to his championship by Barbara Alderman.

Ch. Lorac has proven himself a sire of worth. Bred to Sabrina's Shine Little Star, bred by Marcia Richardson of Sabrina's Maltese, he produced Ch. Simone's King Creole. The lovely male finished quickly, attending just seven shows to gain his title. He was a Group placer from the classes.

A repeat of this breeding produced Ch. Simone's Chemin de Fer. This dog finished in just six shows, garnering three BBs and Toy Group 2nd from the classes, at just ten months. Sabrina was of the Villa Malta, Joanne-Chen, Aennchen bloodlines. Of the same breeding as Ch. Chemin de Fer is Ch. Simone's Dream Walking, owned by Pauline Perry. This lovely bitch was pointed at just six months of age.

Petit Point

Miss Susan Sandlin, of Arlington, Virginia, breeds the Petit Point

Ch. Morning Song's Minuette,
bred by Richard Reid,
owned by Muriel Bittle.

Ch. Lalace's Lorac Dream Walking, bred by
Carol Fellows, owned by Simone Smith and
shown to his title by Barbara Alderman.

Canadian Group-winning Ch. Marsh's Disco
Dancer, breeder, owner, handled by Muriel
Bittle.

171

Maltese. Her breeding program is kept on a small scale as she has a full time job in addition to her kennel duties. Every dog in the breeding program at Petit Point is of show quality. The only dog which does not have championship points at Petit Point is Peersun's My Valentine, whose coat was cut down when she was acquired.

The first Maltese at Petit Point was acquired in 1979 from Kathy DiGiacomo's Kathan Maltese. His name was Ch. Kathan's Petit Point Alfie (Ch. Kathan's Peppermint Twist × Ch. Su Le's Bittern). He finished at 14 months, owner-handled, and has proven a successful sire.

Miss Sandlin's second Maltese also came from Kathan Kennels, Ch. Kathan's Petit Point Sugaree (Ch. Kathan's Rhinestone Cowboy × Kathan's Rhapsody in Blue), bred by Margaret Wehanger. Ch. Sugaree finished at 11 months, with back to back majors.

The third Maltese was also acquired from Mrs. DiGiacomo, Kathan Petit Point Blu Velvet (Ch. Su Le's Bluebird × Angie Baby), bred by Mr. and Mrs. N. Kenny. Velvet was shown only a few times in the United States, winning a three-point major at six months. She was then sold to Columbia, South America, where her show career was continued.

Miss Sandlin's fourth Maltese, Peersun's My Valentine, bred by Shirley Pearson, was acquired as a brood bitch. She has proven herself a good producer. Bred to Ch. Alfie, the resulting get were both show successes—Petit Point Pique and Ch. Petit Point Poker Chip.

A repeat breeding of Ch. Alfie to Ch. Sugaree was done and resulted in the first homebred champion at Petit Point, Am., Can. Ch. Petit Point Sugar Blues. A second repeat resulted in the bitch, Petit Point Berceuse.

Elkins Maltese

Florence Elkins of Wyandotte, Michigan, established her Elkins Maltese in 1973 with the acquisition of Meri Miss Pixie of Eng (Joanne-Chen's Dancing St. V of Eng × Miss Happy Birthday of Eng), from Anna Engstrom's Eng Kennels.

Her first breedings were done with dogs of the Su Le line. The first get produced at Elkins Maltese was Elkins Petite and Jeweliana. Out of four different breedings, one was quite successful. Elkins Amethyst Beauty, bred to BIS Ch. Su Le's Martin, produced Ch. Elkin's Treasure of Love, whelped July 10, 1977. This was the first Elkins champion. Also sired by Best in Show Ch. Su Le's Martin, and out of Elkins Amethyst Beauty, was Ch. Elkins White Ice. Ch. White Ice finished with three majors, breeder-owner handled.

An outcross between BIS Am., Can. & Bda. Ch. Oak Ridge Country Charmer and Elkins Jewelette produced Ch. Elkins Charmer's Twinkle, Ch. Elkins Florian Fantasy, and Elkins Patrician Purity, all littermates.

Elkins Dewdrop is dam to Ch. Misty Morning Breeze, bred by Beatrice Naysmith.

Naysmith Maltese

Mrs. Beatrice Naysmith of Camden, Michigan, was unaware of the Maltese until 1973. At that time, she and her husband attended the Detroit Kennel Club show. While there, they became fascinated by the little white dogs of Malta.

Upon her return home, she shared the news of her "find" with her mother, Mrs. Florence Elkins. Mrs. Elkins subsequently purchased her first Maltese, Meri Miss Pixie of Eng. Mrs. Naysmith's first Maltese, Elkins Dew Drop, was out of this bitch by Ch. Su Le's Whip-Poor-Will. She was acquired in 1975.

Mrs. Elkins had, by this time, become active in the fancy and the show ring. Mrs. Naysmith began to accompany her mother to dog shows.

Mrs. Naysmith bred her first litter in 1976, and included her first champion, Ch. Naysmith's Strut N Stuff (Ch. Elkins Treasure of Love × Naysmith's Honeydew). At six months, Strutty had a four-point major. He finished with three majors. This included a five-point major from the puppy class. Ch. Strutty became a champion at 11 months of age, and later proved himself a quality stud.

Mrs. Naysmith has introduced the Dazzlyn bloodline into her bloodline. She owned Ch. Dazzlyn Dictator, bred by Mrs. Underwood. Ch. Dictator was WD at the 1977 AMA Specialty.

Mrs. Naysmith also introduced the Villa Malta line into her breeding program with dogs acquired from Francis Wright.

Two other champion Naysmith Maltese are Naysmith's Little Whisper, sired by Ch. Strutty, and Elkins Lil' Squirt of Naysmith, a grandson of Ch. Oak Ridge Country Charmer.

Sanibel

Manya Dujardin has a 20-year background in the purebred dog fancy. Her interest in Maltese commenced in 1977. In the first litter of Maltese bred at her Sanibel Kennels, in Oxford, Connecticut, she got Ch. Sanibel Timothy Truelove.

Mrs. Dujardin follows the practice of linebreeding, occasionally inbreeding, followed by an outcross. Her resulting get are between four and eight pounds.

What attracts Mrs. Dujardin most to Maltese breeding is the fact that of the many breeds with which she has had experience, the Maltese is outstanding in that there is no predisposition to genetic defects (liver or kidney disease, epilepsy, cleft palates, PRA, undulating Patellas, etc.).

Sanibel Maltese are kenneled outdoors. They are extremely hardy and never sick.

Mrs. Dujardin has enjoyed a close relationship with Mrs. Ruth Hager of Nika Maltese. They have co-owned several dogs together.

Maltara

Marjorie and Myron O'Hare of Clearwater, Florida, have bred the Maltara line of Maltese for a number of years, using a blend of the Sun Canyon and Joanne-Chen bloodlines. Noted of their breeding are Ch. Maltara's Show Boat, Ch. Maltara's Show Impress, Ch. Maltara's Show Imp and Ch. Sun Canyon Sugar Imp. Ch. Maltara's Show Off is co-owned by the Bianca Maltese.

Kandida

Mrs. Peggy Hogg has been involved in the Maltese fancy for many years. She began showing Maltese in 1969, as a professional handler. She has shown many Maltese to their championships, too many to list.

She is especially known for having shown some of the top-winning Maltese specials in the history of the breed. Her charges have always been superbly conditioned and groomed to perfection.

Included among the specials Peggy has guided to their noteworthy wins is Ch. Joanne-Chen's Maya Dancer, a dog bred by Joanne Hesse and owned by Mamie R. Gregory. Peggy handled this dog to more BIS wins than any other dog in the history of the breed, totalling 43. Ch. Maya was top Toy dog two consecutive years, as rated by all systems. Ch. Maya was rated #2 dog in the nation one year. He was awarded the *Quaker Oats Award* two years, twice won the Westminster Toy Group and has a Maltese Merit Award for having sired numerous champions.

Ch. Cuddledoon's Mayadoll Prince, a Ch. Maya son, was owned by Dr. and Mrs. Nelson King. Shown only a few months, he won three all-breed BIS.

Ch. Marees' Tu-Grand Kandi Kane, owned by Nancy Shapland, won 11 all-breed BIS. He had 47 Groups and received the *Quaker Oats Award* for Top Toy after being only shown one year.

Ch. Malone's Snowie Roxann, also owned by Nancy Shapland, and bred by Jennie Malone, was a top-winning bitch. She won 15 all-breed BIS, 52 Group 1sts and BB at several Specialties.

Using the Kandida prefix, Mrs. Hogg plans to continue her interest in the breed by breeding on a limited basis, in conjunction with Mrs. Nancy Shapland. Their first Kandida Maltese, Ch. Kandida's Casper, finished undefeated.

174

The top winning Maltese of all time, Ch. Joanne-Chen's Maya Dancer, owned by Mamie Gregory, with his handler Peggy Hogg.

Multiple BIS-winning Ch. Malone's Snowie Roxann, bred by Jennie Malone, owned by Nancy Shapland and handled by Peggy Hogg.

175

Al Jon

Miss Alma Jones, of Short Hills, New Jersey, has been in Maltese since the early 1970s. She uses the Al Jon prefix. She began with an Aennchen–Joanne-Chen bred bitch, which she showed to its championship, Ch. Mike-Mars Lovely Lady. She purchased several other Aennchen bloodline dogs, including Aennchen's Sova Dancer. She recently bred a bitch of Cari and Joanne-Chen bloodlines to Ch. Aennchen's Ethanbet Snow Dance, and a superb male resulted.

A lovely male was acquired from the Myi Maltese, Ch. Myi's Super Seeker, which was owner-handled to his championship. Ch. Seeker has proven himself an excellent stud.

Carlinda

Martha Di Giovanni and her daughter Linda have been breeding and exhibiting Maltese for a number of years. Located in Staten Island, New York, their dogs bear the Carlinda prefix. Their original stock was of Cari-Joanne-Chen bloodline. They have bred and exhibited several champions, including the noted BIS dog Ch. Carlinda's Journey to All Star. Also of note at Carlinda are Ch. Carlinda's Latest Sensation, Ch. Carlinda's Latest Fashion and Carlinda's Secret Dream of Ja Ma, co-owned with Mr. and Mrs. M. Whitman.

Nika

Ruth Hager, from Madison, Connecticut, uses the Nika prefix. With daughter, Jackie, this veteran fancier is a familiar figure at Northeastern dog shows.

Mrs. Hager has enjoyed associations with several other breeders over the years, most notably, Mrs. Marge Stuber of the Primrose Maltese. More recently there have been associations with the Tenessa Maltese of Mr. and Mrs. S. Feldblum and the Sanibel Maltese, owned by Mrs. Dujardin.

Noteworthy of the Nika Maltese are Ch. Primrose Desdemona and Ch. Primrose Goddewyn, bred by Mrs. Stuber; Nika's Whodat, co-owned by Jacqueline Reilley; Ch. Sanibel Woofer of Nika and Ch. Sanibel Spring Pepper of Nika, co-owned by Mrs. Dujardin.

Lyndale

The Lyndale prefix identifies Mrs. Lillian Harrington, of Vestal, New York. Her bloodlines are mainly Villa Malta, with some Cari, Joanne-Chen and Primrose representation.

Included among the Lyndale Maltese are Ch. Lyndale's Miss America, owned by Jean Carioli; Ch. Gaylord of Primrose Place, bred by Marge Stuber and Ch. Villa Malta Miss Stacey, bred by Marge Rozik.

Melodylane

Freeman and Mary Purvis, of Centerville, Iowa, have been dog fanciers for many years, their main interest being in Yorkshire Terriers.

In 1980, they acquired Group-winning Ch. Gayla Joanne-Chen's Muskrat Luv, a stud dog, from Mrs. Darlene Wilkinson's Gayla Maltese. They then became involved in Maltese and continued to use their Yorkshire prefix, Melodylane.

One of the first Maltese litters produced at Melodylane produced Ch. Melodylane Dear Abby Luv and Ch. Melodylane Raggedy Ann Luv, sired by Ch. Muskrat Luv.

Ch. Andy was owned by Chip Constantino and AKC judge, Norman Patton, of Missouri. His career began with his owner handling, winning the Puppy Sweepstakes at the Houston AMA Specialty in August, 1981. He was also RD at the same show. The Purvises specialed Ch. Andy for a time, winning several Group placements. After being acquired by Messrs. Patton and Constantino, the dog was handled by Mr. Tim Lehman to top honors. Within four months, Ch. Andy had eight all-breed BIS and 18 Group 1sts; later his total stood at 26 Group 1sts and nine all-breed BIS.

Ch. Dear Abby was WB at the 1981 AMA Specialty for a five-point major. A third littermate, Ch. Melodylane Once 'N Luv with Amy, finished with back-to-back four-point majors.

Pat Sharit

Mr. Pat Sharit of California has been a very active member of the Maltese fancy for many years. He has had association with B. June Pozzi, of the Bejune's Maltese, and Larry and Judy Slaalien, of the Jular Maltese.

Included among his dogs are Group placing Ch. Ro-J's Bojangles De Chablese; BIS Ch. Bejune's Tomfoolery, co-owned with B. June Pozzi; and Ch. Tomfoolery's daughter, Ch. Montara's Ms. D. Meanor O' Ju Lar, co-owned with the Slaaliens.

Ju Lar

Ju Lar's Maltese have been bred since 1970 by Judy and Larry Slaalien, in Portland, Oregon. Their first litter was whelped in 1970. The Slaaliens acquired several dogs from Jari Bobbilot's Moderna Maltese, namely Ch. Mysta Myt of Moderna and Group placing Ch. Ju Lar's Betcha Myt of Moderna.

One of the greatest rewards to come to their Maltese was their brood bitch, Ch. Ju Lar's Victoria being named top brood bitch at the 1982 AMA Specialty in Las Vegas. Ch. Victoria took the class, being the first *trimmed* Maltese ever shown. Her get included Ch. Montara's Ms. D. Meanor O' Ju

177

Ch. Nika's **Bonus**, the first homebred champion for owner, Ruth Hager.

Ch. Primrose Desdemona of Nika, bred by Marge Stuber, owned by Ruth Hager.

Ch. Gayla Joanne-Chen's Muskrat Luv, multiple Group winner, owned and handled by Freeman and Mary Purvis.

BIS-winning Ch. Bejune's Tomfoolery, co-owned by Pat Sharit and B. June Pozzi.
Courtesy AKC Library

Ch. Melodylane Dear Abby Luv, WB at the national AMA Specialty, bred, owned and handled by Freeman and Mary Purvis.

Ch. Gayla Joanne-Chen's Muskrat Luv, shown winning the stud dog class at the AMA national Specialty in 1982. His get are: Melodylane Bouncy Buttons Luv, Ch. Melodylane Good Ole Boy Luv and Melodylane Happiness Is Luv.

Ch. Ju Lar's Victoria, shown winning the brood bitch class at the 1982 AMA national Specialty, with her get, Ch. Montara's Ms D Meanor and Ju Lar's Phillip.

Am. & Can. Ch. Ju Lar's Betcha Myt of Moderna, owned by Judy Slaalien, and Ch. Ju Lar's Kaese, owned by the Brownleewes and Judy Slaalien (left).

Am. & Can. Ch. Ju Lar's Andrew, bred and owned by Judy Slaalien.

Lar, co-owned with Patrick Sharit, and Ju Lar's Philip, sired by Ch. Moppet's Dream Weaver.

Westwood

Doris and her mother, Jane Wexler, breed the Westwood Maltese near Cleveland, Ohio. Their bloodline is based upon the Su Le, Joanne-Chen and Villa Malta bloodlines.

One of their top producing bitches, Ch. Wexler's Lily Love MMA, was bred to Ch. To the Victor of Eng, producing a litter of two champions, Ch. Westwood Magic Moonbeam and Ch. Westwood Wishing Star. Another champion out of Ch. Lily Love, Ch. De Tetraults Love of Westwood, was owned by Virginia Davey.

Added to their breeding program as studs were Ch. Kathan's Viceroy Mr. Blue and Ch. Villa Malta Timothy, bred by Marge Rozik.

Lennard Reppond

Mr. Lennard Reppond of San Leandro, California, has been in the Maltese fancy since the 1960s. He has owned and shown a number of noteworthy Maltese, and has maintained a steady interest in the breed.

Mr. Reppond owned and showed the 1966 Group winner Ch. Enrico, a BB winner at nine months. His record included 30 BBs and 21 Group 1sts. Ch. Enrico was top Toy in the Western United States in 1967, according to *Kennel Review.*

Other dogs of note associated with Mr. Reppond are Ch. Seafoam's Gypsy Dancer and Ch. Myi's Morning Glory, bred by Beverly Passe.

Bienaimee

Mrs. Blanche Tenerowicz of East Hampton, Massachusetts, purchased her first Maltese from Claudette Le May's Sugar Town Kennels in 1974, Sugar Town Bienaimee. Bienaimee is Mrs. Tenerowicz's kennel prefix. She also acquired Ch. Joanne-Chen's Mino Maya Dancer. This dog has become her foundation dog. Ch. Mino was shown by Miss Daryl Martin, daughter of Rena Martin, breeder of Martin's Puff Maltese, based on the Joanne-Chen bloodline.

Mrs. Tenerowicz has bred a number of champions that finished with Miss Martin on the lead.

Heartland

Mrs. Mary A. La Bach founded her Heartland Maltese in Nicholasville, Kentucky. The first bitch at Heartland was Mary's Cotton Petite Amore (Ch. Boreas Rex × Boreas Coelestia).

A linebreed mating produced Mary's Cotton Small Wonder. Acquired

Ch. Myi's Morning Glory,
bred by Beverly Passe and
owner handled by Mr.
Reppond.

Multiple BIS-winning Ch. Our
Enterprizing Be Be, owned
and bred by Susan Grubb,
handled by Annete Lurton.
Courtesy AKC Library

from the Le Grand Maltese of Mrs. Helen Johnson was Le Grand's White Magnolia (Non-Vel's Pokoi of Le Grand × Ch. D' Arelene's Dark Eyes), a bitch. With the acquisition of another bitch, Noble Faith's Gem of Heartland, the Heartland prefix was established.

Mrs. La Bach began exhibiting when she acquired Ch. Sun Canyon Devil Dancer O K Y (Ch. Halos Mini Mite Dancer × Sun Canyon Felicity). This dog finished before he was a year old and was followed by Ch. Snow Fire of Merry Ho (Ch. Su Le's Man-O-War Bird × Merry Ho's Serendipity II), which finished handily. Ch. Snowfire sired the next Heartland champion, Ch. Heartland's Toby Toot, out of Le Grand's White Magnolia.

Acquired from Mrs. Sue Kuecher was Ch. Tampier's Gayla Amanda (Ch. Windsong's Hey Mr. Banjo × Tampier's Glad's Mr. Dumplin'). A favorite at Heartland, she finished handily.

Tampier's Maltese

Sue Kuecher has the Tampier's Maltese, located in Oak Lawn, Illinois. Mrs. Kuecher had an association for a time with Mrs. Darlene Wilkinson. The dogs produced during this association bore the Tampier's Gayla prefix.

Mrs. Kuecher acquired Ch. Joanne-Chen's After the Lovin from Mrs. Joanne Hesse. Ch. After the Lovin was WD at the 1980 AMA Specialty. He is serving as a major stud force at Tampier's, already having sired champion get.

Ch. Tampier's Love Me Tender, known as "Elvis," was bred by Mrs. Kuecher and is co-owned by Kris Collins of Krystal Maltese. Ch. Elvis is by Ch. After the Lovin, out of Tampier's Glad's Lil' Dumplin'. Ch. Elvis won a five-point major the first time he was shown at eight months. He finished at ten months with three majors and was Best Junior Puppy in the Sweepstakes at the 1981 AMA Specialty. He is already proving his worth at stud, having sired his first champion get, Ch. Tampier's Appassionata, bred and owned by Mrs. Kuecher.

Ch. Appassionata (Ch. Tampier's Love Me Tender × Joanne-Chen's Feelings) was Best Puppy at the 1982 AMA Specialty. He finished with three major wins, including one for five points.

Krystal

Mrs. Kris Collins breeds Krystal Maltese in Glendale Heights, Illinois. She enjoys a close relationship with Mrs. Kuecher and her Tampier Maltese. She co-owns with Mrs. Kuecher Ch. Tampier's Love Me Tender.

Ch. Krystal's Logical Charm, co-owned with Mrs. Kuecher, won the Bred-by-Exhibitor class at the 1982 AMA Specialty. Ch. Krystal's Inside Moves, bred by Mrs. Collins, is owned and was shown by Simone Smith and Marlene Greenberg.

Merry Ho

Mrs. Mary Hohs breeds the Merry Ho Maltese near Cleveland, Ohio. Her foundations are Joanne-Chen and Su Le.

An important stud force at Merry Ho is Ch. Su Le's Man-O-War Bird. Dogs of note from Merry Ho include Ch. Merry Ho's V.W. Rabbit and Ch. Snowfire of Merry Ho. Mrs. Hohs has the distinction of having sold the popular entertainer, Liberace, his pet Maltese.

Our Enterprizing

Susan Grubb maintains Our Enterprizing Maltese in Norwalk, Ohio. Her kennel is noted for producing multiple BIS Ch. Our Enterprizing Be Be.

Ch. To the Victor of Eng was bred to her bitch, Joanne-Chen's Kandi Bon Bon, and on June 1, 1977, Be Be and her four littermates, orphaned at birth, were given little chance to survive. The litter was bottle-fed; all survived.

On June 1, 1979, her second birthday, Be Be won her first BIS at Crawford County KC, Bucyrus, Ohio. She went on to win two more Bests.

Be Be is now retired and at home to take part in the Enterprizing breeding program.

Bianca

Marynelle Clark of Dublin, Ohio, has been an avid Maltese fancier for many years. Her closely linebred Bianca line began with her first litter in 1955.

The foundation of Bianca Maltese was based upon some noteworthy Maltese, including Ch. Idnar's King Midas, Ch. Sun Canyon Drummer Boy, Ch. Fairy Fay's Figaro, Ch. Bobbelee Brag-A-Bout, Ch. Aennchen's Shikar Dancer, Ch. Shabudi of Kismet, Ch. Valentino of Maltacello, Ch. Patrick Al Mar of Villa Malta, and others of the Villa Malta bloodline.

Early Bianca dogs include Stentaway's Pageboy and Stentaway's Page Girl, bred by Mary Hechinger. Ch. Maltara's Show Off was owned and shown by the O'Haras and bred by Mrs. Clark. Ch. Bianca's Maltara Coat Machine, bred by Mrs. Clark, was also owned by the O'Hara's Maltara Maltese.

Descended from Bianca Maltese is Ch. Holly Doll O' Rolling Glenn, owned by the Glenns. Her son, Ch. Rolling Glenn Caesar Augustus, finished his championship at Westminster with a five-point major.

Yorkfold

Mrs. Frances Geraghty and son Bob have been active Maltese fanciers in Ohio for many years. They are primarily known for their Yorkfold

Multiple BIS-winning Ch. Maree's Tu-Grand Kundi Kane, bred by Anne Wright, owned by Nancy Shapland, handled by Peggy Hogg.

Ch. Su Le's Screech Owl, owned by Jerri Walters, Kathy DiGiacomo and Barbara Bergquist.

Ch. Carlinda's Journey to All Star, bred by Martha and Linda Di Giavonni. The Carlinda Kennels are based on the Cari, Joanne-Chen bloodline.

Yorkshire Terriers. However, several noteworthy Maltese have been bred or campaigned by them, including the famous Ch. Alpond's Sky Rocket, Ch. Yorkfold the Caucasian and Ch. Yorkfold Zorro.

4

The Maltese
Around the World

The Maltese Dog in Canada

The first Maltese to be registered with the Canadian Kennel Club were recorded in 1899. They were a bitch, Gipsy, whelped in 1895 and a dog, Jumbo, whelped in 1897. Both dogs, sired by Bob out of Gipsey, were bred by Mrs. Cook of Toronto.

James McNaught, of Toronto, bred a dog, Tiny (Jacko × White Diamond), whelped in 1900. Miss Goldsmith registered this dog with the CKC in 1902.

The American breeder Miss Gertrude Roon exhibited her Baby Boy at a dog show in Toronto in 1902. Maltese continued to be exhibited at Canadian shows from 1903 until 1913. However, during this same period no Maltese were registered with the CKC. In 1914, two English imports were registered by Mrs. Short, of Brixton Maltese, St. Thomas, British Columbia, an active fancier of the period. These were, a dog, Major Meneris of Brixton, whelped in 1910, and a bitch, Bunty of Brixton, whelped in 1912.

Several dogs of the Brixton bloodline were used in the United States as foundation stock for the Melita Kennels of Anna Judd and the Fretona Kennels of Mrs. Freerkson, both located in Seattle, Washington. Mrs. Helene Studebaker Henderson also imported several Brixton Maltese.

Mrs. Judd registered several dogs with the CKC as well as with the AKC, as did Mrs. Henderson. The first two Maltese in history to earn both

American and Canadian titles were Mrs. Judd's Ch. Melita Cupid and Mrs. Henderson's Ch. Studebaker Namur.

From 1913 to 1930, one of the most active Canadian fanciers was Mr. Raymond Card. Mr. Card showed Maltese in England before moving to Canada, and brought several dogs with him when he relocated. During this period, he finished an amazing five dogs for their Canadian titles.

From 1923 to 1941, Mrs. Skidmore of Nova Scotia was actively breeding and exhibiting. The origin of her foundation bloodline is not known, although she purchased a bitch from Mrs. Peaster in Philadelphia. Mrs. Skidmore showed her Tiny and Snowbird to their Canadian championships.

Also from Nova Scotia was Mrs. Andrews. She imported into Canada two Maltese from Miss Bancroft's Hale Farm line, Invictus and Dewdrop, in 1939. Maltese of her breeding became noteworthy, and several were imported back into the United States, to be used as foundation stock in American breeding programs.

Two such dogs were Skytop Sunrise and Skytop Lassie, acquired by Hannah Mee Horner. Another American breeder to acquire Maltese from Mrs. Andrews was Mrs. Agnes Benson of Merrilynn Kennels in Cleveland, Ohio.

A Canadian breeder of Maltese in the 1950s was Mr. Matt Smith. His interest commenced as a child in England. Mr. Smith immigrated to Canada and established himself in the Maltese fancy. In 1937, he acquired Group placing Tiny, a bitch, and from Miss Neame in England, he imported Invicta Milo as a stud for Tiny.

After the conclusion of World War II, Mr. Smith imported several more dogs from England. From Miss Neame's Invicta Kennels, he acquired a dog which she had shown in England. He had been named Best Puppy at an English Maltese Specialty show at 11 months. In Canada, he became BIS Canadian Ch. Invicta Demetrius. He was never defeated in the classes.

From Mrs. Bentley he acquired Leckhampton Dawn, which also became a Canadian champion. Bred to Ch. Demetrius, Ch. Dawn produced Ch. Pliny of Valetta.

Miss Elizabeth Kelly, daughter of Mr. Smith, bred the Shirlene's line of Maltese in Vancouver, British Columbia. Her foundation dogs were also of Miss Neame's English Invicta bloodline. Notable among the Canadian Shirlene champions are Beau Ideal, who finished at eight months of age; Flicka, which weighed 2½ pounds; Little Duchess and Snow Flurry.

After the conclusion of World War II, most breeding stock imported into Canada came from Villa Malta Kennels. There were several Canadian breeders who achieved admirable results with their Villa Malta imports. Among them were Mary Margaret Annand, of Toronto. Her foundation Villa Malta dogs included Shawn and Princess Carmni, as well as

Canadian Ch. Brigid of Suirside. Ch. Brigid was exhibited at the 1952 Westminster show. In a field of 17 Maltese, including the two top Maltese of the era, Int. Ch. Invicta Dina of Questover and Ch. Electa Pampi, owned by the Villa Malta Kennels, Ch. Brigid was BB.

Poodhall

Former professional handlers, Hans and Andrena Brunotte, began breeding Maltese through their Poodle client, Mrs. Justin Morgan, who bought her first Maltese from Dr. Calvaresi in 1959. This dog, Am., Can. Ch. Fidino of Villa Malta, became Canada's top-winning Maltese in 1960. His most outstanding win was a BIS under Alva Rosenberg, when Maltese were not doing great winning.

Mrs. Morgan then bought Am., Can. Ch. Gina of Villa Malta, who was top-winning Maltese in Canada for 1961 and 1962. She had four BIS and 16 Group 1sts, won on both sides of the border. In 1963, the Brunottes handled Mrs. Pendleton's Am., Can. Ch. Pendleton's Peachytu to four Group wins in Canada. In 1964 and 1965, Am., Can. Ch. Poodhall Diana of Mar-a-Mor was Canada's top Maltese. She was followed by Am., Can. & Bda. Ch. Poodhall Euripides, who was the top Maltese in Canada for 1966. He won his American and Canadian championships as a puppy.

When Mrs. Morgan died she left all her dogs to the Brunottes. They continued to breed and show them and finished 19 homebreds; many were Group winners. They were strongly bred Villa Malta bloodlines; Fidino was a son of Musi of Villa Malta. Their second and third stud dogs were great-grandsons of Musi.

Revlo

Revlo Maltese, of Prince Albert, Saskatchewan, became permanently registered in the early 1960s under the management of Douglas and Mary Olver and Miss Elaine Mitchell, co-owner and handler.

The Olver's foundation stock was purchased from Faydon Kennels. This stock was Jon Vir linebred. They imported Invicta breeding from Mrs. V. Wormon, Floriana Kennels of London, England. Imported were two bitches and two males. One of these males was Floriana Mdnia, known as the "Doctor." The Doctor's sire was Dido of Yelwa. He was out of Juliette Maybush. He became a Canadian champion at 11 months, and an American champion with all major wins. After finishing, he took 21 Group placements, and was among the top ten Toys of Canada in 1967, 1968 and 1969.

At the same time they used Am. Ch. Windrifts Fantabulous, owned by Mrs. Vivian Edwards, at stud. This Ch. Aennchen's Shikar Dancer progeny produced three generations of champion bitches. A Fantabulous daughter was acquired and brought to Revlo for breeding.

Multiple BIS-winning Am. & Can. Ch. Gina of Villa Malta, top Maltese in Canada 1961 and 1962, owned by Mrs. J. Morgan, shown by Andrena Brunotte.

Am. & Can. Ch. Fidino of Villa Malta Canada's top winning Maltese in 1960 owned by Mrs. J. Morgan, handled by Andrena Brunotte.

Best in Show and multiple Group-winning Can. Ch. Poodhall Kronos, bred and owner-handled by Mrs. Brunotte.

Mrs. Olver purchased a male by Am. & Can. Ch. Sun Canyon Matinee Idol II from Mrs. Palmersten. He became Ch. San Su Kee Little Bit-O-Idol, Canada's #1 Toy in 1979. Ch. Bit-O-Idol was a C.A.C.I.B. International champion, and also an American, Mexican and Canadian champion. His final record included four Canadian all-breed BIS and 19 Group 1sts.

In 1968, the Olvers acquired Jamie, Am., Can. Ch. Mike Mar's Sirius of Revlo. Ch. Jamie was a Ch. Mike Mar's Devil Dancer son. His dam was Ch. Alpond's Shine Little Star. He was top Maltese in Canada in 1972, sire of 14 champions, Canadian and American. Ch. Jamie also won the 1973 AMA Specialty, held in Seattle, Washington.

Ch. Jamie sired many champions, including Am. Ch. Revlo's Sir of Batoche, and Am., Can. Ch. Revlo's Bangladesh, known as Dash. He was number four Canadian-bred Maltese in 1974 and was BW at Westminster in 1974.

Also included as offspring from Ch. Jamie are Am., Can. Ch. Revlo's Louis Riel, a Canadian BIS winner. Louis' dam is Can. Ch. Revlo's El Alamein II. She was shown nine times in Canada and had one BIS, seven Group 1sts and two Group 2nds. Ch. Revlo's Do-Dee of Fluff won from the puppy class 13 Best Puppy in Groups, six Best Canadian-bred in Groups, three Best Puppy in Show, one Best Canadian-bred in Show, and two Group 1sts, along with many placements. Revlo's top brood bitch was Ch. Revlo's Star of Midway.

Ch. Star of Midway bred to Ch. Ringleader gave Mrs. Palmersten Am. Ch. San Su Kee Star Edition, #1 Maltese in the United States in 1974 and the first half of 1975. He was BB and Group 3rd at Westminster in 1974. This bitch also gave Mrs. Palmersten Am. Ch. San Su Kee Starshine, WB at Westminster in 1976, and repeated the win at the national Specialty that same year.

In a repeat breeding of Ch. Ringo to Ch. Star of Midway, the Olvers retained Am., Can. Ch. Revlo's Ringo Star of Midway. In 1982, she became #1 Toy dog and #6 of all breeds in Canada. She was awarded two Canadian Group 1sts from the puppy classes enroute to her championship. She earned her American title in just five shows and was RB at the 1978 AMA Specialty.

In 1975 the Olvers purchased Ch. Revlo's Little Chief of Villa Malta from Marge Rozik.

Four Halls

Four Halls Maltese, of Vancouver, British Columbia, started in 1968, when Glenna and Vicki Fierheller purchased their first show dog from Joanne Hesse. She was Am. Ch. Joanne-Chen's Shieka Dancer (the last Ch. Shikar daughter). Sheika was their first Canadian champion and went

Multiple Canadian BIS winner Int. Ch. San Su Kee
Little Bit-O-Idol. On the right is handler, co-owner
Elaine Mitchell and co-owner **Mary Olver.**

Am. Ch. Revlo's Sir of Batoche (Am. &
Can. Ch. Mike Mar's Sirius of Revlo ×
Madama Kristina), owned by Carole
Thomas. He is the sire of champions,
including the 1982 Sweepstakes
winner, Ch. Marcris Marshmallow.

An important, early stud at **Revlo**
and top Maltese in Canada, 1969,
English import, Am. & Can. Ch.
Floriana Mdina.

Am. & Can. Ch. Mike Mar's Sirius of Revlo, owned by Mary and Doug Olver.

Ch. Revlo's Mauresa Enchantress, full sister to Ch. Ringo Star.

Mary Olver and Ch. Revlo's Bangludesh being congratulated by the former Prime Minister of Canada, the Hon. John J. Diefenbacker, after a Best in Show win.

Am. & Can. Ch. Revlo's Louis Riel, a top Canadian winner.

Ch. Revlo's Ringo Star of Midway, multiple BIS winner with Bests in both Canada and the United States.

on to become a BIS winner. She was #2 Maltese and #10 Top Toy in Canada, 1969.

The foundation bitch at Four Halls was Joanne-Chen's Sweet She Dancer (niece to Ch. Maya Dancer), which they purchased from Marcia Hostetler. She produced Am., Can. Ch. Four Halls Conversation Piece, a BIS winner in Canada, and Can. Ch. Four Halls Ouvrage D'Art.

Ch. Conversation Piece is their first homebred BIS winner, sired by Can. Ch. Maltacello's Friendly Ghost. She was Canada's #1 Maltese and #4 Toy for 1978, and has produced three champions.

As of 1982, Four Halls bred or owned 17 champions, including two BIS winners, five Group winners, nine Group placers, and four American champions.

Four Halls has had success with Joanne-Chen stock, with a bit of Maltacello and Mike Mar added.

Normalta

Very active in the fancy in Canada for a number of years were the Normalta Kennels, owned by Norm Thompson and Fred Kramer, located in West Vancouver, British Columbia.

Their first top winner was BIS Can. & Am. Ch. Snowbelle's D'Arcy. Ch. D'Arcy was #3 Maltese in Canada in 1969.

Their next top winner was bred by Mrs. Berquist's Su Le Kennels, Am., Can. Ch. Su Le's Sparrow (Ch. To the Victor of Eng × Ch. Primrose Di Di Ray of Su Le).

The Group-winning Am., Can. Ch. Moppet's Bolero of Normalta (Ch. Snowbelle's D'Arcy × Can. Ch. Whisper's Jona, CD) was bred by Lynn Weir, with whom the dog was co-owned. The Moppet's line of Maltese owned by Lynne Weir is based upon the Normalta breeding.

The Canadian fancy was indebted to Messrs. Thompson and Kramer for having published a magazine featuring Canadian Maltese. The magazine, *For the Love of Maltese,* was financed with their own private funds.

Moppet's Maltese

The initial breeding stock at Moppet's Maltese Kennels, owned by Lynn Weir of Surrey, British Columbia, came from the Normalta Kennels. Noted of the Moppet's champions are Am., Can. Ch. Moppet's Starshine, CD, and Am., Can. Ch. Moppet's Dominique, CD.

Also of note are Moppet's Chehalis and Velvet. The noted Ch. Moppet's Bolero of Normalta was bred by Mrs. Weir. He was owned and shown by Norman Thompson and Fred Kramer.

194

Can. Ch. Four Halls
Creme de la Creme,
bred and owned by
Glenna Fierheller.

Ch. Joanne-Chen's Sheika Dancer, owned by
Glenna Fierheller.

Am. & Can. Ch. Four Halls Conversation Piece,
multiple BIS winner, bred and owned by Glenna
Fierheller.

195

Snospark

Peter and Patty Scott established their Snospark Maltese in Ontario. The Scotts have based their breeding on Ch. Aennchen's Shikar Dancer descendants.

They have purchased several dogs from Vivian Edwards' Windrift Kennels in Florida.

Their most recent winner, Ch. Snospark's Tempest Tease is by Ch. Le Shiek Dancer du Barrie. Ch. Le Shiek is sired by Ch. Aennchen's Shiko Dancer, out of Ch. Southern Tease of Windrift, a Ch. Shikar granddaughter.

Tempest Tease was whelped by Can. Ch. Windrift's Amari Dancer. Amari is a bitch which the Scotts acquired from the Windrift Kennels. Ch. Amari is sired by a Ch. Shikar grandson, Ch. Conquest's Mr. Chips, out of Windrift's Cotton Candy.

Chatelaine

Leslie Kerr, located in British Columbia, breeds the Chatelaine Maltese. She has the Moppet's bloodline, as well as several American imports from the Dil Dal, Primrose and Su Le bloodlines.

Noted among her dogs are Chatelaine Starlight (Am., Can. Ch. Moppet's Starshine, CD × Schamonix Azure Dee) and Su Le's White Scooter.

Litter brothers, Can. Ch. Chatelaines Subaru, which had Group placements on the way to his championship, and Chatelaines Scerroco, were sired by Am. Ch. Su Le's Whip-Por-Will. Their dam was Schamonix Azure Dee.

Bannon

Mrs. Maureen Bannon of Calgary, Alberta, imported a lovely Maltese from Mrs. Agnes Cotterell, of Cotterell's Maltese in Boise, Idaho.

Can. Ch. Cotterell's Regan of Rascal was first shown when he was ten months old. At his first show, he was BB, Group 3rd and Best Puppy in Group. The following day he was again BB. Ch. Regan earned his Canadian championship title at 13 months and was BB 13 of the 14 times he was shown; he also has a Group 2nd and two Group 3rds. Ch. Regan is sired by Am. Ch. Al Dor Little Rascal.

Tissagables

Sharmion Aune Foucault, of Montreal, has bred her Tissagables Maltese for a number of years. Her first bitch was from Nyssamead Kennels, Ch. Nyssamead's Disa.

Another of her famous dogs was top-winning Am., Can. Ch. Artamis

196

Multiple Group-winning Ch. Snospark Taste of Honey, owned by the Scotts.

Can. Ch. Cotterell's Regan of Rascal, bred by Agnes Cotterell and owned by Maureen Bannon.

of Tissagables. Mrs. Foucault enjoyed a close relationship with Mrs. Jean Carioli of the Cari Maltese. Several puppies and stud services were acquired from Mrs. Carioli's Kennels on Long Island.

The Maltese Dog in England

The Maltese was a favorite of Patrician Romans. Since England was once the Northernmost frontier of the Roman Empire, the influences of Rome certainly must have been felt there. The Roman nobility in England probably brought their Maltese with them when they conquered and governed, just as they had brought the Mastiff. However, there is no written record to support this fact.

Oral tradition has the breed introduced into England during the reign of Henry VIII (1509-1647). There is, in fact, no written or pictorial record of the breed in England, until the reign of Queen Elizabeth I, when her personal physician, Dr. Caius, specifically mentions the *Dog of Malta* being present at the Royal Courts of England. It would seem odd, though, that the Maltese dog would not be present on the scene in England, as there is definite record of his existence in Continental Europe since the 13th century.

Mary Queen of Scots (1542-1567) kept many Maltese, imported from Lyon. Tradition has it that it was a Maltese which accompanied this ill-fated Queen to the block.

It is chronicled that in 1680 a Spanish ship was sunk off the Isle of Skye. The vessel carried a Maltese, which was recovered and brought to the Island. There the Maltese was crossbred with local Terriers, producing the forebears of the now extinct Clydesdale and Paisley Terriers. These two variants of the Skye Terrier sometimes carried drop ears, as does the Maltese.

The daughter of James I of England, Princess Elizabeth (1596-1662), was as fond of dogs as was her grandmother, Mary, Queen of Scots. She is noted as having kept the Maltese, among many other small dogs.

The history of the breed in England remains documented by pictorial representation from the time of Dr. Caius until the reign of Queen Victoria. Such luminaries as Sir Joshua Reynolds, Hogarth and others included the Maltese dog as a subject matter in their oil paintings.

By 1830, the Maltese had become nearly extinct in England. This is documented by Sir Edwin Landseer's painting titled, *The Lion Dog of Malta, The Last of His Tribe.*

Two Maltese were imported into England in 1841 from the Philippines by Capt. Lukey. They were intended as gifts for Queen Victoria. They never were presented to her, due to their condition as a result of their nine-month voyage to England.

These two dogs, Cupid and Psyche, were given to Capt. Lukey's brother, a dog breeder. Cupid and Psyche were bred and produced Psyche, owned by Miss Gibbs. At 20 months, Psyche was pure white and weighed 3¼ pounds. This dog was exhibited at the dog show held in 1859 at Newcastle-on-Tyne.

The recorded history of the Maltese as a breed began in 1862. In that year, 20 Maltese were shown at one show, and more than 40 at another. A noted breeder at that time was Mr. Mandeville, who owned and bred the celebrated Lilly, Fun, Mick and Fido. Fido was a name Mr. Mandeville used on several dogs of his breeding, over a period of eight years. Others of note during this time were Mr. Haxton's Patti and Mr. MacDonald's Prince.

The Kennel Club of England was established in 1873. One of the first tasks of that newly formed body was to create a Stud Book. Between 1859 and 1873, 24 Maltese breed were recorded.

The first dog show sanctioned by the Kennel Club was held in London, in June, 1873. Prinny, owned by Mrs. Blackman and Polly, owned by Mr. Whitlock, were the winners.

Others of note during these early years were Mopsey, owned by Mr. Monck, whelped in 1865, and sired by one of Mr. Mandeville's Fidos. Patchill, owned by Mr. Dewey, was also sired by one of Mr. Mandeville's Fidos.

Beginning in 1874 with stock from Mr. Mandeville and Mr. Jacobs, Lady Giffard bred Maltese for a decade. She was the first English breeder to achieve pure white, silky coats that trailed on the ground.

Notable of her breeding were Hugh, his litter brother Lord Clyde, and a litter sister Queenie. One of her early Maltese was Brendaline, which she showed to the age of 19 years. The famous brood bitch, Blanche, was whelped in 1882.

English Maltese and breeders of note from the mid-1880s until 1900 include Mr. Watt, of the Lilly White Maltese, which included Prince Lilly White and Flossie; the Normacot Kennels owned by Mr. Leese; Ch. Pixie, owned by Mr. Jacobs; Little Count, owned by Mr. Fish; Ch. Prince Lilly White II, bred by Mielner; Boo Boo and Vee Vee, owned by Mrs. Langston; Ch. Maid of Honour, bred by Mr. Rayment; Floss and Lu Lu, owned by Mr. Pettit, Mrs. Palmer and Mrs. Morrison.

These noted Maltese exhibited prior to 1900 were much smaller than those currently exhibited in England. Many coats were curly or wavy, and many ears were set on rather high, as opposed to the current desire for a low set ear.

In 1902, Maltese other than white were introduced. Classes at dog shows were provided for them and entries were made until 1913, at which point they disappeared.

The standards for these two varieties varied slightly, the colored variety being smaller (8½ pounds top weight) than the pure white variety

An engraving of one of the Maltese named "Fido," owned and bred by Mandeville.

Portrait of a royal personage of the House of Lyme with her Maltese dog, dated 1615.

The Maltese, as he appeared prior to 1900 in England. This print appeared in *Modern Dogs,* published in 1899, by R. Lee.

The Lion Dog of Malta, The Last of His Tribe. Sir Edwin Landseer's painting documenting the near extinction of the breed in England, 1830.

Queen Elizabeth I of England in the Garden of Wanstead, with a Maltese dog at her skirt, by Marc Gheeraerts the Younger, 1578. From the collection of the Duke of Portland, Welbeck Abbey.

Another "Fido" of the era. This one the property of Mrs. L. Mandeville of London.

"Psyche," owned by Miss Gibbs of Morden, England, as he appeared in *Dogs and Their History,* by E. Ash, in 1895.

An oil portrait of the Maltese dog, "Hugh" with a Pomeranian. "Hugh" was bred and owned by Lady Giffard of Red Hill in 1875.

(12 pounds top weight). The white dogs were required to be pure white in color, without any color whatsoever in the coat. The colored variety could be any of several colors, including solid black, fawn, slate, blue, brown or black and tan. The parti-colored variety was required to be heavily marked, the more the better.

The leading breeder of English colored Maltese was Mrs. Hamilton. Her top winning specimens were seven-pound, fawn colored Nitza and five-pound blue Princess Duski. The availability of colored studs in England was scarce. This forced the cessation of her breeding these dogs.

From the beginning of the new century until 1914, there were several Maltese kennels of note in England; during this period, many English Maltese were exported to other countries including Europe and South America, Canada and the United States. The top winning Maltese of this time was Major Mite, owned by Mr. Leese. Also outstanding was Ch. Snowflack, owned by Mrs. Card.

Due, in part, to World War I, by 1920 there were few Maltese, or Maltese breeders in England. A very few Maltese are noted in the period between 1920-1922, and none between 1923 to 1926. Tydfil, owned by Mrs. Taylor; Oliver Twist, owned by Mrs. Partridge; and Snowflake of Esperance, bred by Mrs. Horowitz, were exhibited in the first two years of the decade.

Harlingen

Snowflake of Esperance was owned by Miss Van Oppen, who after her marriage became Mrs. C. Roberts of the famous Harlingen Maltese Kennels.

Mrs. Roberts decided to use bloodlines of other countries to strengthen the then-dwindling British stock. From Germany, Mrs. Roberts received the following Maltese which bore the Harlingen prefix: Mizi, Dolly, Eve, Mercon, Miracle, Mirette, Daydream, Delight, Joy, Ladybird, Rex and Snowfall. From the Netherlands, she acquired Snowqueen and Peter, both of which bore the Harlingen prefix.

With these imports and a few remaining Maltese descended from English bloodlines, the foundations for the modern English Maltese were laid. One of the German imports, Harlingen Polly, was bred to the last of the best English stud dogs, King Billie, producing Ch. Harlingen Snowman. This one dog served as the foundation of many modern English Maltese bloodlines. Ch. Snowman was a top-winner from 1927-1930; he had the distinction of being a breed winner at Crufts. His final record included 17 Challenge Certificates before his death at ten years of age, in 1936. This record remains unbroken.

The English Maltese fancy is indebted to this lady and her foresight in strengthening the quality of the breed. Several of her imported dogs were sold to other English Maltese breeders. One of these dogs, Mizi, was exported to the United States.

Harlingen Dolly was bred to Invicta Perseus, producing Eng. Ch. Harlingen Moonbeam and Am. Ch. Harlingen Sun Ray, which was owned by Mrs. Virginia Leitch of the United States.

The Harlingen Kennels are active to this day. Mrs. Roberts has been joined by her daughter, Alice, in the promulgation of the breed. They were both licensed by the Kennel Club to judge Maltese at Championship shows.

Invicta

Miss M. M. Neame was active in the Maltese fancy since 1925, when she purchased two Maltese imported by Mrs. Roberts' Harlingen Kennels. They were the Dutch Harlingen Snowqueen and the German Harlingen Joy. She began her Invicta bloodline in 1927. Miss Neame used the best English stud dog then available, King Billie, with Snowqueen. This produced her first homebred brood bitch, Rapunzel.

The first stud dog, Invicta The Card, was acquired from Mrs. Bridges. Bred to Harlingen Joy, Invicta Joker and Invicta Jest were produced. These two dogs were the most influential forces in the Invicta Maltese Kennels.

Miss Neame bred over 20 English champions and as many which were exported to other countries, where they achieved their championship titles.

Noted of her top producing stud dogs were Invicta Perseus, who sired five champions, and Ch. Invicta Dollar, sire of 11 champions to be found not only in England, but France, Spain, Canada and the United States, as well. Sent to the United States were American champions Invicta Plover, owned by Bertha Watkins; Tobias of Maybush, owned by Mrs. Peck; and Invicta Nicker, noted as being the best English Maltese imported into the United States at the time (late 1950s), owned by Elvira Cox.

By the late 1960s, Miss Neame had disposed of all but one of her dogs. All but three of the last stock she possessed were given to Mrs. Pat Day, of the Saumarez Maltese Kennels, which remained active through the 1970s.

Leckhampton

Mrs. J. C. Briely established her Leckhampton Maltese in 1937. The numerous Leckhampton champions descended from Invicta dogs of her sister's bloodlines, most noteworthy of which was Ch. Leckhampton Larkspur.

In 1954 Miss Warman imported her first Maltese from the island of Malta. This bitch, Floriana, was bred to a dog of Yelwa breeding, and the Floriana Maltese Kennels began.

Miss Warman subsequently introduced the Invicta and Rhosneigr bloodlines into her breeding program. From this combination sprang the famous Am., Can. Ch. Floriana Mdina, known as the "Doctor," owned by Douglas and Mary Olver of Canada.

Maltessa

Miss D. Sheppard, of the Maltessa Kennels, trained as an assistant to Miss Neame. Miss Sheppard's Maltessa Maltese were active during the late 1940s through the 1950s.

One of Miss Sheppard's breeding was exported to Sig. Nadya Colombo of the Electa Maltese Kennels in Italy. Noted champions of Maltessa breeding include Minuette and Ruffles.

Gissing

Mrs. C. Hunter began her Gissing Maltese Kennels in 1945 when she acquired her foundation dogs from Miss Neame's Invicta Kennels. Her first stud dog of note was Ch. Invicta Phaon. Mrs. Hunter retired, and moved both herself and her dogs to Portugal in 1968.

She had been a noted exporter of Maltese. One, Ch. Prince of Gissing, became a Japanese champion. Amphion Prince of Gissing was sold and exported to Messrs. Oberstar and Ward in the United States where he was shown to his American championship.

Another breeder of note of this era was Mrs. Blanche Mace of the Yelwa Kennels.

Vicbrita

Mrs. Margaret White established her Vicbrita Maltese in the early 1950s, when she imported a bitch from South Africa. To this were added the Gissing, Harlingen and Invicta bloodlines. Mrs. White's efforts were aided by the addition of her daughter, Gillian, in 1958. This enabled Mrs. White to concentrate upon the breeding aspect of their kennel, while Gillian oversaw the exhibition of their dogs.

Most famous of the stud dogs at Vicbrita is Ch. Vicbrita Fidelity, who sired over a dozen champions.

Her dogs have been in demand by Maltese breeders in a number of countries. They have been exported to Italy, Sweden, Japan, South Africa, Australia, Canada and New Zealand. Many became champions in their newly adopted countries.

Many Vicbrita Maltese were exported to the United States. Among them were: Ch. Vicbrita Rozeta, owned by Mrs. Marge Stuber; Ch. Vicbrita as Always, sired by Ch. Vicbrita Fidelity; and Ch. Vicbrita Tranquility, owned by Dorothy Tinker. Also owned by Mrs. Tinker was

Ch. Ellwin's Sweet Charity, bred and owned by Mrs. L. Lewin.

Ch. Snowgoose Valient Lad, bred and owned by Mrs. V. Herrieff.

Ch. Invicta Orion.

Ch. Vicbrita High Society, July 1966. One of Margaret White's prized Maltese from her Vicbrita Kennel, which produced many fine English champions, some of which were exported to the United States and Canada.

Ch. Vicbrita Tobias, one of her top-winning dogs, and Vicbrita Claire and Vicbrita Felicity.

Ellwin

Mrs. L. Lewin founded the Ellwin Maltese, using dogs of the Vicbrita bloodline. As of this writing she is still active in the fancy. Mrs. Lewin has had winners at Crufts, including Ch. Ellwin Victoriana, by Ch. Vicbrita Fidelity. Other Ellwin Maltese of note include Ch. Ellwin's Sweet Charity and Ellwin's Royal Envoy.

Other English Breeders

Mrs. M. C. Sturgiss of the Francoombe bloodline has been active in the fancy since the 1960s. She is currently licensed by the Kennel Club to judge the breed.

Other current kennels of note include Mrs. V. Herrieff's Snowgoose bloodline. Most noted of their breeding is BIS Ch. Snowgoose Valiant Lad, Toy Group winner at Crufts in 1983.

Included among their other six generations of line-bred Maltese is Snowgoose Yousef of Villarose.

Others of note in the English fancy at the time of this writing are Mrs. C. Hemsley of the Abbyat Maltese, and her Abbyat Oberon; and Mrs. M. E. Townes, breeder of the Regencylodge Maltese. She held a winner at the Crufts 1983 show, in Regencylodge Snow Karnino.

The title of English champion is very difficult to acquire. It must be earned in strong competition with the best each Maltese breeder or fancier has for competition.

A Challenge Certificate is awarded to the winner of first prize in the Open Class at a championship show. In order to earn the title of champion, a dog must win three Challenge Certificates, under three different judges at three different championship shows.

If a dog is campaigned, after receiving his championship, his record will include the number of Challenge Certificates he is awarded.

The Maltese in Ireland

In 1922, one Maltese was registered in the Irish Kennel Club's Stud Book. This was the first time a Maltese appeared there. No more were registered until 1935.

Some early Maltese breeders included Mrs. Gordon Fraser, Mrs. J. B. Farrell, and Mrs. Joan Felice.

Suirside

The largest number of Irish champions registered with the Irish

Kennel Club have been bred by Mrs. Felice of Carrick-on-Suir. Her first Maltese, Willow, was bred by Mrs. Gordon Fraser. She later imported Invicta Aglaia from Miss Neame in England. Her breeding program was founded with these two dogs. Subsequently she acquired one other dog from both Mrs. Fraser and Miss Neame.

Maltese of the Suirside bloodline were not only winners in Ireland, but in England and the United States, as well. Mrs. V. Leitch acquired Show Man, Blossom and Rosabelle of Suirside. These were the first dogs ever to be sent by air from England to the United States.

Miss M. M. Aunand of Toronto, Canada, owned and showed Am., Can. Ch. Brigid of Suirside, BB at Westminster, 1952 and the first Irish-bred Maltese to hold titles in the United States and Canada.

Mrs. Felice had most nearly left Maltese breeding when she was supplied with new stock from the Floriana and Yelwa Kennels in England, as well as some American stock descended from her original bloodlines.

The Maltese in Scandinavia

In Sweden the Maltese is considered a very unusual breed. There are about 100 registered a year, and an average Swedish dog show will draw only about seven or eight exhibits.

There is very little information available in Sweden on the fancy, thus making it hard to find books or other printed material about the breed.

The origins of the Maltese in Sweden have been obscured with time. The Swedish Kennel Club established their Stud Book in 1903, but the first Maltese did not appear in it until 1914. The first entry was Printz. He was followed by Dorrit and Rixi.

The first Swedish breeder to import English stock was Julia Althin, who imported Harlingen Duke in 1928, from Mrs. Roberts.

In the decade from 1930 to 1940 the Toyhomes Kennels, owned by Aina Rossander, was most noted, using Invicta English imports as its foundation.

One of the oldest Maltese kennels is Av Barbette's Maltese having bred over six generations.

The Av Barbette Kennels were established in 1938 by Mrs. Ella Hagelthorn. Her first stud dog, Ch. Lill-Man av Barbette, was of the Maltessa and Invicta bloodlines. He sired 42 registered get. Mrs. Hagelthorn bred several dual Swedish and Finnish champions.

There are about a dozen breeders of the Maltese dog today in Sweden, but only a few of them specialize in the Maltese dog only.

Sweden does not have any particular noted bloodlines, other than the Av Barbette's Kennel. Many dogs are imported from England. Dogs imported are from the better known English Maltese breeders, including

Ch. Bo-Peep with Moonbeam of Suirside and Judy of Suirside, 1966.
Courtesy AKC Library

Int. Ch. Tamino av Barbette, top Maltese in Sweden, 1977.

those from the Vicbrita, St. Erme and Sucop's bloodlines, as well as several others.

Others of the most active Maltese kennels in Sweden are: Beldan's, Parall's, Hinebrocker and Colon Bines.

There appears to be a decline in the number of breeders in Sweden at this time. In Finland, however, the breed is quite popular, and there are many involved in the fancy there.

Of the Scandinavian countries, Finland quite likely leads in breeding and exhibiting Maltese. Finnish dogs have quite superior coats, therefore many are imported into Sweden from Finland as well as from England.

The largest dog show in Sweden is held in Stockholm. This show has drawn slightly larger entries of 15 or so Maltese. The quality there has been good. Some winners at the Stockholm fixture have been a bitch, Briarcliffe Snow Pixie, an English import bred by Jean Murphy, which has been awarded Best of Breed, and Meriadaes Fabian, a dog from the Hindackeus Kennels owned by Mr. B. Wauserius of Sweden.

The standard for the Maltese dog is exactly the same in all countries of Scandinavia. It is quite different than our present standard.

It requires the following:

> The Maltese is a tiny dog. The body is short and well composed. The head, most like a terrier, Skye Terrier, but much smaller. The eyes are small and black, with black eye rims. The ears possess long silky hair. The nose is black, the lips are black, the nails and pads are black. The coat is snow white, long, straight and silky. The tail falls as a plume on the back. The weight is three to six pounds, the smaller the better.

The Maltese in Italy

With the evidence of his existence being documented by historians, writers, poets and artists, the ancestors of the Maltese dog have been present on the Italian Peninsula since the time of the Roman empire.

The modern Maltese is represented in the works of the most prominent Italian artists beginning as early as the 1400s. In these works, several members of the Maltese family are clearly represented.

The Italian Stud Book was established in 1898. The first Maltese, a bitch named Chula, was registered therein in 1901.

In the early days of dog shows in Italy, the Maltese was exhibited in mixed classes with other breeds, including the Bolognesi, the Bichon and Avanesi (Havana Silk Dog—see CHAPTER 1).

These elegant little dogs were kept by the nobility, as well as by ladies and gentlemen of Italian society. Giuseppi Verdi, noted operatic composer, was one such person. His Maltese dog, Loulou, was said to have

Several Electa champions bred and owned by Sig. Nadya Colombo. Left to right they are champions: Electa Ketty, Electa Pitin and Electa Baby.

Head study of Ch. Gemma Lionello, bred by Prof. Tamagnone.

Ch. Electa Cinzia, bred and owned by Sig. Nadya Colombo.

accompanied him and his mistress to operatic rehearsals, as well as to the opera and theatre.

Irene Vicini-Rosso was the first person noted to have bred Maltese, for a decade, beginning in 1922. She is known to have used foundation dogs from Monaco and Austria.

England and Austria were the main source of the Maltese dog into Italy for some years before World War II. After the war, England continued to supply new stock to the country. Noted of the pre-war Maltese fancy are Lina Lorenzetti of Turin, Amalia Borsoni of Florence and Maria Biagi of Verona. All of the dogs bred by these ladies were principally out of Austrian bloodlines.

Electa

Most illustrious of the Italian breeders, though no longer active, was Sig. Nadya Colombo, of Milan. Based upon the English Invicta and Fawkhalm bloodlines, her dogs came to be the most beautiful Maltese in Europe. There was a worldwide demand for her breeding.

In just 15 years of breeding, Sig. Colombo's Electa Kennels had produced nearly 30 Maltese champions. Imports into the United States included Laila, Brio, and Pampi, among others. Her dogs were noted for their superb pigmentation and luxurious, silky coats. These coats seemed to be of better quality than others produced in any other nation, by any other Maltese Kennel.

Sig. Colombo retired from breeding Maltese shortly after producing her last champion, Ch. Electa Dandy, whelped in 1951.

Gemma

Professor Bianca Tamagnone bred her Gemma line of Maltese from the early 1950s through the 1970s. Int. Ch. Electa Pucci, her first champion, was later joined by several English Vicbrita and Invicta bred dogs. She finished several champions, including her famous Ch. Gemma Lionello.

Professor Tamagnone is the noted author of the Italian book on the Maltese dog, *Il Maltese, Il Bolognese e Il Volpino Italiano*.

The Maltese in Australia

The "Malts," as the Maltese dog is known in Australia, seem to be indeed lovely, possessing deep, full pigmentation, pure white, straight coats of superb length, and exhibiting the same bright, alert, lively expression which is so typical of the American Maltese. The Australian "Malt" is usually quite a bit larger than his American cousin. The Australian standard, in dealing with size, specifies not over ten inches from the ground

211

to top of shoulder. This would presumably permit the showing of a smaller specimen, but it would seem that the Australian judges prefer larger dogs.

There are seven territories or states in Australia, of which the commonwealth is made. Six states have their own kennel organization, with their own regulations. The various kennel organizations work with one another using reciprocal agreements.

In the state of Victoria, the Kennel Control Council operates out of Melbourne. In New South Wales the Royal Agricultural Society Kennel Club operates from Sydney. In Queensland the Canine Control Council operates out of Brisbane. The Southern Australia Kennel Club operates from Glenelg. The Western Australia Kennel Club presides in Perth. There is no kennel association in the Northern territory. The island of Tasmania, off the South East coast of Australia, has the Kennel Club of Tasmania operating from Queenstown.

Since each states holds jurisdiction and registration powers for its own territory only, when a breeder uses a stud dog from another state, it is a very difficult procedure to register the get. There is a great deal of difficulty involved, and occasional long waits which last until the produced puppies are well on in age.

In addition, each state has its own requirements for earning a championship certificate. All states are currently on a point system similar to that used in the United States.

Western Australia

There has been only one breeder of Maltese noted in Western Australia. Mrs. E. de Pallette has been active in the breed since 1932, when she acquired her first dogs of the Invicta bloodline while still living in England.

Mrs. de Pallette established her Whiteinch Maltese in England and did well at the shows. In 1949, she and her husband emigrated to Western Australia. With them they brought five Maltese. Of these, two were of the Invicta bloodline, one was of Sigroc breeding, one was from the Suirside Kennels in Ireland, and one was of her own Whiteinch breeding.

From these she has continued to breed her stock in Australia.

Victoria

Victoria has known the Maltese for a very long time. It is estimated that the breed first arrived there in the 1880s. At that time all dog records were kept by the Victorian Poultry and Kennel Club, which exists to this day. The current records of the breed, however, date from the 1930s. Up until the 1950s there was only one breeder of note operating in Victoria, Mr. H. V. Wilson, who imported Leckhampton stock from whence his breeding stemmed.

Today, one of the largest Maltese clubs in Australia is located in Victoria, having approximately 100 members. The Victorian Kennel Control Council provides that the Maltese Club of Victoria must yearly hold one championship show and one parade show, as well. The championship show is likened to an American point show. Their parade shows are similar to match shows held here. A parade win gives no championship points, but provides a training ground for puppy hopefuls.

Parade shows also serve as training grounds for would-be judges, who must officiate at a specified number of such competitions before they are considered being granted a license to judge at championship shows. Aspiring judges must also have been exhibitors for at least five years.

The Victoria Maltese Club may also hold a limited parade show, wherein only club members may exhibit. These are mainly social events within the club. As in this country, champions may not be exhibited in competition at parade shows.

The most prestigious event in dogdom which occurs in Victoria is the Royal Melbourne Show, a ten-day event. The last day culminates with the selection of the final three winners, Best in Show, Best of Opposite Sex to Best in Show, and Best Puppy in Show. Afterward, everyone celebrates at a large cocktail party, for which tickets of admission are sold. Members of the general public may attend this party. Various awards are presented at this event, including those for Top Toy Dog, Top Dog all breeds, Reserve Top Dog, etc.

Currently active in the fancy in Victoria are Mrs. T. Pamment, who is owner of Ch. Blizzard Snow Sheen, which was awarded the Top Dog award in 1968. Other noted Maltese in Victoria include Ch. Leckhampton Moonraker and Ch. Moswyn Snowraker.

The current fancy in Victoria is graced by American Maltese Association member, Mrs. G. Hodges of Essendon, Victoria. Also of note is Miss Lyn Harrison of Kew. Her Maltese, Ch. Sir Thomas, retired from the ring at six and a half years of age. His record included 30 BIS.

South Australia and Queensland

There have been no active Maltese fanciers located in South Australia since the 1920s.

Queensland, on the other hand is quite an active center for the fancy. One of the earliest Maltese breeders there was one Mrs. Pike, who imported the Invicta bloodline into Queensland in 1938.

Currently located in Queensland are Mrs. Delia Skinner, who exhibits and breeds her Maltese. Mrs. Skinner maintains an active membership in the American Maltese Association.

Mrs. Skinner's Ch. Kreswick Lil' Sweetheart, at four and a half years, has been bred just once, producing a litter of two champion sons. These are

Multiple BIS-winning Ch. Sir Thomas, pictured here at 6½ years of age.

Multiple BIS-winning Ch. Cosyvista Moon Dew, owned by Mr. T. Tancred.

Mr. William Farnelle, noted pianist and breeder of the Oelrich Maltese in New Zealand.

rather small for Australia, weighing 3½ and four pounds each. They are in great demand at stud because of their small size, in a country where many Maltese are quite large.

Mrs. Skinner notes that her Maltese coats grow quite slowly, due to the tropical climate in North Queensland.

Also from Queensland is the noted Mr. T. Tancred. He has done much to improve the breed there by imparting his knowledge, which is considerable. Mr. Tancred owns Ch. Cosy Vista Moon Dew, a multiple BIS dog, and a big winner at the Royal Brisbane fixture.

The Royal Brisbane show is similar to the Royal Melbourne show, in that it is a ten-day affair. Wins at this fixture carry much prestige with them. In 1972, there were 2,506 dogs entered at this show. As of 1980, the entry was up to 4,798.

Tasmania

A number of Maltese have been exhibited at the Tasmanian shows, although there are no recorded breeders there. The show regulations in Tasmania are quite stringent. An exhibitor is prohibited from bringing a comb or brush into the show ring with their exhibit. Further, it is not permitted to "bait." This indeed seems a severe restriction, especially to the longer coated breeds. It prompts one to wonder why such a regulation was ever at all necessary.

Some Australian shows are rather isolated, with sparse entries in some breeds. It is possible to gain challenge points, in some states, without ever having competed against another specimen of the same breed. However, about 80% of the exhibitors at dog shows in Australia reside in areas close to large cities. At most dog shows held in these areas, a large number of all the breeds, especially Maltese, is represented. At these shows, challenge points are most difficult to obtain. Making an Australian champion can be a difficult task.

The Australian government has very stringent importation laws both for dogs and dog products. Many Australian breeders admire American stock, and would like to import dogs from us. However, the time and expense of doing so is discouraging. Laws governing the importation of fine-quality dog products such as those used in the United States are also so prohibitive as to make such an enterprise or effort futile.

The Maltese in New Zealand

There is evidence that Maltese were first introduced into New Zealand in the early 1900s. However, records of the first registration with the New Zealand Kennel Club date from 1933 when Ruffles was entered, owned by Mrs. J. McDonald.

Although much admired by New Zealanders, the breed did not flourish until the 1950s. It was then that the first imports began to arrive. From Australia came the Wimpole, Whiteinch and Maswyn bloodlines. From England came Maltese of the Yelwa and Invicta bloodlines. Some of the Suirside dogs from Ireland were also imported.

These early imports were quite large, larger than is preferred there today. These dogs, for the most, weighed ten pounds or more. Dogs of this size tended to have voluminous, profuse, dense coats.

Despite their large size, these dogs were considered attractive show dogs with no better specimens available to compare them to. They enjoyed many good wins in the show ring.

The bright, alert, very easily trained and intelligent Maltese were great successes in the obedience rings in New Zealand. They held their own in competition against larger breeds, earning many CDX and UD titles.

In the 1960s, several more English imports arrived from the Rhosneigr and Lepu Kennels. These added bloodlines caused a great advancement in the breed.

However, the next decade had to be spent in achieving better size, type and quality. Also imported into New Zealand in the 1960s were a pair of Vicbrita Maltese from England. They were Ch. Vicbrita Edelweiss and Ch. Vicbrita Specialty. These two Maltese were of a small size, and quite highly refined in type. They caused quite a stir in the fancy at the time, as this type of dainty toy Maltese had been unknown in New Zealand until their arrival.

These two were followed by Ch. Vicbrita Thesius, Ch. Vicbrita Vitality and Ch. Vicbrita Excelsior, all of which added to the genetic complexion of the Maltese in New Zealand.

It would appear that the standards the Maltese breeders of New Zealand have set for themselves are now quite high. Some of the more successful breeders have enjoyed requests for their stock from other countries. However, the 1980s find some of the older breeders still preferring the larger, older-type dog. Often at the shows in New Zealand, there is a considerable variety of types and sizes of Maltese being exhibited.

In comparison to England and the United States, dog shows held in New Zealand are not large. The average one-day championship show will attract approximately 1,000 entries. The largest dog show to be held in New Zealand is the "National" Dog Show, which is a three-day event. This show will draw an entry of 3,000 dogs.

The system for gaining the title of champion in New Zealand includes winning eight Challenge Certificates. These certificates must be won under at least five different judges. In England a championship must be won with three Challenge Certificates, but the competition there is far greater.

New Zealanders, as with the Australians, are very seriously hampered in their presentation of the Maltese by lack of good quality grooming products and preparations, due to stringent import restrictions. The variety of preparations and products have increased, though rather slowly, over the years, but compared to what is offered and available in other countries, the sampling is minimal.

The latest arrival from England to New Zealand is Ch. Vicbrita Park Royal. This dog earned a Challenge Certificate at the Windsor Championship show in England. He is a grandson of the famous Ch. Vicbrita Tobias, which was exported to Mrs. Tinker in America. Ch. Park Royal is also a half-brother to the top-winning Ch. Vicbrita Sebastion in England.

Many of the New Zealand fancy admire greatly and would like to import American stock for breeding. However, the New Zealanders are faced with the same sort of difficult importation regulations as the Australians have. This includes first a six-months quarantine in England, with kennel bills plus shipping charges. Then the dog must be shipped (by air or sea) to Australia or New Zealand where the animal must be quarantined for an additional four months. All of the aforementioned shipping charges must be paid by the importer, as well. The long quarantine period can also be stressful for dogs.

As with Australia, there are no importation restrictions in shipping dogs from either New Zealand or Australia into the United States.

Noted breeders of the Maltese dog in New Zealand include Mrs. A. Windley, considered to be the first breeder of Maltese in New Zealand, beginning in 1913. Also included are Mrs. Hannah, Mrs. Coogan, of May Forest Maltese, Mr. and Mrs. Pogsen of the Aetavady Maltese, Mrs. Wood of the Seven Acres Maltese and Mrs. Morrison of the Valmain Maltese Kennels established in 1954.

Mrs. L. Commins imported the first Maltese into New Zealand in 1951. Mrs. Parsley is perhaps one of the most productive breeders in New Zealand, having registered more puppies of her Clyde's breeding than any other breeder in the country. This breeding program was eventually acquired by Mrs. Williams.

Mrs. H. Wilson founded her Lautana Kennels in 1955, with dogs acquired from Mrs. Commins.

Mr. William Farnell acquired his first Maltese from Mrs. Commins, as well, a year later in 1956. Mr. Farnell is one of the most celebrated pianists in New Zealand. He was later joined by Mr. Douglas Darcy Wright in founding the Oelrich Maltese Kennels in Remuera, Auckland, New Zealand.

Noted among his breeding is Oelrich Harlequin (Ch. Oelrich Tobias × Oelrich Emily), a dog heavy in the Vicbrita bloodline. Harlequin was shown only twice in 1976, and was a BB winner at six months and has made other good wins.

Other breeders of the Maltese in New Zealand worth note are Mrs. C. Lockwood of the Oat-Lea Kennels, Mrs. B. Towers of the Silverlodge

Kennels, Mrs. N. Simpson of the Carabelle Kennels, Mr. and Mrs. Halford and Miss Dolper of the Ranjet Kennels.

Mrs. R. Parker has established herself as the most prominent breeder of the Maltese dog on the Southern Island of New Zealand, Stewart Island. In 1962, she established her Miracle Maltese Kennels there.

It would appear the Maltese fancy on both Islands of New Zealand is in a healthy state of improvement and growth, with the fancy there striving to perfect their stock.

The Maltese in Japan

There have been Maltese dogs in Japan for many years. They are held in high esteem by the Japanese people. Unfortunately, there is no account of when the Maltese actually arrived there.

It is likely that he arrived at some point in ancient times, brought from China or the Philippines. Unfortunately, there were no records kept about these dogs, nor dogs in general in Japan, until well after World War II.

There exist presently in Japan, two kennel clubs, the Japan Kennel Club and the Japan Dog Federation. These organizations award champion certificates and put on championship shows. However, there are no stud book registers kept. Such records are left to the individual breeders and owners.

Many Japanese Maltese of good quality and of very small size were brought back by visitors to Japan, before World War II.

During and shortly after that war, due to many adverse conditions, the ranks of Maltese were decimated. However, it was not long before their numbers were once again on the rise. Today, the Maltese is the #1 dog in Japan, in numbers, as well as in the hearts of the Japanese people.

The publisher of *Japan Dog World* since 1948, Mr. T. Soki was very instrumental in the revival of the purebred dog fancy in Japan, particularly the Maltese.

Several dogs were imported from England for breeding purposes, as well as from the United States and Australia. One of the first was Am. & Eng. Ch. Vicbrita Frivolity.

The bloodline, however, making the most impact upon the Maltese fancy in Japan was the Aennchen bloodline. Although Aennchen herself never sold a dog to Japan, many dogs bred by her, or descended from her breeding were sent to Japanese breeders to become top producers.

The first of the Aennchen bloodline to arrive in Japan was Ch. Aennchen's Mastyr Dancer, sold there by Mr. Michael Wolf. Ch. Mastyr Dancer became the top producing stud in Japanese history, siring many champions. At one point, all champions being shown in Japan were Ch. Mastyr sons or daughters. Ch. Mastyr was imported into Japan by Mr.

Aiko Kobayashi. One of these get, Ch. Iris of Shukenson, out of Jap. Ch. Edith of Shukenson, had five BIS. He too was owned by Mr. Kobayashi, and was #1 Maltese in Japan in 1971. At one Specialty having an entry of 360 Maltese, all of the dogs entered were descended from Ch. Mastyr Dancer.

Another force in bringing the Aennchen's Dancer bloodline into Japan was Mr. Akira Shinohara of A.-S. Gloria's Maltese located in Osaka, Japan. Mr. Shinohara is a member of the Kennel Club of Japan. Mr. Shinohara's interest in the Aennchen bloodline began in 1965, when he saw a photo layout in *Popular Dogs,* featuring Ch. Aennchen's Shikar Dancer, and several other Aennchen champions.

Since Aennchen had refused to sell dogs out of the country, Mr. Shinohara felt it would be a near impossible task to acquire dogs of her breeding to be brought to Japan. Finally, several Americans who possessed dogs from the Aennchen bloodline were willing to sell to Mr. Shinohara. He thus acquired the bitches, Am. Ch. Acnnchen's Susi Dancer and Mar-T's Tiny Snow Dancer.

In May, 1966, the first litter of pure Aennchen bloodlines was whelped in Japan. By Ch. Aennchen Mastyr Dancer out of Ch. Aennchen's Susi Dancer were two males and two females. These became a great attraction to the entire fancy in Japan. All four get became BIS winners. Among them were A.-S. Gloria's Snow Dancer Junior and A.-S. Gloria's Snow Princess. Ch. Snow Princess was acquired by the Villa Bay Kennels, where he became a top stud, siring many lovely puppies.

Mr. Shinohara then acquired the record holder for the most BIS wins, Ch. Anna of Aromatic Peak. Mr. Shinohara went to great effort to acquire this bitch, as he thought her to closely resemble Ch. Aennchen's Poona Dancer.

Mr. Shinohara imported another dog of the Aennchen bloodline, Ch. Mike Mar's Shikar's Replica. This dog was bred to Ch. Anna producing three more BIS champion bitches for A.-S. Gloria's Maltese, namely, Snow Queen, Snow Jewel and Snow Hi Lady. All were successful producers.

Still Mr. Shinohara was not completely satisfied with his breeding program. From the first time he had seen the photo of Ch. Shikar Dancer, he had desired to own, if not Ch. Shikar himself, an inbred descendant of his.

Ultimately, in 1966 his dream was fulfilled when he acquired Ch. Joanne-Chen's Shikar Dancer, a closely inbred Ch. Shikar Dancer son. This dog brought his kennel many champion get, and much admiration from the Japanese fancy. Mr. Shinohara's entire breeding program became geared to this one dog.

Mr. Shinohara also imported the lovely dog, Ch. Joanne-Chen's Sweet He Dancer and Ch. Joanne-Chen's Aga Lynn Dancer, a bitch. Ch.

219

BIS Japanese Ch. Fuji Mizaud White Sally, shown taking a BIS. Miriam Thompson (Sun Canyon) sold Mrs. Nagasawa Am. Ch. Sun Canyon Jasmine II, in whelp to Ch. Sun Canyon Double-O-Seven. Four puppies were whelped in Japan, one was the bitch pictured here.

Ch. Joanne-Chen's Shikar Dancer, age ten years, owned by Akira Shinohara.

Sweet He also produced some outstanding get at A.-S. Gloria's Kennel, though of different type than of Shikar's get. Three more BIS A.-S. Gloria's champions were produced, Snow Select Boy, Snow Shikar Dancer and Snow Samanthar. Ch. Select Boy was the result of breeding Ch. Shikar to Ch. Susi. The latter two champions, Snow Shikar and Samanthar, were sired by Ch. Shikar out of the Aga Lynn bitch.

Mr. F. Kobayashi had been breeding Maltese well before Mr. Shinohara and was his prime competitor in the show ring. Mr. Kobayashi's death made available Ch. Mastyr Dancer progeny, BIS Ch. Petty Sie of Shukenson. This bitch was acquired by Mr. Shinohara and bred to Ch. Shikar, producing Best in Show Ch. A.-S. Gloria's Fanfare.

In the spring of 1972, Mr. Shinohara imported Ch. Joanne-Chen's Siva Dancer, one more closely linebred Aennchen stud, to strengthen the Aennchen bloodline at A.-S. Gloria's. The addition of Ch. Siva's breeding, especially on the maternal side of the pedigree, was an enhancement to his linebred, inbred Aennchen bloodlines.

Also acquired was a daughter of the famous Ch. Joanne-Chen's Maya Dancer, namely Ch. Joanne-Chen's Mayan Dancer. Ch. Mayan was bred to Ch. Shikar producing a litter of two, a dog and a bitch.

In 1974, Ch. Joanne-Chen's Sweet Man Dancer joined the stud force at A.-S. Gloria's. New stock has been continuously brought into the A.-S. Gloria's Kennels, and to those kennels associated with it, in the hopes that they would contribute to the improvement and refinement of the Maltese dog in Japan.

In 1974, Mr. Shinohara sponsored a Ch. Joanne-Chen's Shikar Dancer lineage Specialty show open to direct descendants of his Ch. Shikar. The total entry at this show was 116 dogs, an astounding number for any Specialty show.

In 1980, Mr. Shinohara introduced a new strain into his breeding program. From Dean and Beverly Passo he purchased Am., Can. Ch. Myi's Sun Seeker, a Group-winner in the United States and a BIS winner in Canada. Later, after Ch. Sun Seeker's show career had ended, Mr. Shinohara acquired another dog, Ch. Myi's Siin Seeker.

One other Maltese breeder, fancier of note is Mr. Hideo Ito, of Tokyo. Mr. Ito is a popular judge of Maltese both in his own country as well as in the United States, where he officiates in the ring frequently. Mr. Ito is also an official of the Japan Kennel Club.

Mr. Ito has imported eight American champion Maltese, some of which he acquired from Mrs. Jean Carioli's Cari Maltese. They were of the Aennchen, Joanne-Chen bloodline.

Mr. Ito is dedicated to the advancement of the breed in his country. The author and Mr. Ito have spoken on numerous occasions both in Japan and the United States on many aspects concerning the Maltese dog. These conversations have proven mutually enlightening.

Dr. Kiyoshi Kawase, DVM, is owner of the Kawase Veterinary Hospital in Tokyo. He has developed a great interest in the advancement of the Maltese dog through his association with Mr. Hideo Ito. Many hours were spent by this author in enjoyable and enlightening conversations with Dr. Kawase, both in Japan and in the United States. Both Dr. Kawase and Mr. Ito are frequent visitors at the Westminster show. Dr. Kawase is also a member of the Japan Kennel Club.

5

An Introduction to the Maltese Standard

An EXACTING STANDARD may be a very useful tool, helpful in establishing certain values and expectations. With regard to the dog, a standard is the description of characteristics peculiar to a breed. Each breed standard is therefore a delineation of the corresponding breed. The American Maltese standard has been established to be as precise a blueprint of the Maltese as possible. It helps give a more perfect description of the Maltese to the mind's eye of the Maltese fancier.

The Maltese has been, for more than twenty-eight centuries, the little aristocrat of the canine world. Breeders have been dedicated to the perpetuation of this lovely breed. Throughout the centuries, there have been particular characteristics that have remained unique to the Maltese. This uniqueness is tied genetically to other factors in the breed. Dedicated breeders and fanciers of the Maltese dog must strive to maintain a high standard, based upon centuries of tradition, lest we wind up with dogs that are considered by some to be "sound" but are totally lacking in the centuries-old qualities that set the Maltese breed of dog apart from all others.

It is useful, therefore, before approaching today's official American Kennel Club approved standard, to be acquainted with the descriptions of the breed dating from the earliest times in recorded history, to those of dog authorities writing about 100 years ago. Since the breed is ancient, it is of special interest to consider what has been written by the earliest naturalists and the original authors of natural history. Among those who have discoursed on the Maltese dog are included the founders of the systems by which animals, and dogs in particular, are classified.

Perhaps the first descriptive prose on the Maltese was penned by Aristotle (384–322 B.C.) in his book on Zoology. In Box IX, chapter VI, in his description of a type of weasel, which was known as the Itkia, he speaks of the animal as being "about the size of a Maltese dog, of the little, tiny sort."

The following account regarding the size and type of the Maltese dogs found in Turkey was penned by Asterius (325–405), the Bishop of Amasia, writing in the fourth century. In part his account read:

> As I said something before about the prize dogs of Laeonia, I must also say something about the dogs that are left to shift for themselves in the street. The best of them are employed for hunting in the country; but the Turks who live in the towns do not keep domestic dogs, and the dogs have no special masters, except the very little tiny Maltese and Polonian ones, which are much prized, and which the women of good family rear for pleasure. The others make their bed in the streets, and never leave them day or night.

There is little additional description of the Maltese dog from this time until the time of Elizabethan England. The Maltese dog appears in the writings and accounts of several noted authors during that time span.

In 1570, Englishman John Keyes (Caius) published his classifications of the known breeds of dog in England. Keyes was a medical doctor, who later became the first physician to Queen Elizabeth I of England. Before this, he had traveled to Padua, Italy, to pursue his studies. There he met the Swiss naturalist, Konrad von Gesner, who prompted him to edit the table of dogs mentioned earlier. Later, von Gesner would come to include this account of British canines in his *Historia Animalium.*

Keyes wrote his work in Latin, and even his name was Latinized, becoming Johannes Caius. His work was entitled *De Canibus Britannici.* In 1576, an English translation of this work was published. This was the first attempt at a systematic classification based upon the practical principles of the utilization of the dog. Dogs of the "gentle" kind were shown to be exclusive property of the gentry. Dogs of the "homely" kind were assigned to guard rural dwellings and flocks, and dogs of the "currish" kind were assigned to persons of lower social rank, and to clownish entertainments, whence they derived the name "toy."

The Maltese dog came under the first classification. It was called *Canes Delicati,* and known as the "Spaniel Gentle," or "Comfortor." The following is his passage on the Maltese:

> There is also among us another kind of highbred dogs, but outside the common run of these dogs, namely those which Callimachus calls Meltei from the Island of Melita in the Sicilian strait, whence that kind chiefly sought after for the amusement and pleasure of women. The smaller the kind the

more pleasing it is, so that they may carry them in their bosoms, in their beds, and in their arms in their carriages. That kind of dog are altogether useless for any purposes, except that they ease pain of the stomach, being often applied to it, or frequently borne in the bosom of the diseased person (easing pain), by their moderate warmth (lit. by the moderation of their vital heat). Moreover it is believed from their sickness and frequently their death that diseases even are transfered to them, as if the evil passed over to them owing to the intermingling (lit. likeness) of vital heat.

In the late 1500s, two other English naturalists, Abraham Fleming and William Harrison, based their works upon the publication and systemization of John Keyes. In the main, they simply repeated what Keyes had written. They did, however, add some observations of their own.

Fleming wrote that the Maltese, which he referred to as an Island Dog, was curled and rough all over, with the face and all parts of their bodies covered by long hair. He further wrote:

> Of the delicate, neat and pretty kind of dogs called Spaniel Gentle, or Comfortor, in Latin Melitaeus, or Fotor. . . . There is besides another sort of gentle dogges in this our English soyle but exempted from the order of the residue, the dogges of this kind doth Callimachus call Melitaeus of the Island Melita in the sea of Sicily (which at this day is named Malta an island indeed). These dogges are little pretty proper and fyne and sought to satisfie the delicatenesse of daintie dames and wanton womens wills instruments of folly for them to play and dallie withall to tryfle away the treasure of time to withdraw their minds from commendable exercions . . . with vaine distractions.

Harrison, in 1588, had this to say of the Maltese:

> Of the delicate, weak, and pretty kind of dogges called the Spaniel Gentle, or Comfortor, . . . the third sort of dog of the gentle kind is the Spaniel Gentle, or Comfortor, or as the common term is the hound, and these are called Melitei of the Island Malta from where they were brought hither. These are little, pretty, proper and fine and sought out far and near to satisfie the nice, delicacie of daintie dames and wanton womens wills, instruments of follie to plaie and dallie withall in triffling away the treasure of time . . . a sillie poore shift to shun their irksone idleness. These sybaritical puppies the smaller they be and thereto if they have a hole in the forepart of their heads the better they are accepted, and the more pleasure they provoke as meet plaie fellows for mincing mistresses to beare in their bosoms to keep companie withall in their chambers, to succor with sleepe in bed and nourish with meat at bord, to lie in their laps and licke their lips as they lie like young Dianaes in their wagons and coaches: and food reason it should be for coarseness with finenesse hath no fellowship but featnese with neatnesse hath neighborhood enough. . . . It is thought by some that it is verie wholesome for a weak stomach to beare such a dog in the bosom, and though some suppose that such dogges are fyt for no service, I daresay by their leaves they be in a wrong boxe.

The most descriptive passage to be written was by Ulysses Aldro-vandus. The Maltese appears in volume II of his twenty-volume work, *A History of British Quadrupeds*. These volumes were published after his death in 1605. He wrote:

Blondus reports that the name 'Maltese (or Melitensis) little dog' is derived from the island of Malta, which is situated opposite to the promontory of Pachymos (Sicily). In agreement with this statement Strabo writes that in former times little dogs, which were born on the island of Melita (Malta), situated in the Adriatic Gulf, have been the pet dogs of women. Today Malta is no longer famous for its dainty little dogs, as only poor shepherds live there.

In our times Blondus added that these dogs came from Spain. Gesner says that the most elegant dogs are bred at Lugdum (Lyon) in France; these dogs are sold at a price of ten denarii or gold drachmas. This however does not surprise Aldrovandi; he reports to have observed that a little dog of this type was sold at Bologna for 400 pounds of Bolognese money. In some Italian places these dogs are called 'Boltoli,' because, though their body is small, they are said to be ferocious and irascible like venomous toads (rubetae), which however the Italians call 'bota.' Aldrovandi considers the aforementioned gentle, aristocratic little dogs somewhat overbred, delicate and to a certain extent exotic.

Blondus says that there are two types of these delicate dogs; he found that some of them have longer hair and others have shorter hair. Bolognese breeders of Maltese dogs call those with longer hair 'nothi.' [Aldrovandus illustrated both types.] As to the colour, Blondus mentions white and black ones. Today however reddish or white ones are favored. According to Blondus, this type of dogs is one foot or half a foot long, and the dog is all the more precious if its size does not exceed that of a mouse.

In general their size is that of a weasel called ferret. The dog must be kept small. Therefore it is confined to a basket and is also fed therein. If it were moved too often it would become excited and grow too much. The growth of these dogs is also prevented in some other manner. There are some people who take the fresh rind of a wild fig tree and apply it to a swollen liver or spleen; then the rind is exposed to heat until it becomes dry and that point the swelling of the intestines has usually disappeared. Marcellus Empiricus reports that the same artificial method is used in order to prevent the growth of these little dogs. Furthermore these little dogs are of such a type that they need very little and extremely delicate food. People enjoy these little dogs to such an extent that queens gave them the small portions of their food in golden vases. Therefore it is not astonishing that Martial wrote:

'Issa is more gentle than all the girls,
Issa is the most favored pet dog of Publius.'

Albertus reports that the physical condition of female Maltese dogs is such that they often die when they bear puppies more often than once. The breeders of these dogs however do everything they can in order to get progenies, so that they can have profits. Therefore they buy the male dogs when they are still small. If they are not inclined to have sexual intercourse, feeding them with salted fish. Furthermore the breeders twist the mouth of the new born puppy with their fingers so that it is more attractive for the dog fancier to behold. If the breeders want the new litter to become more hairy, they strew the places where the pregnant mothers lie continuously with wool. If these mothers have the wool permanently before their eyes, they will give birth to puppies with manes like lions. Porta reports that it occurred that a female dog which had lain on the skin of a ram during its pregnancy, produced an offspring with an elegant mane.

Another Englishman, E. Topsel, based what he wrote, in part, upon the works of Strabo, adding his own observations, in 1607:

> There is a towne in Pachynus, a promontory of Sicily called Melita, from whence are transported many fine little dogs called Melitei canes; they were accounted the jewels of women but now the said towne is possessed by fishermen and there is no such reckoning made of these tender little dogs, which are not bigger than common ferrets or weasels, yet they are not small in understanding nor unstable in their love for which cause they are also nourished tenderly for pleasure, whereupon came the proverb 'Melitea Catella' for one nourished for pleasure, and Canes Digno Throno, because princes held them in their hands sitting upon their estate.

> Other nations have no common name for this kind that I know. Martiall made this distich of a little French dog, for about ten crownes and sometimes more. They are not above a foot long and always the lesser the more delicate and precious. Their head is like that of a cony, short legs, little feete, long taile, and white colour, and the haires about the shoulder longer than ordinary is most commended. They are of pleasant disposition and will leape and bite without pinching, and bark prettily, and some of them are taught to stand upright, holding up their forelegs like hands to fetch and carry in their mouths that which is cast unto them.

Two centuries after Dr. John Keyes had compiled the first systematic classification of the dog, the great French naturalist Buffon, or Georges Louis Le Clerc, authored in 1777 his *Historie Naturelle General en Particuliere*. Within this work was his *Ordre des Regenes de la Nature*, basing his organization of canine varieties on the various types of ears, classified by shape, position and stiffness. The name for the Maltese dog used by Buffon was the Bichon or Chien de Malta. Of that breed of dog, he wrote:

> These dogs were very fashionable a few years ago, but at present they are hardly seen. They were so small that ladies carried them in their sleeves. At last they gave them up, doubtless because of the dirtiness that is inseparable from long haired dogs, for they could not clip them without taking away their principal attraction. So few remain that I could not find one to make a drawing of and the illustration on Plate XL is a copy of a drawing in the large and beautiful collection of natural history miniatures in the print room of the

King. So far as we can judge from this illustration it seems that this dog has the muzzle of the petit barbet, and the long glossy coat of the spaniel on the body. That is why they gave it the name of 'Bouffe' [puffed]. It is also called the Maltese dog, because the first specimens came from Malta. There is reason to believe that they belong to the family of poodles, and to that of the spaniels, as shown by the shape of the body and the coat and colour.

Writing works based upon *Aelian's Zoology,* at about the same time as Buffon was Jostoni, or Joannes Johstonus. Of the Maltese dog he wrote the following:

> Maltese dogs are so-called from the island of Malta, which faces Pachynus, a promontory of Sicily. They are either short-haired or long-haired, or maned. Blondus praises those that are black and white; today the red and white varieties are regarded as valuable. In size they resemble the ordinary weasel. That they may become small, and remain so, they are shut up in boxes, and are fed there. They are fed on the choicest foods. If they conceive many at a time, the bitches suddenly die. That they may be born with shaggy coats, their keepers line the places where they lie with sheepskins, that they may always have them before their eyes. At Lugdunum (Lyon) in Gaul they are sold for ten gold pieces each. At Bononia (Bologna) the larger sort are sold for forty pounds. They are great pets with women.

An English naturalist of the same period, Oliver Goldsmith, in his volume, *A History, Earth and Animated Nature,* included this passage dealing with the Maltese breed of dog:

> The Lion Dog (Canis Leoninus). These, are small species of the spaniel. The first is supposed to have sprung from the intercourse of the little spaniel with the smaller water dog. It has hair, all over the body, extremely long and silky, and generally pure white. The other has long silky hair about the head, neck, shoulders, and extremity of the tail; but on the other parts of the parts it is short, giving the little animal a leonine appearance. It is probably bred between the little spaniel and one of the naked varieties.
>
> The lap-dog, at the time of Dr. Caius was of Maltese breed; at present it comes from different countries; in general the more backward or extraordinary these are, the more they are prized. Of these of the foreign kinds, I shall mention only three; which are more remarkable than any of the rest. The lion-dog greatly rsembles that animal in miniature, from whence it takes its name. The hair of the forepart of the body is extremely long, and tufted at the point, so that, in all these particulars, it is entirely like the lion. However, it differs very much from that fierce animal in nature and disposition, being one of the smallest animals of its kind, extremely feeble, timid and inactive. It comes originally from Malta, where it is found so small that women carry it about in their sleeves.

From the island of Malta itself, in 1805, came a book with clear reference to the dog bearing that island's name. Of that breed, Louis de Boisgelin wrote:

> There was formerly a breed of dogs in Malta with long silky hair, which were in great request in the time of the Romans; but have for some years past greatly dwindled, and indeed are almost extinct. Buffon calls these dogs bichons, and describes them as mongrels between the small Spanish dog and the little Barbet. Linnaeus gives them the name of Canis Familiaris Maelitacus; and says that to prevent their growing too large, their spinal bone must be rubbed with spirits of wine mixed with oil, giving them at the same time very little to eat. These dogs were greatly admired by both Greeks and Romans. Aristotle mentions them as being most perfectly proportioned, notwithstanding their very small size; and Imon describes the Sybarites as going to the bath attended by little Maltese dogs.

By the mid to late 1800s the dog fancy in Britain had grown to great proportions. With this keen interest in the purebred dog fancy came numerous dog "authorities" all of whom became noted authors on subjects relevant to the dog. Among those who included discourses on the Maltese dog in their printed material were H. D. Richardson, the Rev. Thomas Pierce, otherwise known as Idstone, the celebrated Stonehenge (John Henry Walsh), who edited a dog journal called the *Field,* Mr. H. W. Huntington, Rawdon B. Lee and Henry Webb.

The writings of Richardson, in particular, are of interest, as he more than the others discoursed in detail his observations upon the breed in 1847. Noting that the Maltese was a "small Poodle type dog, possessing silken hair, rather than a wooly coat, and the short turned-up nose of the Pug," he continued:

> It is usually black, but sometimes white—in any case it should be one colour. An uncle of mine had one named 'Lion', who although under five pounds weight, killed an enormous rat in a few seconds, in my presence in the Hill-street Baths, Edinburgh.
>
> This dog was well-known to the ancients, is figured on many Roman monuments, and was described by Strabo. His small size, the want of strength in proportion to his courage, have, however, long reduced this spirited little dog to the condition of a mere lap dog; and as he has been superseded by, perhaps, prettier, and at all events more easily obtained pets, he has now become almost extinct. Landseer has not long since, introduced one into a splendid painting as 'The Last of His Race.'

Noted English authorities continued to keep the breed before the public's eye throughout the 1890s and early 1900s. In 1904 the noted

English dog writer Gordon Stables called the dog the "Maltese Toy Dog," which he felt was a far more accurate appellation than Maltese Terrier, as, he noted, no expert could find any trace of terrier in the breed. In that same year, English dog author Herbert Crompton concurred, noting that earlier the Maltese dog had been known as the "Shock" and "Little Lion Dog."

Here in the United States, the Maltese was judged on the standards and ideals as established by the Kennel Club in England.

The motivating force in establishing a standard for the Maltese dog that was suited to the American fancy was Mr. M. Koerlin. Mr. Koerlin and his wife had acquired dogs of Italian bloodlines. They were instrumental in the formation of one of the first major Maltese dog clubs in this country, the Maltese Terrier Club of America. This club, which later came to be called the Maltese Dog Club of America, was responsible for several successful Maltese specialty shows, held in New York City. Through this active association of Maltese fanciers, a standard was agreed upon. Largely due to the efforts of Mr. Koerlin, the American Kennel Club came to accept the standard authored by this Maltese club, in 1906. The following is that description and standard of points.

Description and Standard of Points

General Appearance — Intelligent, sprightly, affectionate with long straight coat hanging evenly down each side, the parting extending from nose to root of tail. Although the frame is hidden beneath a mantle of hair, the general appearance should suggest a vigorous well proportioned body.

Weight — Not to exceed seven pounds. Smaller the better. Under three pounds ideal.

Color — Pure white.

Coat — Long, straight, silky but strong and of even texture throughout. No undercoat.

Head — In proportion to size of dog—should be of fair length; the *skull* slightly round, rather broad between the ears and moderately well defined at the temples, i.e., exhibiting a moderate amount of stop and not in one straight line from nose to occiput bone.

Muzzle — Not lean nor snipy but delicately proportioned.

Nose — Black.

Ears — Drop ears set slightly low, profusely covered with long hair.

Eyes — Very dark—not too far apart—expression alert but gentle; black eye rims give a more beautiful expression.

Legs — Short, straight, fine boned and well feathered.

Feet — Small with long feathering.

Body and Shape — Back short and level. Body low to ground, deep loins.

Tail and Carriage — Tail well feathered with long hair, gracefully carried, its end resting on the hind quarters and side.

230

Scale of Positive Points

Weight and size 20
Coat 20
Color 10
Body and shape 10
Tail and its carriage 10
Head 5
Eyes 5
Ears 5
Legs 5
Feet 5
Nose 5

  TOTAL 100

Scale of Negative Points

Hair clipped from face or feet 20
Kinky, curly or outstanding coat 15
Uneven texture of coat 10
Yellow or any color on ears or coat 10
Undershot or overshot jaws 10
Prominent or bulging eyes 10
Pig nose or deep stop 10
Roach back 5
Legginess 5
Butterfly or Dudley nose 5

  TOTAL 100

As you can see, the old standard has a scale of positive and negative points, which were deleted from the present standard as approved in 1963.

In the late 1950s and early 1960s there existed in the United States two Maltese dog clubs, the older of which was the Maltese Dog Club of American, and the Maltese Dog Fanciers' Association. An effort was made to combine these two clubs, to establish a parent club, which could then hold American Kennel Club recognized specialty shows.

Due in large part to the efforts of Mrs. Antonelli, this task came to a successful conclusion, with the American Maltese Association being the resultant organization. It then became the task of this new association to establish a uniform standard, acceptable to all concerned, including the American Kennel Club. Mrs. Antonelli spent countless hours acting as liaison between the American Kennel Club and the Maltese fancy. Ultimately, a new standard for the breed was established and accepted by the American Kennel Club in December of 1963. The battle still had not been completed, however. The American Kennel Club had insisted upon retaining several points included within the English standard, such as the requirement for black toe pads, even though the requirement for black nails had been deleted.

Particularly offensive to the American Maltese fancy was the paragraph dealing with the head, as delineated in the new standard, which read: "The muzzle is fine, and tapered but not snipey, its length equal to the length of the skull."

Once again the task fell to Mrs. Antonelli to rectify what the American Maltese fancy considered to be a dreadful mistake. Ultimately, in April, 1964, that section was corrected to read as it does to this day.

Efforts are always being made by one small minority or another to exact changes in the standard. However, this standard has served the breed well for more than twenty years. It has been a stimulus for the healthy promulgation of the Maltese dog, and the increase in registration to numbers undreamed of just a few decades ago. In addition, the breed has enjoyed enormous popularity and success in the show ring. There have been great numbers of Maltese being named Best in Show and Toy Group Winners, as well as countless champions.

It is the opinion of the author that standards should not be changed at the whim of each new generation of the dog fancy. It serves the breed an immensely better service to have the new fancy, as it comes along, work hard to breed to the standard, as it is written and accepted.

This practice ensures the continuity of the breed in the tradition of the many centuries of Maltese generations that have come before us. The easier way, of course, is to change to suit the current mode. However, if the future is built upon the past, it would seem a much more rewarding endeavor to emulate that which has made the Maltese dog so unique and enduring throughout the many centuries.

Here follows the accepted and approved American Kennel Club Standard for the Maltese dog.

6

The Official AKC Standard for the Maltese

General Appearance — The Maltese is a toy dog covered from head to foot with a mantle of long, silky, white hair. He is gentle mannered and affectionate, eager and sprightly in action, and, despite his size, possessed of the vigor needed for the satisfactory companion.

Head — Of medium length and in proportion to the size of the dog. *The skull* is slightly rounded on top, the stop moderate. *The drop ears* are rather low set and heavily feathered with long hair that hangs close to the head. *Eyes* are set not too far apart; they are very dark and round, their black rims enhancing the gentle yet alert expression. *The muzzle* is of medium length, fine and tapered but not snipy. *The nose* is black. *The teeth* meet in an even, edge-to-edge bite, or in a scissors bite.

Neck — Sufficient length of neck is desirable as promoting a high carriage of the head.

Body — Compact, the height from the withers to the ground equaling the length from the withers to the root of the tail. Shoulder blades are sloping, the elbows well knit and held close to the body. The back is level in topline, the ribs well sprung. The chest is fairly deep, the loins taut, strong, and just slightly tucked up underneath.

Tail — A long-haired plume carried gracefully over the back, its tip lying to the side over the quarter.

Legs and Feet — Legs are fine-boned and nicely feathered. Forelegs are straight, their pastern joints well knit and devoid of appreciable bend. Hind legs are strong and moderately angulated at stifles and hocks. The feet are small and round, with toe pads black. Scraggly hairs on the feet may be trimmed to give a neater appearance.

Size — Weight under seven pounds, with from four to six pounds preferred. Over-all quality is to be favored over size.

Coat and Color — The coat is single, that is without undercoat. It hangs long, flat and silky over the sides of the body almost, if not quite to the ground. The long head-hair may be tied up in a topknot or it may be left hanging. Any suggestion of kinkiness, curliness, or wooly texture is objectionable. Color, pure white. Light tan or lemon on the ears is permissible, but not desirable.

Size — Weight under seven pounds, with from four to six pounds preferred. Over-all quality is to be favored over size.

Gait — The Maltese moves with a jaunty, smooth, flowing gait. Viewed from the side, he gives an impression of rapid movement, size considered. In the stride, the forelegs reach straight and free from the shoulders, with elbows close. Hind legs to move in a straight line. Cowhocks or any suggestion of hind leg toeing in or out are faults.

Temperament — For all his diminutive size, the Maltese seems to be without fear. His trust and affectionate responsiveness are very appealing. He is among the gentlest mannered of all little dogs, yet he is lively and playful as well as vigorous.

7

A Discussion of the
Maltese Standard

THE MALTESE STANDARD is used by breeders, judges and fanciers as a yardstick by which they may measure the quality of Maltese dogs. However, standards are just blueprints, or patterns in words. Words can be vague and sometimes difficult and flexible enough so as to be interpreted differently by everyone reading them.

The person who looks at the standard through the eyes of the mechanic rather than those of an engineer will never understand the subtle differences between a good Maltese dog and an excellent Maltese dog. The mechanic knows *how* a good dog should be put together, but the engineer knows *why* a good dog is put together the way he is. The engineer will also appreciate the effect that any slight change might have on the rest of the dog. The actual blueprint that comes before many breeder's and fancier's eye is the winning dog seen in the show ring. Tastes change from time to time. As new breeders become dominant in the ring, the breed goes through evolutionary changes. Sometimes these changes are for the better, other times they are for the worse.

In breeds of dog other than the Maltese, breeders have experienced heartbreak and emotional trauma when faced with animals that are physically unsound because of a breeding program that attempts to exaggerate or improve upon physical qualities that were the current fad in the show ring. This has not happened to the Maltese breed yet. However, it could be just a matter of time before it does, if we have more breeders who are mechanics than engineers. Dogs in competition must be weighed against one another as the sum total of their virtues as well as their faults.

235

Well-balanced dogs winning in the show rings are of much less danger to the future of a breed than dogs with a few outstanding and exaggerated features.

A profound knowledge of dogs is required to interpret any standard. That which lies behind a breed's description is of consequence. As the standard for the Maltese dog is discussed, we shall delve into the background and mechanical factors involved in each separate aspect of the standard. To understand fully what goes into making a superb specimen of the breed and a top winning dog, it is important to get down to the "under the skin" mechanics directly influencing both form and function. In addition, the centuries-old tradition that sets the Maltese apart from all other breeds of dog will constantly be a consideration.

In judging or appraising any breed of dog, there are five useful tools for measuring each dog's conformity to its particular standard. These are type, balance, style, soundness and condition.

Type refers to the combination of distinguishing features which, when added together, make the Maltese unique. The word "type" is frequently abused by fanciers who misuse it as an expression of personal preference. There can be only one correct type within the breed. A Maltese dog, lacking type, has little to offer the breed. However, one excelling in type is a valuable asset, even if he possesses minor flaws. The perfect dog has yet to be bred.

Balance means proportion. A well-balanced Maltese dog possesses neither glaring faults nor one outstanding feature. Balance is pleasing to the eye, with its instant look of rightness, much like a good painting.

Style is a combination of showmanship, personality and elegance. The Maltese dog that possesses an air of pride, eagerness and alertness, in his ancient, aristocratic way, is extremely appealing and very difficult to deny.

Soundness refers to the freedom from disability. Soundness is very frequently used to describe a dog's gait. The quality of a dog's locomotion has little to do with his "sound" condition. It would be better to call a dog that moves properly a "good mover."

Condition refers to well-being. This is a dog with exactly the right amount of flesh, being neither too fat nor too thin. A fat dog is most certainly not necessarily a dog in *good* condition. At the same time, a dog that is lean yet well developed and physically fit is not necessarily in poor condition. A dog in good condition will possess eyes that are bright and clear. The coat will be full, healthy and well groomed.

Some fanciers and judges will tend to place particular emphasis on balance and soundness, for example, while others will express more interest in type. A truly good Maltese will possess a pleasing balance of all the aforementioned qualities. He will win consistently, and receive the admiration of many, no matter which of the preferred qualities are emphasized.

236

To begin, let us consider the *general appearance* of the Maltese:

> The Maltese is a toy dog covered from head to foot with a mantle of long, silky, white hair. He is gentle mannered and affectionate, eager and sprightly in action, and, despite his size, possessed of the vigor needed for the satisfactory companion.

It would seem that the general appearance aspect of the standard is self-explanatory, leaving little room for interpretation.

The Maltese is distinguished in the Toy group by being the only Toy breed possessing a long, silky white coat. The standard is specific in its requirement for a "silky" coat. Silky does not denote a full, puffy, stand-away type coat. Rather, silky suggests an elegant, flowing white coat that falls gently over the body. While the "big" type coats are an impressive sight to see, they are quite incorrect. A more detailed discussion will follow under the section dealing with the coat itself.

A winning Maltese is an immediate attention grabber, due not only to his one most outstanding feature, his elegantly groomed, flowing white coat, but also his vivacious and outgoing personality. He should possess enough energy and personality to fill a 150-pound Great Dane.

The Maltese should be gentle mannered, yet lively and vigorous. For all his regal attitude, he should possess the spunk and stamina to get down and be one of "the boys." However, it should be well understood here that the Maltese should never be "feisty" in a terrier-like manner.

The Maltese is a devoted companion and is always most dedicated to his master. He should, however, not be shy of strangers, nor be in any manner timid. He is eager for the attention of others, although none could ever replace that of his master.

Head

> *Head* Of medium length and in proportion to the size of the dog. *The skull* is slightly rounded on top, the stop moderate. *The drop ears* are rather low set and heavily feathered with long hair that hangs close to the head. *Eyes* are set not too far apart; they are very dark and round, their black rims enhancing the gentle yet alert expression. *The muzzle* is of medium length, fine and tapered but not snipy. *The nose* is black. *The teeth* meet in an even, edge-to-edge bite, or in a scissors bite.

Of the most outstanding aspects of the Maltese dog to which the viewing public and the fancy at large are most readily attracted, the head is one. The standard calls for the head to be in proper proportion to the size of the dog. This is a most important consideration. Dogs that have heads that are too small in size are not in proper balance. Often, dogs possessing this problem have the hair about the head ratted and back-combed to increase volume, and thus size. No amount of teasing or back-combing of the hair can make up for the lack of proper skull size.

On the other side of the question, a dog whose head is too large for the size of his body will never be in proper balance.

The skull itself is slightly rounded. This in no way indicates an apple-shaped head, or an excessively rounded skull top. It is, as stated, slightly rounded, coming up from the stop, rounding out, and then flattening slightly, with the sides of the skull rounding down from the crown.

There is a definite stop, although the angle at which the muzzle blends into the skull is moderate rather than abrupt, as in a Japanese Chin. The skull rises up from this definite stop, and arches toward the top of the skull in a gentle, rounded shape. The foreskull should not protrude beyond the stop, as in the Pekingese and Brussels Griffon.

The ears are rather low set, being set on the head about level with the eye, at the sides of the head. The ear should be long, soft and pendulous. They should lie flat and close to the head. Folded or "button" ears are quite incorrect, as are high-set "terrier-like" ears. The Maltese should have a gentle expression, and any ear but the one called for detracts from this gentle expression. The ears should be heavily feathered with long hair that hangs close to the head. An incorrect ear or ear set will not allow the hair to hang as described. Rather, the dog will have a more fly-away look, reminiscent of the flying nun.

The eye of the Maltese must be rounded in shape and very dark, to the point of appearing to be black. The almond eye of the Poodle or terrier is highly undesirable. An eye that is too small, being "squinty" or "beady" in appearance, is highly undesirable. Equally undesirable is a bulging or protruding eye, such as that possessed by the Pekingese. The Maltese should possess an eye that in size is in proper balance to the rest of his head, and fitted well into his skull. A light eye is highly undesirable and detracts immeasurably from the gentle and alert expression required by the standard.

While the eyes should not be placed too far apart, they should not be set too close together, either. This would add to a terrier-like appearance, which is highly undesirable.

The "points" on a Maltese head are black. These points include the eye rims and the nose. It is also a plus if the lips are black, although such is not required by the standard.

With regard to the eye rims, the standard requires only that the margins of the eyelids be black. Naturally, the thicker this rim of black about the eye, the more the expression will be enhanced. Especially attractive are those eye rims that have the appearance of having been drawn on with a greasy black crayon. Pencil thin, black eye rims are acceptable, in accordance with the standard, but as stated are not as glamorous as the thicker sort.

238

The nose is black, and at its best should look like a chunk of coal set upon the end of the muzzle. Some specimens suffer from "winter nose" or, in bitches, a "season nose." In some specimens of the breed, exposure to sunlight will cause the nose to darken considerably. There may be a lightening of the nose, especially at the edges, in winter on some dogs. Other dogs, however, never experience a darkening or fade. Some individual bitches in season will tend to pink out on the nose and eye rims during the estrus cycle, while others are unaffected.

Much has been written and said of the "halos" a Maltese may or may not possess. The standard itself has absolutely no requirement whatsoever for these halos. A halo is defined as being a darkening of the skin area surrounding the points. This may be any shade from black to a light grayish color radiating out from the points. Many breeders attempt to connect halos with good pigmentation. This connection is erroneous. There are examples of dogs that have possessed heavy halo areas about the eyes and up the muzzle to the point of the stop, while also having incomplete eye rims or weak pigmentation on the nose. This would therefore prove that the dog possessing halos is not necessarily a heavily pigmented specimen.

There have been specimens that possess full complete eye rims, and have one eye with a halo and one without. This is very unattractive, as one eye will look darker and thereby larger than the other. This occurs despite the fact that the eye rims on both eyes are equally as complete and dark.

Some dogs have had very black skin up the nose, lacking these halos from about the eyes. This too is not especially attractive.

However, in both cases, these dogs possess full black points and cannot be faulted.

In some cases, there can be such an overabundance of dark skin that the face will appear to have a smudged, dirty appearance. This tends to detract from the actual dark points. It is an expression that is most unappealing.

Some of the most lovely specimens of the breed had no halos at all. Yet these dogs have had the darkest, richest of pigmentation on their eyelids and nose. Their eyes had that "greasy crayon" look alluded to earlier. In addition, the lips and inside of the mouth have been quite black. Such dogs are equal in pigment to any dog possessing halos, which are in no way called for, mentioned or required in the approved standard.

Present within the breed are two distinct types, and this will be discussed here because of the direct correlation to the Maltese head. There are some specimens that are more terrier-like in appearance, while others are more spaniel-like. The debate upon the issue of whether the Maltese dog was spaniel or terrier was long ago settled and laid to rest by breeders, naturalists and dog authorities of note. The Maltese dog is most definitely not of the terrier family. Therefore, any resemblance to that type is incorrect and undesirable.

239

A well-balanced specimen.

A nicely balanced head.

Proper ears with hair.   Proper ears without hair.

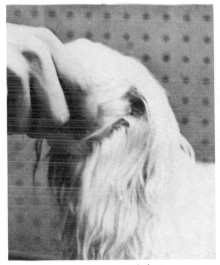

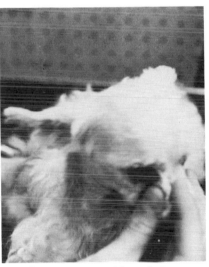

Incorrect ears with hair.   Incorrect ears without hair.

It should be noted here that the Maltese is not a true spaniel, either, even though his type more closely resembles that kind of dog. It has been concluded that the breed is most correctly called the "Maltese Toy Dog."

In the past, especially, and continuing into the present to some degree, the Maltese frequently possessed a long muzzle, perhaps accounting for half the total length of the head. This was usually accompanied by a somewhat narrower skull and a high set and frequently button-type ear. This would tend to give the head a much narrower shape, being definitely terrier in appearance. This is perhaps the most incorrect type of head a Maltese can possess. Conscientious breeders have worked hard to remove this influence from the breed.

It is important to remember that the Maltese is not and should never be bracheocephalic (Pekingese, Pug, etc.) in type. The most proper skull-to-muzzle ratio would be approximately three-fourths skull to one-fourth muzzle. This ratio allows for a pleasant balance and appearance.

Just as muzzle length has had a very important impact on the Maltese head, the width of the muzzle is also important. Since the standard calls for a fine and tapered muzzle, a muzzle that is wide and boxy down to the nose would be contrary to proper type. The key word here is "tapered." At the same time, a muzzle that is extremely narrow and snipy (as in a Pomeranian), even though the length is correct, would present an unbalanced head.

The description of the bite is self-explanatory. Teeth are very important to a dog's health, appearance and well-being. A muzzle that is either too short or too narrow will not provide enough bone for the teeth to be seated securely. In the case of the show dog, this could lead to premature tooth loss resulting in early retirement from the show ring.

The dentition should be kept healthy and clean, free of tartar. This is easily achieved at home, if the dog is trained from a young age to allow the scaling procedure to be done. Keeping the teeth and gums of the Maltese in good condition will also add to the longevity of the teeth.

Neck

Neck—Sufficient length of neck is desirable as promoting a high carriage of the head.

Since the neck of the Maltese is singled out and described, it should be obvious that it is a very important aspect adding to the over-all balance of the dog. A Maltese should never appear to have his head screwed into his shoulders. Rather, it should be quite gracefully arched, in the manner of a swan, although it is not quite as exaggerated as that.

The neck should really be considered along with the front quarters, since all of the muscles that draw the front legs forward depend upon the neck for base support, either directly or indirectly.

Good shoulder "layback" contributes to the reach of the neck and correct head carriage. The layback of the shoulder also will provide a pleasing transition of the neckline into the withers and topline. If there is poor shoulder layback, the muscles will be poorly developed. Such a neck will then join the withers abruptly, and the neck will appear skinny and short.

The correct Maltese should possess a neckline setting well into the shoulders. He should carry his head up high, in a regal manner.

Body

> *Body*—Compact, the height from the withers to the ground equaling the length from the withers to the root of the tail. Shoulder blades are sloping, the elbows well knit and held close to the body. The back is level in topline, the ribs well sprung. The chest is fairly deep, the loins taut, strong, and just slightly tucked up underneath.

The appearance of the Maltese should be compact, or "cobby." He should be square from the point of the withers to the root of the tail, and from the point of the withers to the ground. Since the actual body length extends somewhat forward from the shoulders, known as the withers, the Maltese dog is actually slightly longer than he is tall. This slight additional length of body allows the Maltese to coordinate drive from the rear with reach from the front.

However, a well put together Maltese will have the appearance of being much more compact and shorter in body than he truly is. Well laid back shoulders and properly angulated hindquarters create an illusion of shortness because the distance between the two assemblies is short in comparison to the total dog. A well-developed rib area will also help to make the dog appear to be shorter than he really is.

A Maltese that is taller than he is long will often lack proper angulation in the front, the rear or both front and rear. This type of body construction can cause a dog to crab, or sidewind, and will often cause roaching of the spine as well. He will do this, especially when gaiting, to avoid leg interference.

The ideal layback of shoulder will be at a 45 degree angle. The shoulder reaches its maximum efficiency at that point. A 45 degree angle has 38% more surface area than a straight 60 degree angle shoulder blade. This angle shoulder blade will be two-and-a-half times more efficient in its function. A properly sloping shoulder blade gives wider spread to muscles and provides more area for muscle attachment. It also provides the Maltese

Profile view of
a downface
Maltese.

Incorrect downface, snipy, expression.

A square dog with excellent tail set and carriage, a nice arch of neck, with head carried high. The topline is level, and the dog exhibits proper ear set and proportion of head (¼ muzzle, ¾ skull).

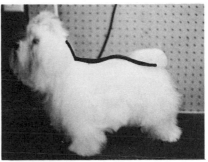

Incorrect topline, high in the rear or down at the shoulders.

Incorrect topline showing a roach. This dog lacks neck and leg. It is long and low, and despite the head carried up, the neck is too short to give an elegant appearance. The tail is carried in an incorrect "screw" or pig-tail. This dog lacks good over-all balance.

An incorrect, "soft" back or sagging topline.

An incorrect "sloping" topline, the shoulders (withers) are higher off the ground than the root of the tail.

245

with greater reach and power in his front quarters. It is often said that a dog cannot step beyond his shoulders. There can be no rear drive unless the front can take care of it. The shoulder serves as the foundation for the entire front assembly. It is as important to the Maltese as it is to the Great Dane. The weight it supports is the same in proportion to that of the Great Dane. The concussion that the front quarters absorb when a Maltese jumps from one's lap is just as severe, proportionately, as that of a large dog leaping a six-foot hurdle.

The elbows of the Maltese should be held close to the body, to allow the leg to reach out in a straight line, thus minimizing the waste of energy.

The back should be level in topline. This means that the topline should be the same height from the ground at the withers (shoulders) as it is at the root of the tail. The line down the back following the spine should be dead level, devoid of any humps or depressions in that level line. There are several topline faults most frequently found in the Maltese. These include the roached back, or a topline that has a "hump" that may be quite slight or rather severe. This "roach" or hump will usually occur over the area of the loin of the dog, just behind the ribs. This roached back condition may be the result of a short-backed leggy dog or a dog that is too long in the loin.

Another common fault is the "soft" back. This is the exact opposite condition of the roached back. Where a roached spine will curve upward from the ground, a soft back will create a depression downward in the topline, toward the ground.

Soft backs are not positive and firm during movement, as a good topline should always be. Soft backs may be inherited or they may be the result of poor muscle health due to lack of exercise. A topline such as this will often sag permanently as the dog grows older.

Power generated by the back legs is delivered forward through the back. There can be no question that a straight firm back will be much more efficient than one that is curved or soft.

Another incorrect topline condition seen in the Maltese, which is no more correct than the roached or soft back, is the sloping topline. A sloping topline is one which is devoid of a roach or dip, but which slopes downward toward the tail from the withers. Many spaniels possess this type of topline. While a sloping topline may be correct on a Cocker Spaniel, it is totally and completely incorrect on the Maltese. This topline usually carries with it a highly angulated rear construction, which is far from that which is desired or required by the Maltese standard. In considering a Maltese dog, one should always bear in mind that both the front and rear construction are moderate, and the topline, invariably, level.

The ribs should be well sprung, and the chest fairly deep to provide ample working space for the heart and lungs. There may be a slight depression at either side of the rib cage, at the elbow. This will allow for the elbows to fit in closely to the ribs. The ribs will then spring out from behind the elbow. There is a tendency for many Maltese to possess less chest capacity than is desirable. Such specimens have "sausage-like" bodies in shape, and are far from desirable. The loins should be taut and strong, with a *slight* tuck up underneath. The loin is an unsupported bridge between the front and the rear. This area must be firm, and the construction underneath it slightly arched to provide optimum support. This is one of the first areas to lose functional strength in the obese or over-conditioned show dog.

Tail

Tail—A long-haired plume carried gracefully over the back, its tip lying to the side over the quarter.

The tail of the Maltese must be carried well up and over the back. The tail should rest on the back, or lie on either side.

One of the most common faults with the tail of a Maltese is a low tail set that causes a "flag" tail, or one that stands up straight in the air. This "flag" tail may or may not curve slightly, however it never touches firmly on the back. A flag or gay tail is a gross fault in the Maltese, as it is completely detracting to the overall balance and beauty of the Maltese.

Low tail sets that curve over to touch the back are also incorrect, although not as offensive as the gay or flag tail. A low tail set will tend to give a longer look to the back, as well, thus destroying the compact or cobby look desired. These types of incorrect tails are serious faults, indeed, since they are dominant traits passed on to future generations.

The screw tail, pig tail or double-curled tail is also incorrect, although not as offensive as a flag or gay tail. The vertebrae in a screw tail are often malformed. Since the tail is a continuation of the spinal column, it could possibly be the sign of other spinal defects that cannot be seen.

Legs and Feet

Legs and Feet—Legs are fine-boned and nicely feathered. Forelegs are straight, their pastern joints well knit and devoid of appreciable bend. Hind legs are strong and moderately angulated at stifles and hocks. The feet are small and round, with toe pads black. Scraggly hairs on the feet may be trimmed to give a neater appearance.

The Maltese is one of three Toy breeds whose standard calls for fine bone. Obviously, then, it is very important for a Maltese to possess fine bone. To understand why this is so important to the breed we need to consider the axiom, "Form follows function." The Maltese for all these many centuries has been bred as a dog kept by the gentry, carried in sleeves and bosoms and in the arms of their masters. A dog bred for such a function must be light, and most certainly refined in his physical nature. Fine bone

An incorrect gay or flag tail.

Incorrect low tail set and poor carriage.

A correct front, elbows held in close to the body, the leg bone straight. The toes are pointing straight ahead, the feet properly trimmed.

An incorrect front with toes pointing out in an "east-west" stance.

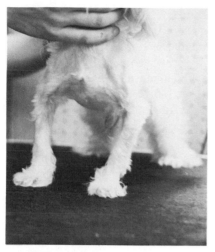

An incorrect "harp" front, out at the elbows, with curved bone, toes pointing out, in an "east-west" stance.

An incorrect "cowhocked" rear.

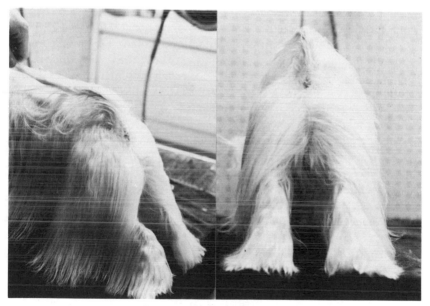

Two views of a proper rear.

certainly requires a dog of lesser weight and size. It attempts to assume that no stocky, coarse specimen of the breed should ever be introduced into the gene pool. By stressing this requirement for fine bone, the standard attempts to ensure that the Maltese will never become a dog so large and coarse as to cease to be able to do that which he was created to do.

The forelegs should be straight, with well-knit pasterns, so that the pad is under the center of gravity. If it is not, the foot and pastern will take quite a beating with every step. Crooked legs occur most frequently in the heavily boned Maltese.

The pastern should be free of appreciable bend. However, it is far better for the pastern to be slightly sloped rather than dead straight. A slightly sloping pastern will cushion the impact of the foot hitting the ground. This usually will keep company with a good front.

The hind quarters should be moderately angulated in the stifle and hock so that when the Maltese is standing, his feet will be slightly behind the rear quarters. This will allow the rear legs to move with long, smooth, sweeping strides. The straight stifled Maltese is not uncommon. This defect will frequently be accompanied by sub-luxating patellas.

Heavy, coarse stifles are extremely objectionable, and should be heavily faulted. The patella bones and tibia bones should meld at the stifle in a sleek, fine and elegantly refined joint. In feeling these bones, one should not be reminded of what one would expect in putting one's hands on a coarser boned dog, such as a Shih Tzu.

The feet should be small, compact and round. This type of foot is perfectly built for the toy dog that bounds about the house, since it is less subject to injury and does not require as much muscular effort as a longer foot.

With regard to the coat on the legs, the standard requires that the legs be nicely feathered. They should not be moth eaten or skimpy in coat. A nicely coated leg will add to the overall balance of the body's hair coat.

The standard notes that the feet may be trimmed to give a neater appearance. It should be noted here that this is *the only place* in the standard that allows for the trimming of the Maltese. The Maltese is an *untrimmed breed,* as prescribed by the standard. Further discussion shall follow under the section dealing with the coat.

It is noted that the toe pads are required to be black. This requirement did not appear in the original standard that was in effect from 1906 to 1963. It was added to the present standard by the American Kennel Club, which took the requirements from the English standard. It is curious that the requirement for black nails in the English standard was passed over, yet the black pads requirement was retained. It would seem that a connection between the pigment of the points and that of the pads was being drawn. Some breeders try to establish such a connection. In reality, there is none. The pigmentation of the points and that of the foot pads are quite independently inherited and genetically controlled. Dogs with coal-black pads may be completely devoid of pigmentation on their points, and vice-versa.

It is rather amusing when one observes a judge making a *large* point of the black pad requirement in the show ring. This is especially so, when one considers there are so many other points in the standard that are immensely more important to the breed than whether or not the foot pads are black.

It would be ludicrous to fault an outstanding specimen of the breed because of the lack of complete pigment on a pad. This seems even moreso when it is considered that this requirement was never thought important by the members of the fancy who conscientiously worked to establish the present standard.

Coat and Color

Coat and Color—The coat is single, that is, without undercoat. It hangs long, flat, and silky over the sides of the body almost, if not quite to the ground. The long headhair may be tied up in a topknot or it may be left hanging. Any suggestion of kinkiness, curliness, or wooly texture is objectionable. Color, pure white. Light tan or lemon on the ears is permissible, but not desirable.

A Maltese in full coat is truly a remarkable sight to behold. It attracts all, both novice and seasoned pro. In effect the Maltese coat makes him stand out above all the other breeds in the Toy Group. The author shares the opinion of the knowledgeable, long-time members of the fancy that the Maltese dog is a head and coat breed, first, before all other considerations.

The Maltese coat is in a class by itself, unique in dogdom. It is lustrous white silk. It is unfortunate, however, that many unknowledgeable people consider quantity the only essential in meeting the exacting letter of the standard. More than equal consideration must be given to the actual quality and texture of the hair coat than to the amount of hair the dog possesses. Anyone can recognize a big coat or a lot of hair. However, it will take a true student of the breed to evaluate quality and texture. Coats that are kinky, wooly, cottony or that possess undercoat and guard hairs should be very heavily penalized.

A true silky coat will fall against the body as described by the standard—long, flat and silky over the sides. There may be some suggestion of wave, but this will in no way be caused by the hair coat. Rather, it will be the true silk conforming to the armature of the body beneath it. The coat thus molds itself to exhibit the dog's body. The true silk coat should enhance and exhibit the finely structured body beneath it, not cover it in a mass of puffy hair. A true silky coat is not sparse. Quite the contrary, although there will appear to be a lack of volume upon touch, the amount of hair will be quite surprising. With a good silky coat, there will be many fine silken hairs per square inch of body surface. Such hair, even without preparation, will have a pearly silky gleam. These coats will be cool to the touch, as with silk.

In years gone by, before the advent of synthetic fibers, it was pure silk that was worn in tropical climates, due to its cooling properties. A handful of proper Maltese coat will possess this same cooling quality.

When a handful of proper coat is lifted up from the body of the dog and dropped, it will fall limply back to the sides of the dog, like gleaming silk. If it remains otherwise, i.e. remains standing away or puffed out, it will not be proper coat texture.

In addition to lacking the gleam and gloss of a true silky coat, a wooly or cottony coat will be coarser to the touch. Its tensile strength will be much less than that of the true silk coat.

Some true silk coats may take a bit longer to develop than the cotton or wooly types, but the wait is worth it. Unfortunately, genetically, the improper type coat is dominant over the correct silky coat. It therefore requires extra careful effort on the part of the breeder to develop the ability to consistently produce proper coat texture.

The only trimming allowed by the standard is to the feet, to remove scraggly hairs, and thus give a neater appearance. The standard requires only that the hair cover the body and reach almost, if not quite, to the ground. However, with modern hair care products and the development of better grooming techniques, coats may now reach what would be considered, several years ago, remarkable length.

Today, it is unusual to see a Maltese whose coat does not touch the floor. There are some specimens that, no matter what the care given, will never attain this length of coat due to improper genes for coat growth. However, as stated, this is today quite an uncommon situation. It is unusual to see a Maltese whose hair coat does not reach the ground. An excessively long coat may prove troublesome to movement, at outdoor dog shows, especially. A long coat will drag behind a dog, giving him the appearance of being either much longer or much bigger than he is in actuality. Because of these reasons, some trimming of the coat may be performed.

It is important to always bear in mind that the Maltese dog was bred to be a lap, bosom and sleeve dog. Therefore, excessive locomotion was never a factor in his development. This in no way is meant to suggest that a Maltese should not be capable of healthy and sound self-locomotion. He should definitely be capable of walking, running and even climbing stairs. Yet, one should never lose sight of what the dog is, and what he was bred to do. The Maltese was not bred for all these centuries to be exhibited in a show ring. Indeed, in other nations he is exhibited untrimmed. The glory and the birthright of the Maltese dog is his coat. The trimming of the root of the tail, Poodle fashion, may help to correct a poor tail set, or even help to shorten a back that is too long. However, it remains that the Maltese is not a trimmed breed, as explicitly stated in the standard. The feet may be trimmed. Any other excessive trimming to any and all parts of a Maltese dog's coat remains most undesirable, incorrect and should therefore be avoided and penalized.

The color of the Maltese is pure white—as white as the driven snow. A pure white dog is much preferable to a dog with color in his coat. The standard allows for lemon or light tan ears. Often, puppies will possess colored ears. This color usually will lighten with maturity. Puppies will sometimes have spots of lemon in the coat as well. Usually such lemon spots will disappear with maturity. If they do not, they are undesirable, and any specimen over a year of age possessing such lemon spots must be penalized.

Many dogs that have blackish or greyish patches on their bodies will have corresponding colored coats growing from these spots of pigment on the body flesh. However, no link may be made between these and coat color, as some heavily pigmented dogs will be pure white, while others will have color. This is most likely a genetic throwback to a time, not so very long ago, when the Maltese was bred in colored varieties. Occasionally, a Maltese may be seen to have black hairs mixed into his white coat. This, too, is a genetic throwback to the colored Maltese bred in the early 1900s, as well as at many other points throughout his history.

Size

Size—Weight under seven pounds, with from four to six pounds preferred. Over-all quality is to be favored over size.

The Maltese must weigh seven pounds or less, i.e. from one pound up to seven. The preferred weight is from four to six pounds. The standard is quite explicit in this account.

Many eight, ten and twelve pound Maltese have been exhibited in the ring, especially within the past half dozen years or so, and these have done more than their fair share of winning. This phenomenon is not limited to the Maltese breed. Because many other members of the Toy Group have begun to exceed size and weight limits, the Maltese has tended to do so as well, much to the grave detriment of the breed, and to the dog fancy in general.

It is so frequently heard, "In order to compete and win in the Toy Group I (we) need a larger dog." This philosophy is totally abhorrent to the entire concept of the sport of purebred dogs. In addition, it leads to the breeding and exhibiting of specimens of the breed that are totally incorrect in type. Has anyone the right to alter centuries of tradition in order to win at a dog show? The answer is, of course, no.

An incorrect cottony coat. It is straight in appearance, but is thick and coarse to the touch. This type of coat will stand away from the body, rather than hang long and straight.

A correct coat will have a pearly shine, fall loose and straight and will be cool to the touch.

An incorrect wooly coat will have actual kinks in it, as does lamb's wool. This type of coat is dry and coarse and will stand away from the body.

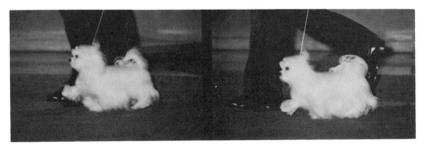

These photos exhibit the proper jaunty, smooth-flowing gait desired in the Maltese.

254

The standard remains clear and firm, undaunted by time and those who would change it to suit their fleeting momentary aspirations. Credit must be given to certain of the Toy breeds that have maintained true Toy stature, and still maintained healthy promulgation as well as highest honors in the show ring. Those breeds include the Yorkshire Terrier, the Pomeranian and the Chihuahua. If these breeds have proven that bigger is not better, perhaps the current Maltese fancy can look to them for inspiration.

When the Maltese standard was changed in 1963, the three pounds or under ideal was changed to read: "Over-all quality is to be favored over size." Unfortunately, many have interpreted this to mean larger specimens are to be favored over smaller ones. No such preferential treatment ever was intended. Rather, what was meant to be achieved was that all Maltese of the proper size and type should be considered equally. History and tradition tell us that both the larger and the smaller Maltese have always been with us, from the earliest of times. In very ancient times, and up until 1963, the very tiny Maltese were most favored. The 1963 standard was meant to give equal opportunity to many more Maltese dogs. It was not instituted to allow the Maltese to grow beyond correct proportion, as prescribed by the standard. Nor was it meant to institute prejudice against the smaller Maltese. Correct type should always remain the priority in judging and breeding the Maltese. Once again, any dog over seven pounds is of incorrect type and should be very heavily faulted.

In concluding this dissertation on size, mention should be made of the smaller bitch. Many breeders are hesitant to own such a bitch, and likewise, many judges refrain from giving awards to the smaller bitch, due to breeding considerations.

With regard to the owner-breeder, such considerations are never thought of by the Chihuahua or Pomeranian breeder. A small, sound bitch may certainly be bred, and will whelp as naturally and freely as any larger bitch, sometimes even more easily. Your author would not have a bloodline were it not for such bitches.

With regard to the dog show judge passing on an entry of this sort, it is the duty and obligation of the judge to pass upon the type, soundness and quality of such a bitch. It should be of absolutely no import to the judge whether or not the bitch ever is bred. The breeding ability is not what is being judged, especially since the ability is totally unknown to the judge at the time he is passing upon an entry. What the judge should pass upon is the exhibit before him in the ring, without any outside considerations.

Gait

Gait—The Maltese moves with a jaunty, smooth, flowing gait. Viewed from the side, he gives an impression of rapid movement, size considered. In the stride, the forelegs reach straight and free from the shoulders, with elbows close. Hind legs to move in a straight line. Cowhocks or any suggestion of hind leg toeing in or out are faults.

The gait is fairly adequately defined by this paragraph. Additional notes may be made with regard to the front. Front movement is most obvious when a Maltese gaits, as the hair separates and leg movement may be closely observed. The reach of the forelegs should be straight out in front. There should be no excessive outward swing. Such an exaggerated swing to the front, which is also called "swimming," is caused by a very poor front construction, usually a harp front. A harp front is one that will be out at the elbows. The legs will be excessively curved in bone, in the shape of a harp. The legs come toward the center of gravity under the dog. Usually, the feet will be east–west, or that is, toe out in opposite directions from the center of gravity. Such a poorly constructed front will cause a great deal of wasted energy in the locomotion of the dog. There will be an actual wide, outward swing of the front legs as the dog propels himself forward.

Poor rear movement is usually hidden by the trailing skirt of a dog in full show coat. However, the educated eye can spot improper drive in the rear. Usually, there will be an excessive swivel-type action accompanying a poor rear assembly. There may also be something other than a smooth flowing action in the rear accompanied with poor rear locomotion.

As noted in the standard, the Maltese propels himself quite rapidly on his own. The Maltese should therefore always be walked and never run around the show ring. Excessively fast gaiting is very undesirable, not only for the aforementioned reason. In addition, running a dog would also serve to hide any flaws in movement, which would otherwise be evident if the dog were properly walked through his paces. The Maltese possesses a lively, animated, self-confident and rather regal demeanor while he is being gaited. Running a Maltese about a show ring does nothing to enhance this picture, but rather detracts considerably from the desired picture of the Maltese in motion.

Temperament

Temperament—For all his diminutive size, the Maltese seems to be without fear. His trust and affectionate responsiveness are very appealing. He is among the gentlest mannered of all little dogs, yet he is lively and playful as well as vigorous.

The Maltese personality is unique among the Toy breeds. This temperament is one of his most outstanding characteristics. A good Maltese temperament is a most important factor in judging whether a

Maltese is of good breed type. The shy or overly aggressive specimen has a personality defect, which may well be inherited by his progeny. Therefore, a Maltese possessing a shy, timid or withdrawn personality or one that is feisty to the point of viciousness should be penalized severely when weighing a dog's merits against those of other specimens. As stated, the Maltese is vigorous as a breed. If the dedication to his health and sound promulgation continues to be observed this fearless, responsive, diminutive dog should continue to grace the human race for all the centuries to come.

8

Selecting a Maltese

$\mathbf{T}$HE MALTESE DOG is one of the most perfect breeds of dog to be kept by man. He was bred so that his sole function in life would be that of a companion to man. He serves in this capacity better than most any other of the family of purebred dogs.

Know What You Want

One of the first considerations in the acquisition of the Maltese dog is whether he is to be a pet, a showdog or used in obedience training. There certainly is no reason why a Maltese pet dog cannot serve in more than one function. Many a Maltese pet has gone on to become a conformation champion of record, an obedience champion or both. Many Maltese remain simply dearly loved and cherished pets.

The Right Age

The age at which you acquire your Maltese puppy may be determined by the plans you have in store for him or her. Show-quality puppies are usually purchased at between four and six months of age, or older. A pet puppy should be ten weeks of age, or older.

Choice of Sex

If you have it in mind to breed your Maltese, this would be a determining factor in the selection of the sex of your dog. The female Maltese (bitch) may be just a fine pet or she may also be bred. If she is to be a mother, and have a show career as well, it is suggested that she be shown to her championship before being bred. Motherhood can be very damaging to her coat, and will probably leave her out of show condition for quite some time.

It should be noted here that indiscriminate breeding is a very unwise idea. What the world needs least are more unwanted puppies. Quality puppies are usually the result of breeding programs of dedicated breeders. These breeders are not breeding solely for the purpose of creating new Maltese puppies. Rather, they are working hard at improving and perpetuating the finer qualities of the breed. In essence, the ethical breeder, whether he or she possesses a large kennel operation or a small hobby kennel, is breeding the Maltese in order to produce show stock of superior quality. Since not all puppies produced are always of show quality, there may upon occasion be several pet puppies to be placed.

Considering the female (bitch) strictly as a pet, one must remember that she will usually have a season, or estrus, twice yearly. This can be a great inconvenience. If your bitch is to be only a pet, you may want to consider neutering her. There are breeders who will require that a pet bitch be neutered, or never bred.

A male (dog) Maltese will be a perfect pet. The dog tends to be somewhat more affectionate and gentle in demeanor than is the average bitch.

Children in the Home

A breeder should use great discretion when selling a Maltese puppy to a home with toddlers and very young children. Small dogs and young children can be a poor combination. Such a combination can often end in a badly maimed or dead puppy. It is usually best to wait until children are old enough to be somewhat responsible before allowing a Maltese dog to be part of the household. Maltese are especially good companions to single people of any age, and loving couples and families, as well.

Where to Find a Maltese Puppy

It is always a much better idea to purchase your puppy from a breeder—not just any breeder, but a breeder who specializes in the Maltese. In buying from a breeder, you will be certain of the environment and quality of care your puppy has had. The breeder will think of his puppies as part of the family. He has great concern for his dogs, and who will care for them. In placing a puppy, he is allowing part of his home to join another. The concern for the puppy will not end with the sale. A reputable breeder is always available to the new owner, ready to supply advice and helpful information.

If you do not know how to get in touch with a breeder in your area, you may contact the corresponding secretary of the American Maltese Association for a list of reputable breeders, or you may contact the

Will your Maltese be a pet or a show dog?   *M. Martin, Martin's Maltese*

Photo of two Maltese puppies.
Marjorie Martin, Martin's Maltese

Miss Molly Ann Lehman with two San Su Kee puppies.

260

American Kennel Club, 51 Madison Avenue, New York City, New York, 10010. The American Kennel Club can provide you with the names, addresses and telephone numbers of local breeders in your area, as well as the name and address of the secretary of the national breed club.

Your veterinarian could be helpful in locating breeders in your area. All-breed clubs, as well as local Maltese specialty clubs may be helpful in locating Maltese breeders. The names of such clubs may also be obtained from the American Kennel Club.

Dealing With Breeders

When you locate a breeder, you should contact him and inform him of what you are looking for. Most breeders will require information of you, such as: What kind of home environment do you have? Do you have any children? Do you work? Will the dog be left alone for long periods of time? If you have never had a show dog before and are looking for one, some breeders may be reluctant to place a show-quality puppy in your home. Show-quality dogs are not as common as good-quality pet dogs. A breeder expends much effort, time and anxieties in the breeding of his show stock. A dedicated breeder will not want to see a superior specimen of the breed placed in a pet home.

On the other hand, you will never get a show prospect by purchasing a pet. If a dog is sold as a pet, the breeder believes, for a number of reasons, that a pet is all the dog was meant to be. Be honest with the breeder. He has a wealth of knowledge about the breed, and his dogs in particular, at his disposal. It is just as much in the good interests of the breeder to place the right dog in the right home as it is to the purchaser. If the breeder sees that the proper amount of dedication is present, the prospective show owner will eventually receive that which he desires.

Patience is of the utmost importance in acquiring a puppy. Puppies are not like cookies, where several dozens may be baked in a batch and popped out fresh from the oven. Breeding quality dogs takes time. One should not rush into the purchase of any dog, whether it be of show or pet quality.

The Purchase Transaction

In buying a purebred dog one should always be provided with an American Kennel Club registration certificate. Sometimes, however, there may be a lag in time before the breeder receives the blue slip from the American Kennel Club. In such cases, the purchaser may request the registration numbers of the sire and dam of the puppy.

If possible, an outright purchase arrangement for a puppy is more desirable than a purchase that has encumberments attached, such as a pick of the litter clause for the first litter produced, etc. However, on the breeder's side of this issue, at times there may be a good reason for a breeder to demand such an encumberment, such as the puppy being sold is the last bitch produced by a very important stud dog, etc. If there are to be such arrangements associated with the sale of a puppy or an adult dog, be certain that this document is legal and binding. Both the buyer and the seller should retain identical copies of the written agreement.

One final consideration in the purchase of your Maltese puppy is his physical and mental well-being. A puppy should carry a veterinarian's health certificate with him, upon purchase. There should also be a complete accounting of all inoculations he has received, and when they were given. An ill puppy should never be considered for purchase.

An extremely shy Maltese puppy should be avoided as well, especially if the dog is to be shown. Of course, an ethical breeder would not try to foist a dog with poor temperament on an unsuspecting prospective show dog owner. Many times, there will be a slight period of adjustment that accompanies the change of household. However, a bright, alert, outgoing puppy, even in the face of strangers, is much more preferable to one that will cower in a corner and tremble.

9

Knowing About
Your Maltese

The Stud Dog

No matter how hard you search, or how much you are willing to pay, you will never find a perfect Maltese dog. So too in seeking out a male Maltese to be used at stud—none possessing pure perfection will ever be found.

Since there will never be a perfect dog, you must rely upon that which will most suit your likes and dislikes. You should decide upon the general type and the bloodline you wish to use in your breeding program, or with your single bitch. In speaking of bloodlines, we mean the produce of a particular breeder's efforts. Bloodlines may be based upon several types of breeding programs. These include outcross breeding, linebreeding or inbreeding.

An outcross bred dog and his resultant get would possess pedigrees (the family tree) that would have few, if any, ancestors in common to both parents. This might be called a "hit-or-miss" type of breeding program. This hit-or-miss method of breeding may or may not result in litters of value to the fancier. It is difficult, in using a stud dog with this sort of background, to predict with any regularity what the traits of the offspring will be like. Such a stud, or a breeding done in this manner, will draw upon a very large gene pool. As a result, litters resulting from a stud bearing this sort of background may vary greatly. The various members of a litter produced by this type of breeding may vary widely in type and size.

While a total outcross stud or breeding may not be the most desirable

A good stud dog should pass on all his good qualities to his get. Pictured here are Ch. Al Dor Little Rascal and his son, Ch. Cotterell's Rascal's Tid Bit, at four months of age.

to some breeders, they can be of benefit to a breeding program. At times such a breeding might be beneficial in a heavily inbred bloodline, if for no other reason than to insure stamina in the resultant whelps.

An outcross male of outstanding quality may prove to be dominant in his good qualities. That is to say, he will pass his outstanding good qualities on to his puppies, consistently. It would be wise to use such a stud in establishing a linebred or inbred breeding program. Here is an example of a typical outcross bred pedigree:

Ch. Aennchen's Ashur Dancer

Ch. Joanne-Chen's Carime Dancer
Ch. Joanne-Chen's Snow Bunny Dancer
Joanne-Chen's Sweet Gem Dancer
Joanne-Chen's Matcho Man
Ch. Joanne-Chen's Cari High Dancer
Joanne-Chen's Jewel Dancer
Joanne-Chen's Shikar Shaker
Ch. Aennchen's Savar Dancer
Ch. Aennchen's Shiko Dancer
Aennchen's Kara Dancer
Aennchen's Siimi Dancer
Count Elvisio
Aennchen's Padu Dancer
Countess Susana Gatti

In the case of a stud dog that is linebred, both parents are closely related to common ancestors. Puppies resulting from a linebreeding will possess similar pedigrees. This type of stud is useful in producing offspring that are fairly similar in type to their common ancestors. An illustration of a pedigree of this type would be as follows:

Aennchen's Sanjaya Dancer

Ch. Aennchen's Savar Dancer
Ch. Aennchen's Shiko Dancer
Aennchen's Kara Dancer
Ch. Aennchen's Soada Dancer
Ch. Aennchen's Taran Dancer
Ch. Aennchen's Pompi Dancer
Aennchen's Sharika Dancer
Ch. Aennchen's Savar Dancer
Ch. Aennchen's Soomi Dancer
Aennchen's Sharika Dancer
Ch. Ethanbet's Miss Lacey Love
Ch. Cari Joanne-Chen's Love Bug
Miss Muffet XVIII
Bobbelee Lucious Liz

An inbred dog is as closely bred to common ancestors as is possible. In the case of an inbred litter, this is the closest breeding one can attempt. Inbreeding implies a breeding between father and daughter, mother and son or brother to sister or half-brother to half-sister.

Inbreeding and linebreeding are employed by the most successful breeders. Breeders that base their bloodlines and breeding programs upon this type of breeding usually rely heavily upon stud dogs possessing highly inbred or linebred pedigrees. Such stud dogs and breeding programs are one of the surest ways of producing quality offspring due to the highly refined gene pool that is drawn upon. However, this type of stud must be chosen most carefully, with judicious observation of all parental stock. In the case of the inbred litter, the same holds true. It should be clearly understood that all characteristics, both good and bad, are intensified in the breeding of close family members.

Pedigree studies must be done in depth. A thorough knowledge of all the members of the family tree is essential in determining which dogs may be genetic carriers of inherent defects. Such a study must include not only the ancestors, but siblings, as well. Here follows an example of an inbred pedigree:

Aennchen's Kara Dancer

Remo of Villa Malta
Ch. Aennchen's Raja Yoga
G & H Sweeterness
Ch. Aennchen's Siva Dancer
Ch. Aennchen's Raja Yoga
Ch. Aennchen's Puja Dancer
Aennchen's Jon Vir Royal Gopi
Remo of Villa Malta
Ch. Aennchen's Raja Yoga
G & H Sweeterness
Aennchen's GG Dancer
Ch. Aennchen's Raja Yoga
Ch. Aennchen's Puja Dancer
Aennchen's Jon Vir Royal Gopi

After consideration has been given to the type of stud dog, and/or the type of breeding program that is to be pursued, one should look for or acquire a specimen that has as many good qualities as possible. The more good points a dog possesses the more desirable he will be. For the owner of a single brood bitch seeking the services of a stud dog, the considerations should be much the same as for the individual seeking to purchase a stud for a breeding program.

There are a number of desirable characteristics you will want a Maltese stud dog to possess. These include proper size, which is especially important in the Maltese, and good pigmentation, which is equally important. A stud possessing poor pigmentation should never be considered for use at stud.

Since the coat is of such extreme importance to the breed, and is a dominant trait passed on by the stud, it should be of utmost importance in choosing a stud. Be certain the coat is of proper texture and that it has achieved proper length. The ability for a dog's haircoat to achieve length may certainly be inherited. Be certain, as well, that there is a minimal amount of coat color present. Lemon or tan on the ears is permissible, in accordance with the requirements set forth by the standard, although this is not desired. Patches and streaks of color in the body coat, or any resemblance to parti-color markings are highly undesirable. Dogs possessing such coat markings should be avoided in use at stud.

A good bite is extremely necessary to any good stud dog. This is one that is either scissors or level in nature. A stud dog with an overbite—that is, a bite in which the mandible (upper jaw or muzzle) is longer in length than the jawbone—possesses a highly undesirable trait. An undershot bite—a bite in which the jawbone extends out beyond the mandible—is as equally incorrect and undesirable as an overshot bite. Both of these incorrect characteristics are inheritable and highly unwanted. Both should be avoided by the serious breeder and concerned fancier.

A proper tail set is important to the over-all balance of the dog. A nice, high tail set, with the tip of the tail properly resting on the back, at either side, is a must in choosing a stud. Poor tail sets and carriage are highly inheritable. Dogs possessing improper tail sets or carriage should be avoided in use at stud.

Other important characteristics of a Maltese dog to be used at stud are a proper gait, proper bone and angulation in the front and rear, over-all balance, showmanship and personality. These are all qualities that tend to be passed on from one generation to the next and are therefore of paramount importance in the Maltese to be used at stud.

In the case where the services of a stud dog are being sought for a bitch, seek out a stud that excels in every area in which the bitch is faulty. Two specimens exhibiting the same fault should never be bred together. In this instance, it is certain that some of the resulting get would inherit those same defects. In addition, said defects would become extremely dominant in the resultant individuals, having received the genes for the said improper trait(s) intensified by both parents.

The great stud dog is born, not made. He transmits what has been given to him by his ancestors, along with adding something of himself. It therefore is correct to judge a stud Maltese not so much by his own appearance, but rather by the appearance of his ancestors and his get.

While it is a well known fact that the Maltese will grow a better hair coat in cooler climes, heat may be detrimental to a stud dog's reproductive system as well. It has been ascertained that actual sperm counts are lowered and there is an increase in the production of abnormal sperm when a stud dog is exposed to extreme or abnormal heat. However, in mentioning possible abnormalities produced, one should note that it is the bitch (female), not the stud dog, that passes on the defective gene responsible for monorchidism (a single descended testicle) and cryptorchidism (the absence of testicles in the scrotum).

The possible positive effects of sunlight should never be confused with the effects of continued exposure of the stud dog to X-rays and atomic radiation. Such rays and radiation may cause temporary or even permanent sterility in the stud dog. Chemical and hormone therapy for sterility are not recommended, except upon the advice of a veterinarian.

For the stud dog kept in an unwrapped state (more on the wrapping of the coat under grooming), a dry spray-on shampoo product may prove helpful in keeping the hair at the sides of the body clean and free of excessive urine from leg lifting. Such a spray-on shampoo product may be used on the coat after the dog urinates. It should then be brushed out. The hair will become reasonably dry and clean.

Occasionally, the hair coat at the sides of the body may be wiped with a mild clorox solution. This solution will help clean and bleach out the yellow urine staining. In the general day-to-day care of the coat, a small amount of spray-on oil will help to prevent hair breakage, due to the acidic effect of the urine on the hair coat. Of course, putting the hair coat up in wrappers is the most satisfactory solution to the problem.

The Brood Bitch

Puppies with sufficient health and vigor for steady growth after whelping can be produced only by a dam of equal health and vigor. The ideal brood bitch, or bitch to be used in producing only a little or two, should have a wide pelvic structure for easy passage of puppies. If you are not certain of the bitch's proper structure, a simple examination by your veterinarian will reveal whether the pelvic area is of a size large enough to enable easy passage of puppies in a normal whelping. It should be noted that a narrow pelvic structure is inherited and will be passed on by a bitch to her daughters. Such narrow pelvic structures often necessitate cesarean births.

The prospective mother should be in good condition, possessing good muscle tone. If the bitch is physically healthy and strong, and has no history of problems in producing and caring for her puppies, she may be bred every other season for years. However, if you want to breed your bitch solely to recover your purchase price, to make some extra money or to teach biology to your children, please DO NOT breed your Maltese. Every Maltese breeding should be a serious attempt at improving the breed. Many of the

To facilitate whelping, a shorter trim may be useful.

M. Martin, Martin's Maltese

lovely breeds of purebred dogs have been ruined by the avarice and stupidity of careless and promiscuous breedings. The production of too many puppies at one time can present several serious problems, including lots of extra work, the expense of buying extra food, expensive bills for veterinary care and, most importantly, the loss of the individual development of personality in the Maltese puppy. This personality is extremely important and necessary for appeal to the prospective new owners, as well as judges in the show ring.

In preparing a bitch for whelping, she should be bathed and clean, especially her stomach and nipples. Her stomach should be clipped clean of all hair to facilitate nursing. It is advisable to trim down the bitch about to whelp, especially her rear. Occasionally long wet hairs will tangle during the whelping process. Whelps have been known to strangle accidentally in the dam's coat.

Some breeders have attempted to keep a show bitch in coat while delivering and nursing a litter. The coat is saved by putting it up in wrappers. Extreme caution should be exercised if this is done, as the danger of a whelp being caught and strangled in the coat is great.

The hair coat of the bitch that has whelped a litter will usually suffer. Since the major impetus of the bitch's metabolism and energies will be devoted to supplying her whelps with milk rich in nutrients, less of those needed for a healthy coat will be used by her. The coat will become somewhat brittle and weak. It may break easily and there may be some hair loss.

Because of these factors, as well as the imminent danger to the newborn whelps, it is suggested that a bitch due to whelp be cut down in preparation for motherhood.

If a normal delivery is expected, a bitch should not be allowed to remain in hard labor for more than an hour or two before seeking veterinary assistance. In the case of the Maltese dog, the loss of only one puppy can sometimes mean the loss of an entire litter.

In general, cesarean sections are rare among the Maltese. Basically, the broad-headed breeds such as Pugs and Pekingese have a considerable number of c-sections. C-sections definitely do not run in bloodlines, unless one is referring to hereditary factors involving size, etc. Certain conditions in each individual dog, not necessarily just defects, could necessitate a c-section.

Some breeders insist on claiming that a shorter-backed bitch will experience problems in the whelping process. Naturally, these same breeders are constantly espousing the virtues of the longer-backed bitch.

However, the fact remains that the standard for the breed makes no allowances for such structural difference. Rather, it requires that both the Maltese dog and Maltese bitch both be of the same proportions, that is, as long-backed as they are tall. Bitches that are longer-backed are incorrect insofar as the standard for the breed is concerned. In addition, there is no conclusive evidence to support the notion that a longer back in the bitch facilitates the whelping process.

A veterinary exam before the bitch is due to whelp may solve a lot of problems. An x-ray taken about one week before the bitch is due to whelp, especially in the case of a bitch that has not previously whelped, can forewarn of trouble.

The novice breeder, or someone with limited or no experience in the whelping of a litter of Maltese puppies, should rely upon someone who has had such experience, such as a veterinarian or a veteran breeder.

C-sections are usually safe enough in most instances, assuming that the veterinarian performing such an operation is knowledgeable in this procedure and has had experience in the delivery of Toy dogs. Emphasis is placed on the Toy dog here, as the types of problems manifested in the delivery of the Toys can differ markedly from those of the larger breeds. Needless to say, it would be of great benefit to you and your bitch if actual knowledge of the Maltese breed was part of the veterinarian's medical expertise. We relate here the story of the veterinarian who delivered a litter of Maltese puppies, and recommended to the owner that the whelps be put down, due to the fact that all were born albinos. Obviously, this veterinarian had had little or no exposure to the Maltese breed, and was totally ignorant of the fact that usually the pigmentation will not begin to develop until a day or so after being whelped. It is recommended, therefore, that the breeder try to establish a relationship with a veterinarian well before the actual due date of the litter.

The Puppy

From birth, a puppy goes through distinct periods of behavior maturation. The newborn puppy's reflexes are concerned mainly with feeding and movement toward the mother. A rooting reflex will develop and become strong at about one week of age.

A sudden change in puppy behavior begins at three weeks of age. At this point the puppies are able, for the first time in their lives, to learn. They will begin to react to what they see and hear. They will begin to interact with their littermates and to play. For the first time they will begin to notice the human handler. This marks the beginning of the construction of the puppies' personality. Since it is never too early to start playing with your puppies in order to socialize them, three weeks of age would seem a perfect time to begin. You may begin by rubbing and playing gently with them using your finger.

The period of learning and socialization is most acute when the puppy is three to ten weeks of age. Behavioral and perceptual patterns are organized during this sensitive and easily influenced period. It is at this

271

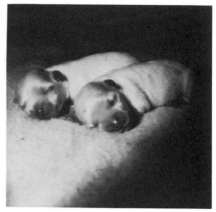

Four hours old.

Ethanbet Maltese

A day-old puppy nursing.

M. Martin

Ch. Martin's Michael-Cid, one day old.

point that the puppies should be moved from the quiet, undisturbed atmosphere in which they have been to a place where they are constantly subjected to people, both familiar and strange.

Since at a later age behavior cannot be influenced quite as easily as at this time, this seven-week period may be the most important in the dog's life. A puppy that does not receive any or limited human contact during the period when the dog is three to ten weeks of age will be physically normal. However, he may exhibit certain schizophrenic characteristics. Such dogs may lose their ability to make positive social contacts with humans. Such dogs are very difficult to train. One need only observe a litter of puppies raised in the woods by a stray bitch to witness the transformation from domestication to wild.

The housebreaking process is much easier with a puppy under ten weeks of age. The task becomes all the more difficult as the dog grows older. During this period, keeping a radio on in the area with young puppies will accustom the puppies to strange noises and noise in general.

Research has shown that overnight isolation of a puppy in a household will increase fear and anxiety, thus reinforcing the social bond with the owner the next day. This treatment will cause slight psychological trauma, but has no lasting negative effect on later behavior.

It appears that aggressive tendencies in behavior are to a certain extent inherited. However, such behavior can be influenced by environmental experiences during very early life. The dog is unique among animals in the extent to which learning can be motivated by a simple reward in the form of a word of praise or an affectionate pat on the head by the owner. Early socialization therefore makes the training of the Maltese dog much easier. Without early experience, a poor response to training and reward is sure to be encountered.

It is a good practice to feed the Maltese puppy three times a day until he is six months of age. Afterward, two meals a day are suggested for those Maltese that are very tiny, or for those with poor body weight problems.

Sometimes, there may be a problem of hypoglycemia in Maltese puppies, especially between the ages of five to nine weeks, and then again at six months of age. Hypoglycemia is a condition in which there is a drastic, sudden drop in the level of blood sugar in the dog. The dog will go into shock and, if not cared for properly, will die. Hypoglycemia is a condition never seen in dogs over one year of age, so it may be said to be a puppy disease. It is likely caused by the uneven spurts in growth of the internal organs of the dog, especially the pancreas. The brain will receive incorrect signals from the pancreas and thus not send out a correct signal for the release of a proper amount of sugar into the bloodstream. Hypoglycemia can be an inherited condition. If a bitch has been hypoglycemic, it is quite likely that she will pass on the propensity for hypoglycemic attacks to her whelps.

The addition of honey or white corn syrup to the puppy's food may help to prevent a hypoglycemic attack. Feeding soft, moist foods may help to prevent a hypoglycemic attack due to their high sugar content. Gatorade or Ringer's lactate with dextrose are good products to use as well. Both of these products contain important electrolytes, which ailing dogs and puppies need.

If you suspect that a puppy may be prone to attacks of low blood sugar, it may prove helpful to contain him in a small area so that he does not use calories he cannot afford to lose in excessive moving about.

The puppy suspected of being hypoglycemic should be kept quite warm, as maintaining proper body temperature takes a tremendous amount of energy in the form of calories, which will be used by the puppy trying to compensate for the loss of body heat. The more calories you can help the puppy conserve in keeping him warm, the better it will be for him.

At the first sign of a hypoglycemic attack, honey or corn syrup may be immediately fed to the puppy, if the Ringer's lactate or Gatorade are not readily available. Signs of an attack are a weakened condition, including wobbly unsureness on leg, frothing or drooling from the mouth and a drain of blood from the head. A check of the gums will show them to be pale, almost a greyish white in color rather than a healthy bright pink.

The puppy's stool should be carefully observed for parasites and worms. Your veterinarian can perform an examination of the stool, checking to see if parasites are present. If necessary, be sure to use a proper dosage of the worming medicine recommended, prescribed or given by your veterinarian. It is important to carefully follow the instructions for administering the worming medicine and administer it only as frequently as recommended.

The importance of having a parasite-free Maltese is of utmost importance. Parasites can take away much of the nutrition your Maltese must receive to develop a proper and healthy coat and physical condition. In extreme cases, if parasite infestation is severe, death may occur.

To help with cleanliness, a small amount of baby oil placed on the rectum will help prevent sticking of the stools and a sore rectum. Be certain to use a minimal amount of oil. Keep an eye out for caked stool, which can be a source of great trouble. If this condition is ignored or neglected, it may become serious enough to lead to the loss of a puppy.

Handling of the Maltese puppy is of utmost importance at an early age, especially to the show prospect. Youngsters should become accustomed to being posed, placed in a stance and handled. Words of encouragement and praise are helpful in this.

Several weeks after the Maltese puppy has been inoculated against communicable disease, he may go out to meet the world. This should be done with discretion, of course. It is not wise to expose a puppy to large crowds of other canines before he is three months of age. City streets are likewise dangerous, as they are the breeding grounds for a myriad of potent and dangerous diseases.

In preparation for his exposure to the world at large, and possibly the show ring, lead (leash) breaking should begin early. About six weeks of age is considered to be an ideal time.

Since a Maltese dog should never wear a collar all the time, he must be conditioned to like the feeling of having something around his neck. A helpful procedure in this regard involves the use of one-inch twill tape. You will need to make a bowline knot at one end. If you do not know how to tie such a knot, a boy scout handbook or a scout himself will prove helpful. Any other type of knot may strangle the puppy. Using an 18-inch piece of twill tape, make the bowline knot at one end of the tape, forming a loop to go around the puppy's neck. This should fit just snugly enough so that the puppy cannot slip his head out. Permit the other end of the tape to hang free. If there are other puppies in the litter, the puppies will use the twill tape to have a tug of war. He will thus learn to accept the tugging of the lead. Keep this twill tape lead on for only about one hour per day, otherwise it will lose its effectiveness.

Another useful technique involves the offering of relished tid-bits to the puppy. Ascertain what sort of treat (bait) will make your puppy excited and happy. This may include chicken, liver, liverwurst, etc. It is helpful to use something that is not messy, especially in dealing with a show dog. Liverwurst, for example, will be quite messy to carry in your pocket. In addition, it will make your hands greasy, which may rub off onto your sparkling clean Maltese, thus spoiling an otherwise radiant appearance. An excellent bait is beef liver that has been well boiled. Dogs love the flavor and aroma. In addition, the liver may be cooked and cut up into individual portions that may be frozen until used.

To use bait, train your puppy to follow you about, excitedly awaiting his treats. Teach your dog to follow along at your side in anticipation of receiving his treat. He will learn to eagerly look up at you, pose, dance, speak and in general exhibit a happily animated and alert attitude.

After doing this for a time, your puppy should gait well beside you as you go across a room, down a hallway or across your fence-enclosed backyard. While in this happy and attentive frame of mind, you will find it easy to slip a lead around your puppy's neck, with his noticing only slightly.

The lead is a leash and a collar in one. At one end is a loop that is used as a collar. It is adjustable by means of an adjustable slip device. This allows a larger or smaller loop, and makes easier the putting on and taking off of the lead. Such Toy dog leads may be acquired from dog supply companies.

Of course, these suggestions are only a part of a complete training program. To make a dog secure and alert on the lead, nothing can substitute for the actual walking of a puppy in a myriad of different and strange environments.

A one-week-old litter.   *Martin's Maltese*

Ch. Aennchen's Arjuna
Dancer's daughter at
ten days.

Two Ethanbet Maltese puppies at four weeks of age.

Ch. Fantasyland Rebecca Lyn, at three months of age.

A three-month-old puppy.   *Pegden Maltese*

A puppy may be called "a show prospect" or "possible show quality" at ten to twelve weeks of age. Usually, what a Maltese weighs at ten weeks of age is about half his total adult weight, within a half pound. Of course, there are some exceptions to this rule.

A puppy may have a perfect bite that will go off when the permanent teeth are cut. A tight tail may loosen with adulthood. Any number of things may go wrong with a dog between the puppy stage and adulthood, which the breeder cannot predict and for which no one may be held at fault. The only way one may be somewhat positive about a dog is to acquire a Maltese that is well over six months of age. However, even at that age, things may go wrong. It should always be remembered that in dealing with living things there can be very few guarantees.

The puppy's baby teeth will begin to fall out usually around the fourth or fifth month of age. The new set of permanent teeth will generally be complete by the time the puppy is six months of age. You may face problems in the change of teeth. This may be an especially important consideration in the case of a show prospect puppy. At times, the primary teeth may fail to fall out, even after the permanent teeth have been cut and are fully in. This frequently is true with the large canine teeth. It is of the utmost importance that these primary teeth be removed as soon as possible if it does not appear that they will drop out of their own accord. Many a good bite and proper dentition have been ruined by allowing the primary teeth to remain along with the second teeth. If you cannot loosen and remove these primary teeth yourself, veterinary assistance should be sought in their removal.

Lead is of extreme danger to your puppy while he is teething. Lead is an extremely toxic substance that accounts for many of the accidental poisonings in small dogs. Puppies are most susceptible since they will chew on almost anything, especially when teething. The most common source of lead is paint. Some paints on the market still contain lead. Linoleum is also a common source of lead. Exercise extreme caution with your Maltese puppy, lest he become one more victim of lead poisoning.

Rawhide chewsticks and rawhide bones are other sources of grave danger to your Maltese. If they are chewed down to a small size, your dog may try to ingest them, especially if they become soft and pliable. At this point, a puppy may attempt to swallow them, with grave consequences. Things such as these may easily be caught in the throat, leading to choking and eventual suffocation. Sometimes an adult dog's life may be saved. However, in the case of an eight-week to three-month old Maltese, it is frequently impossible.

With this in mind, remember always to keep an eye on chew sticks and rawhide playthings offered the Maltese puppy. Throw the chewsticks away when they have been gnawed down to three to four inches in length. Other objects should be discarded before they become small enough to be swallowed.

Am. & Can. Ch. Petit Point Sugar Blues
(left) and Petit Point Malt at ten weeks
of age, owned by Petit Point Maltese.

A litter sired by Ch. Aennchen's Sadana
Dancer.

A San Su Kee puppy at play.

It is helpful to the breeder to keep adequate and detailed records, in addition to those required by the American Kennel Club, if you are planning to establish a breeding program. This will enable you to compare the various records of several of your dogs. Eventually, you will be able to ascertain what is normal and what can be expected of the dogs on your breeding program.

It is suggested that puppies not be totally removed from their original environment much before ten weeks of age. If the dam is of good personality, the puppies should continue to be exposed to and socialized with her. She will pass on much of her positive attitude to her whelps. At ten weeks of age, the Maltese puppy will have absorbed all of what he can from his dam. He will have received the major necessary inoculations, thus making him safe from communicable disease. It is at this point the first "cull" or separation of the litter may be made. Puppies of obvious pet quality should be placed in proper homes. Those of prospective show quality may either be placed in show homes or held back for observation and further development.

In placing the pet Maltese, one should be prepared to face some unusual questions and situations. As a conscientious breeder, the major concern should be the future welfare of each and every Maltese puppy bred. Here then are some typical questions and situations for which one should be prepared.

You may be asked, "Is the Maltese a hardy breed?" The answer naturally is of course the Maltese is hardy. However, let us not take this to the extreme. The Maltese will not be as powerful as a Great Dane, nor will he withstand cold as a heavier coated breed, such as the Siberian Husky.

Another frequently asked question is, "Is the puppy housebroken or paper trained?" Many buyers assume this to mean that even a very young puppy will prove reliable in a different home and environment. The breeder should always be certain to explain that any dog will require further training to adjust to its new home and family routine.

A real danger signal may be present if a prospective new owner states, "Our last dog got real mean." This is usually a clear indication that the family has a history of unsatisfactory relationships with previous pets. Investigate a situation such as this thoroughly. An environment such as this could be very dangerous to any animal, not only a Maltese dog.

Another clear warning sign to the wary breeder is a statement like, "Our dog was killed by a car, and we want another right away." While accidents can happen to all of us, it would be best to find out just how responsible the prospective owners really are. Such homes may allow their pet dogs to roam the neighborhood at will. Such a home is certainly not a proper one for a Maltese.

If the prospective owners happen to mention that they had neighbor problems with their last pet, which necessitated their giving their pet dog away to a home in the "country," beware! These are people to stay away from—far, far, away.

A clear warning signal is readily made apparent when the prospective new owner's story goes something like this: "We only want a pet. We cannot pay very much, but it must be a female because our little boy, age three, has selected a girl's name for his new pet." Oh, really? These people are a must to avoid.

Then, of course, there are the prospective owners who request an older female. They especially want one at a low price, one in need of a good home. They suggest a Maltese that you, the breeder, are not planning to breed again. This is fine, unless they follow up with questions like, "How many litters has she had? How many puppies has she produced per litter? Is she an easy whelper?" Such a home should be totally avoided.

A clear warning of future danger to your Maltese puppy is expressed in a statement such as, "Our son has a personality problem at school. We think a dog will help to settle him down and teach him to be gentle." Watch out! Stay clear of this prospective home. Such children are extremely dangerous to a live pet animal. It would be wise for a breeder to tell such parents, who often have no thought of it, of the possible problems from the pet's point of view.

A most frequently asked question is, "Will you guarantee the puppy?" The answer is, of course, yes. However, what is being guaranteed and for how long? Nearly every ethical breeder will want to guarantee the health and temperament of every puppy sold to be the best possible that can be produced. However, to what extent can this be taken? One often hears of older dogs, which have been properly cared for and immunized, that die of distemper or some other disease at the age of four or five years. At that point, can the breeder be held responsible? There have been instances, for example, where dogs have reportedly died at a year of age of distemper or parvo virus several days after the owner had received a blood titer test of the dog that showed the dog to be immune to the diseases. Then there is the example of the two-year-old dog that suffers convulsions after being given distemper/hepatitis/leptospirosis (DHL) and rabies booster inoculations simultaneously. The new owner claims a disorder such as epilepsy, although no such condition was previously evident. The breeder truly should not be held accountable in such instances.

The best philosophy, therefore, for one engaged in the placement of Maltese puppies and dogs is not "caveat emptor" (buyer beware), but rather, let the seller beware.

A Maltese dog should never become a toy to be played with for a little while and then discarded. The ideal purchase is not made on a whim or on the spur of the moment. It is made, usually, after careful deliberation. It should be made from a breeder who has raised the puppies in his home, rather than from a crowded impersonal and unhealthy kennel. The ideal

Ch. Fantasyland Dream Baby, at three weeks of age and at one year of age.

Ch. Martin's Chanel-Cid, at two months of age and at eighteen months of age.

purchase will be made from a breeder who has raised Maltese for some years. He is one who has exhibited his Maltese with some success. This breeder will be knowledgeable and able to answer most questions. He will not necessarily be eager to sell a puppy to anyone, simply for the money. The conscientious breeder will make himself available to help the new Maltese owner with a number of problems that may arise, especially during the early period of important adjustments. The Maltese puppy should become a family member for many years and should therefore never be chosen in haste.

When a puppy is placed with a new owner, a folder of some sort should accompany the dog. Enclosed in this folder should be a record of all shots administered, weight, wormings if done, when and the results, as well as a diet schedule to carry the dog through his sixth month of age. It may be helpful to include a pedigree with the sale of the puppy. Possessing a pedigree will tend to cause a feeling of pride of ownership of a pet with a family tree.

All puppies may be subject to the inheritance of genetic defects. Some of these defects are rather minor problems, as they will not affect the long, healthy life of a dog. Puppies possessing these types of genetic defects may not become show dogs. However, you will be able to place such puppies in pet homes without any trepidation. Puppies possessing these minor flaws make excellent pet dogs. The prospective owner should have no fears in purchasing such a puppy.

Some genetic defects may be corrected. This, of course, will alleviate the problem in that particular dog. However, it should always be kept in mind that repair of the defect does not alter the gene pool. This defect will be passed on to future generations if the affected dog is used in a breeding program, or bred even once.

Some genetic defects may be quite severe in nature. The question of what to do with a puppy exhibiting a severe problem will have to rest with the individual breeder and his veterinarian.

Some of the genetic defects known or surmised to be inherited would include the undershot jaw or undershot dentition, or the overshot mandible or dentition. These are thought to be the most common of all defects to be passed on genetically. The primary gene effect is a shortening or lengthening of the mandible.

Hemophilia, or profuse bleeding from slight wounds, is very rare in the canine. However, when it does occur it is especially interesting because the clotting defect and its inheritance are likened to the same condition found in man.

Sub-luxated and displaced patellas are serious problems that are transmitted genetically. The only solution is the careful selection and elimination of effected dogs from breeding.

Umbilical hernia may or may not be a genetic defect. If this defect is prevalent in the forebears of the dog, he is likely to have it himself, and likely to produce it as well. However, it is important to note that this defect can be caused by improper handling at the time of birth or perhaps by the cord being cut improperly. Sometimes it may be difficult to know exactly what the source of the problem is. In breeding a dog and bitch that do not display this fault, chances are the whelps will be free of it. If hereditary causes are operative, then a weakness of the stomach muscles will be passed on to the progeny. This will cause the whelps to be prone to umbilical hernia.

Pigmentation in the Maltese predominantly depends upon the whelp's parents' genetic pool. A few fortunate whelps are born with black or greyish eye rims, spotted noses, and/or foot pads. These puppies always mature with the most desirable pigmentation. Usually, however, eye rims, noses and foot pads are pink at birth. At the time the eyes begin to open (ten to fourteen days of age), pigment should begin to appear. Puppies of different bloodlines will show full, deep pigment at a few weeks of age, while others will take up to a full year to develop the desired pigmentation. It can take up to three years, on some Maltese, to develop complete eye rims. It would be wise to breed to a line known for heavy pigment that develops early, even if it means outcross breeding to do so.

Permanent incomplete pigment is a genetic defect. This problem can only be solved by the introduction of superior genes into your dog's gene pool.

The puppy's tail will usually begin to go up and over the back at about the time when the puppies begin to toddle about the nest. By the time the puppy is weaned, the tails will either be good or bad. The tail is an extension of the spinal cord. A poor set of tail is genetically controlled, and should be a prime consideration in your Maltese.

Geriatrics

Unfortunately, we all must grow old, even our beloved Maltese dogs. As with the human, some age quite well. They remain spry, healthy and active until the end. For others, growing old may be quite distressing for both the dog and his owner.

Older dogs have different requirements than do the younger animals. He will sleep more and eat less. His dietary requirements will change. Older Maltese should be fed lesser amounts of protein and calcium, both of which are not beneficial to the geriatric. We are fortunate today to have diets especially formulated with the older dog in mind.

Broken bones, as in the human, are easier to come by in the aged dog. Vision and hearing will be dulled. Some household cleanliness problems may develop that never before existed. It may be a trying time, fraught with worry and frustration. One must keep in mind always the years of joy and

284

Even a Maltese enjoys an easy chair in old age. Ch. Aennchen's Pompi Dancer, whelped 1971, at eleven years of age.

Sometimes a sweater helps, too! San Su Kee Dresden Doll, owned by Peggy Hogg, at approximately twelve years of age.

devotion faithfully given by the little Maltese dog in your care, and bear up with the situation.

The most frequently seen disease in the geriatric Maltese is hyper-adrenocorticism, or Cushing's syndrome. This disease is characterized by excessive thirst, urination and appetite. In addition, abdominal enlargement and generalized hair loss over the abdomen, thighs and back are obvious indications of the disease. The skin of a dog so affected will become thin and darker than is normal, and will frequently have comedones. There is an absence of scratching.

The cause of this unusual disease is as the name implies. Hyper, meaning too much; adreno, referring to the adrenal glands; and corticism, referring to the cortex of the adrenal glands. The adrenal cortex is responsible for producing cortisone. Therefore, Cushing's syndrome is an overproduction of cortisone, which is then released into the dog's system from the adrenal cortex. Once diagnosis is established, treatment, if followed carefully, has proven to be quite effective in treating the causes of Cushing's syndrome.

10

Grooming Your Maltese

BOTH OWNERS AND BREEDERS of Maltese direct much attention toward the improvement of the general quality and length of the dog's coat. The desirable characteristics include improvements of the texture, straightness, elimination of color, rate of growth and strong, healthy hair shafts free of brittle qualities or tendency toward breakage.

To some extent, these qualities are genetically determined. Good quality hair coats are inherited in many bloodlines. Unfortunately, some dogs inherit poor quality coats.

Nutrition, climate, and general care play an extremely important role in the growth of a luxuriant hair coat. This is the type of coat to develop, if show success is your goal.

Of course, many Maltese owners are only interested in having a Maltese to love, without regard for spectacular growth of coat. Many owners of several Maltese keep their dogs in a "trimmed" condition: perfectly suitable for a pet. Further discussion of this topic will follow. However, here, our primary concern is the development of a luxurious length of coat. To begin to understand how this is achieved, some knowledge of the hair and its growth need to be understood.

The Nature of a Coat

In a healthy Maltese, natural oils are produced by the animal itself. These natural oils are secreted by the sebaceous glands as the hair shaft is developing. They are very important to development of a well-conditioned hair shaft, which will attain desired length. The healthy production of oil by the sebaceous glands may be different in every Maltese.

287

Most hair follicles are somewhat perpendicular. This will make the angle of the hair shaft acute to the body on one side, and obtuse on the other.

On the Maltese, the obtuse angle is up toward the back, the acute angle directed down toward the paws. The coat therefore falls naturally downward.

The sebaceous glands of the hair follicle are usually located on the obtuse side of the shaft. A small bundle of muscle tissue is connected to the sheath of the hair follicle, in about the same place as are located the sebaceous glands. When this muscle contracts, the hair is pulled more perpendicular to the dog, giving the dog that "hair on end" look. In humans, we call it "goose flesh." The contractions of this muscle squeeze the sebaceous glands, causing their oils to be extruded into the neck of the hair follicle. From there, the oils travel down the hair shaft, thus conditioning it. The oils also lubricate the skin, keeping it soft, smooth and healthy. Emotional conditions, such as fear and rage, can cause erection of these muscles and their consequent sebaceous secretions.

The fact that hair comes out on a brush or in a comb during the grooming of a hair coat does not necessarily indicate a balding condition. Hair growth occurs in cycles, with alternating periods of growth and rest. The hair shaft continually elongates during the growing phase. The resting phase begins when the germinal cell matrix becomes inactive and atrophies. Finally, the hair will fall out. At this point, the old capila may either become rejuvenated, or a new hair develops.

The Maltese hair cycle resembles that of the human more closely than it does the cycle of those dogs which will shed an entire coat twice a year. The cycle is longer and quite different. All individual hair follicles may be in different phases of their cycle at any given time.

The male sex hormone, androgen, is an important factor in hair growth. In 1942, Hamilton conducted studies which showed that castration, resulting in the lack of male sex hormones, was responsible for the prevention of hereditary baldness. He also demonstrated that the administration of the male sex hormone, to individuals lacking it, set into operation the hereditary tendency toward baldness. However, the presence of the male sex hormone does not cause baldness unless the hereditary disposition for hair loss is present. The conclusion, of course, should never be drawn that male Maltese, or people for that matter, with sparse hair are any more virile than those with a luxurious amount of hair.

Research has been done investigating what effects the cutting of hair has on its growth. Evidence is conclusive that hair cutting has absolutely no effect upon the rate of growth of the hair.

Anthropologists recognize three types of hair: straight, wooly and wavy. Straight hair is characteristically coarse and lank. It is round in shape, when seen from the cross section. Wooly hair is elyptical, or

288

"kidney" shaped in the cross section. Wavy hair will be oval in shape in cross section.

Each individual hair is composed of three parts. A central medulla is composed of soft keratin. The cuticle and the cortex are formed of hard keratin. The pigment present in the cortex cells will give the hair its color, which will depend upon the quantity and quality of melanin pigment present in the cortex. This characteristic is genetically determined.

The influence of proper nutrition on the hair coat must never be overestimated. This is especially true when speaking of the underlying skin and the content and secretions of the sebaceous glands. This secretion is a fatty material called sebum. Sebum oils and lubricates skin surfaces. It acts like a natural cold cream, preventing moisture loss from the skin.

Cold is an important stimulus for this reflex action. Oil helps the body to retain heat, by preventing evaporation. This element in itself is a basic necessity in achieving a good quality coat. Artificial oils added to the coat and coat conditioners are important. They help maintain healthily formed hair, when it becomes too long for the oils excreted by the sebaceous glands to reach all surfaces of the shaft. However, if the Maltese is kept constantly in a warm, dry atmosphere, seldom allowed outside and seldom exposed to the cold, the reflex oil secretion may never occur. Or, if it does occur, it will be infrequent. If this happens, the point at which the hair arises from the follicle could lack the protective natural oil coating. This would result in excess dry spots on the hair shaft, which are weaker than the well-oiled portions of the hair shaft.

As growth of the hair shaft continues outward from the body, these weak spots, multiplied in thousands of Maltese hairs, may appear as brittle, thin areas on the hair shaft, eventually resulting in brittle breakage.

Helping Nature

Of course, the most desirable condition would be for the entire hair shaft to be lubricated for maximum protection. The question arises, how many breeders and exhibitors are absolutely certain that their coat oils, sprays and conditioners are reaching each and every hair shaft, completely?

One essential factor needed for a healthy production of sebum is the accumulation of fatty material, called cytoplasm, in these glandular cells. In order for this to happen, there must be an adequate amount of fat in the diet. This is where nutrition comes to play an extremely important role in the hair coat's proper development.

While amounts of dietary protein are essential to the formation of the protein hair shaft, essential fatty acids and vitamins are also necessary for the adequate production of sebum, and other substances vital to the assurance of adequate hair protection and healthy growth.

It is possible to achieve a long coat or a thick coat, or even textured

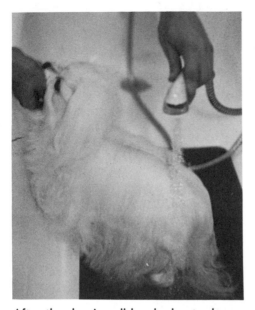

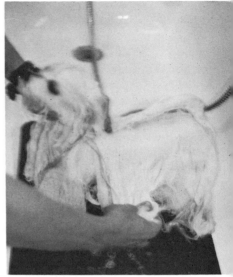

After the dog is well brushed out, place a drop of mineral oil in each eye for protection. Place him in the tub. Be sure to use a rubber mat to prevent slipping and injury. With warm water, wet down the dog from head to tail. Try not to lose the center part down the back when doing this.

Use enough shampoo to fully lather th entire dog well. Never "rub" shampoo in the coat. Rather it should be worked i using a squeezing action.

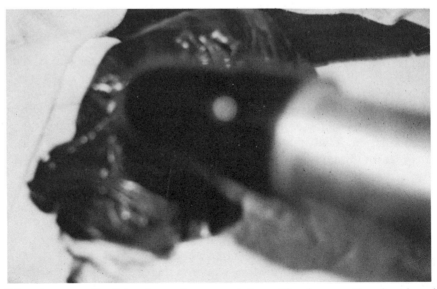

Condition the coat after it has been shampooed clean. The dog may then be placed in plastic bag and towels, and put under a dryer.

coat using genetics in breeding, and artificial conditioners on the hair shafts. However, the combination of these factors in one Maltese would be impossible without adequate nutrition.

Presented here are but a few of the most important variables which can affect a Maltese coat. Careful attention to all is the best way to assure coat quality and over-all health. The serious breeder must blend his experience with the experience of other breeders, publications, scientific reports and reports of researchers who study these phenomena. He should do this in order to make any necessary improvements in his breeding stock.

Shampooing

Shampoo soaps are formed by combining an alkali with an oil or fat. The oil used may be of vegetable origin, such as almond, peanut, coconut, olive, castor and palm nut. The fat used may be animal fat, lanolin, tallow and synthetic compounds. Most shampoos contain varying amounts of the same fatty acids. Therefore, the shampoo soap formed varies with the substances used.

Shampoos with a high pH factor, which are highly alkaline, are especially damaging to all types of hair, making it dry and brittle. The proper pH balance for a Maltese coat is around the pH five level. Human hair is usually nearer to a pH level of seven. For this reason, it would be wise not to assume that a product which works well on human hair will do the same on a Maltese coat.

Nitrizine paper is useful to a Maltese fancier in this regard. It may be purchased from your local pharmacist and used to ascertain the pH level in any product you may want to use in the care of your Maltese coat. The paper is dipped into the product. It will change color. There is a chart on the nitrizine paper package which you may use to determine the pH level of any product you are planning to use. Anything below seven on the chart is acidic. The lower the pH, the greater is the degree of acidity. Anything from seven to 14 on the chart is alkaline. The higher the pH, the greater is the degree of alkalinity.

The Maltese coat should be shampooed as often as necessary. This can be determined only by working with each individual.

In shampooing a dry, brittle coat, avoid using any shampoo containing alcohol. A liquid cream shampoo, consisting of heavy white liquids, should be used on this type of hair. These cream shampoos are mostly emulsions. They often contain oily compounds that make the hair feel silky and soft. An egg shampoo is also recommended for this type of hair coat.

For very delicate, fine hair, an acid balanced (non-strip) shampoo should be used. This type of shampoo is mild in action, contains conditioners, and is low in alkaline content.

If you have a Maltese with a tendency toward an oily coat, purchase a shampoo which has a high concentration of soap or detergent. Be careful not to overuse this product, as it can dry out and damage your dog's hair coat quickly.

An effective homemade shampoo formula, especially effective for a show bath to remove oil, combines:

> 1½ cups Lux or Ivory Detergent
> 1½ cups of water
> ¼ cup of glycerin
> ¼ cup of vinegar

Old-fashioned laundry bluing, or any of the kinds of shampoo you may choose to use, may be added to this. It is especially effective in brightening a dull coat.

Plain shampoos may contain a liquid soap or a detergent-based product. These shampoos seldom contain lanolin or other special agents that may be used to leave a gloss on the hair. If a liquid soap is used, it should be followed by an acid rinse to counteract its alkaline reaction on the hair.

If the Maltese coat is especially dirty or oily, it may be necessary to shampoo it twice. Otherwise, one shampoo usually gives the desired results. It is not necessary, as some believe, for the shampoo to have a high sudsing action to be beneficial to the hair coat.

Thoroughly rinse all lather out of the coat after the last shampoo. It is important to remove every trace if the hair is to be in superb, sparkling condition.

There are many qualities of water. Chemically, water is composed of hydrogen and oxygen. Depending on the kinds and quantities of other minerals present, it can be classified as either *hard* or *soft* water. It is important to know the kind of water that is available, whether it is hard or soft, in order to select the right products to achieve the desired results.

Soft Water—Rain water, or water that has been chemically softened, contains very small amounts of minerals, and therefore, lathers freely. For this reason, it is preferred for shampooing the Maltese coat.

Hard Water—contains certain minerals, and, as a result, does not lather very freely. However, it can be softened by a chemical process and made suitable for shampooing.

Minerals are present in all kinds of water; the more minerals, the harder the water. In soaps, there are more fatty acids. The minerals and fatty acids combine to form a soap scum which dulls the hair and makes it difficult to comb.

It is impossible to remove all the soap curds from the hair with ordinary water.

Special acid rinses now on the market actually remove soap curds from the hair, thus making brushing the coat easier, and at the same time, adding brilliance to the hair.

The main ingredients of prepared acid hair rinses are:

Citric acid—from the juice of the lime, orange, or lemon.
Tartaric acid—obtained from residues in wine making.
Acetic acid—present in vinegar.
Lactic acid—Lactose, or sugar of milk.

Acid rinses are used to dissolve soap curds, separate the hair, and make it soft, pliable, and bright. Most acid rinses, whether solid or liquid, are dissolved in water before they are used.

There is another approach to maintaining the proper acid balance of the skin and hair. Apple cider vinegar is a natural product distilled from apple cider. A teaspoonful added to the dog's drinking water twice a week will aid in growing a good-textured, shining coat. Sometimes, however, it may be difficult to encourage a dog unaccustomed to the sharp added taste, to drink water so offered.

For the dog who hates the bath, in between regular baths, or for quick clean-ups without the need of a wet bath, baking soda may give good results. Rub the baking soda lightly into the coat. Then thoroughly brush it out from the coat. The baking soda not only cleans, but it deodorizes, as well.

Conditioning

The proper care and treatment of hair requires the use of many products. Certain products remove excess amounts of natural oils and moisture from the hair, causing it to become dry and brittle. As a result, hair conditioners are required to help restore some natural oils and moisture. A Maltese with naturally dry, brittle hair will benefit from regular conditioning.

Conditioners are primarily designed to coat and restore damaged hair. They are available in cream and liquid forms. The formulation of the product varies with the manufacturer. It may contain lanolin, cholesterol, moisturizers, sulfonated oil, vegetable oils, proteins, or various combinations of these. Most conditioners should be applied to hair that has been shampooed and towel-dried.

There are two general groups of hair conditioners available. The selection of the type to be used depends on the texture and condition of the hair and the results to be achieved.

Instant Conditioners—These are applied to the hair, allowed to stay on from one to five minutes, and then rinsed out. They usually have an acid pH; they do not penetrate into the hair shaft, but add natural oils and moisture to the hair. These products are what their name implies—*instant*. They may make the hair coat feel good to the touch, for a day or two after the application. However, since they do not penetrate into the cuticle, they cannot condition the most important part of the shaft.

Protein Penetrating Conditioners—These utilize hydrolized protein (very small fragments) and are designed to pass through the cuticle, penetrate into the cortex, and replace the keratin that has been lost from the hair. They improve texture, equalize porosity, and increase elasticity. The effects of the penetrating conditioners will gradually be of benefit to the hair shaft. When you first use a product such as this, the positive effects may last for only a short time. However, as the hair shafts attain a better condition, more strength and elasticity, you will be required to do such treatments less frequently.

There are many conditioners available, made both for dog and human use. Some work best when heat is used to help the beneficial ingredients penetrate the hair shaft.

Some conditioners will require that you apply more of the product than others. Some conditioners are very thick. If applied too liberally, they may be difficult to remove from the hair coat. Unfortunately, since each Maltese hair coat varies, the only way to determine the correct amount of conditioner to use on each dog is by trial and error. However, no matter how much or how little conditioner is applied to a coat, each strand of hair should be covered, from root to end.

The heat process used to enable these products to work best is a rather simple procedure. After applying the conditioner of your choice, place the entire dog in a plastic bag, exposing only the foreface. Cover with warm towels, and place under a dryer for about ten minutes, or for whatever time is recommended.

Hot towels may be used alone, without the plastic bag. Two very hot, damp towels, which have been well wrung out, should be placed over the dog, and then covered with a dry towel to hold in the heat. Follow the same directions as in using a plastic bag.

Another kind of penetrating conditioner does not require heat to enable it to penetrate the hair shaft. One product of this type is called Fermodyl. There are several classifications of this type hair conditioner. Each one is made for a different type or quality hair, i.e. dry, brittle, curly, etc.

This type conditioner is applied after the dog has been shampooed and a creme rinse has been used on the coat. After the creme rinse is out of the coat, towel dry the dog and apply the conditioner. Do not rinse it out. Proceed to blow dry the coat.

Creme Rinse

A creme rinse is a commercial product with a creamy appearance, and it is used as a last rinse. It tends to soften the hair, add luster, and make tangled hair easier to comb.

To be effective, creme rinses depend on one or more chemicals. They have one property in common—they coat the hair, sealing in moisture. Some substances adhere to the hair shaft and are not washed off by ordinary rinsing. The result is that the hair has a nice soft feel, and is much easier to brush and handle.

A creme rinse does not have the same function as an acid rinse. Creme rinses are slightly acid in reaction because of the ingredients used. However, the acidity is so low that, in the dilutions used, it would have no effect as a soap (curd) remover. There are any number of excellent prepared products, made for both dogs and humans, available.

If you are using a new product, whether it be a shampoo, conditioner or creme rinse, be certain to test it, to ascertain the results by using the product. Never test use any product immediately before a dog show.

Preparation of the Show Coat

The show coat should be brushed, or at least inspected, every other day. The amount of care required will depend upon the type and condition of each individual coat.

The factors which come into play include how badly and how quickly the coat mats. In other words, the rule of thumb in maintaining a coat in superb condition is, brushing and grooming must be done whenever necessary.

A Maltese must be brushed thoroughly from head to tail, paying attention to every part of the dog. Special care should especially be given to those parts of the dog which tend to mat more easily than others. This includes behind the ears, under the elbows, and at the rear quarters. Effective brushing is done carefully, without pulling and tugging at the coat. This only serves to rip out and break coat. Attaining a superb show coat on your Maltese will require much time and patience. As you eventually become accustomed to brushing your dog's coat, the time spent at the task will diminish.

Before bathing your Maltese, all mats should be completely removed. Water will cause mats left in the coat to tighten and become extremely difficult to remove.

When the bathing regimen is finished, lightly towel dry your dog, and follow with a blow dryer. Best results can be achieved by using a dryer set upon a stand. This will allow you to easily direct the stream of air where you want it to go. Always use a warm setting on the dryer. Hot air may tend to dry out a coat excessively, causing it to be brittle and easily broken.

The procedure you use in drying your Maltese will determine the dog's finished appearance. Even a well-conditioned dog can have an undesirable finished appearance if dried improperly.

Brushes for a Maltese coat should be made of pure bristle, preferably set in rubber. Also, a pin brush may be effective. These are brushes made of

You may use hot, damp towels rather than a plastic bag, when conditioning the coat.

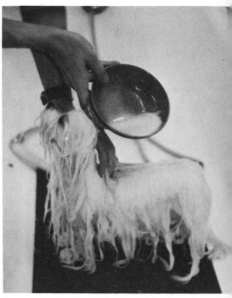

A creme rinse may be used before blowing the coat dry. It should saturate the entire coat, head to toe, and then be rinsed out well. Omit the creme rinse if the Maltese is to be oiled.

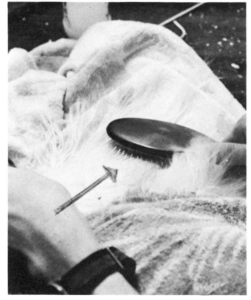

When blowing the coat dry, always brush out and away from you (follow arrow).

Save the head until last. Blow the head dry using straight strokes.

296

long, steel plated, non-rusting pins set in rubber. Never, never use a slicker brush. These tear out and destroy the silky coat of the Maltese. Nylon bristle brushes break hair as well, and should be avoided at all times.

The Maltese should be layer-brushed dry. Begin at the hindquarters, working forward, to about the shoulder. Do the left (judge's) side last. Turn the dog over, and proceed in the same manner, blow drying from the hindquarter up to the shoulder. Be certain all the layers of the coat have been dried thoroughly on both sides.

As you work, the part of the dog which has not yet been blown dry should be kept damp. A damp towel draped over the wet areas of the dog will help.

If you are uncertain about the proper technique in brushing a Maltese, either ask a knowledgeable breeder-exhibitor to demonstrate the technique for you, or watch how it is done at a dog show or a grooming seminar.

Blow dry the entire main body coat and tail first, saving the head hair and front fall for last.

Remember that the proper way to hold a brush is by its handle. The handle is there to be held, so be sure to do so. While you are brushing, be certain not to put an upward flip at the end of each brush stroke. Each stroke of the brush should be long and straight, completely removed from the hair before the brush is raised. Be certain to brush away from you. If you brush toward you, you will be likely to achieve short, incorrect strokes with an upward curve at the end of each stroke. This upward curve will cause breakage to the ends of the hair shaft.

Combs used on the Maltese should be made of steel. The teeth should be long enough to reach through the hair to the skin. For general use the teeth should be moderately spaced. A fine tooth comb is used to remove matter which collects at the inner corner of the eyes.

After you have dried your Maltese you may use a steel comb to comb through the coat, making certain the Maltese is thoroughly dried, and completely devoid of mats. The part should be made perfectly straight at this time, beginning at the tip of the nose, over his skull to the occiput, down the center of the neck, and following the spine down the center of the back, ending at the root of the tail. You may use a steel-ended rat tail comb, a knitting needle, or something of this sort to achieve this.

After the part is correct and straight, and the hair coat is laying as you like it, a finishing preparation may be applied lightly to the top of the coat.

Oiling and Wrapping

Again, it must be heavily stressed that the care of a Maltese must be tailored to each individual. Good coats will require less maintenance, and much less frequent attention. The poorer the coat quality, the more work required in the maintenance of the coat.

After a show, your dog should be given a shampoo bath, conditioning, if necessary and a creme rinse. This is done immediately after a show to remove dirt—the major cause of matting, to correct coats.

Many coats require an artificial oil added to keep them in good condition, soft and pliable and not brittle. Some dogs require no artificial coat oil. These are quite fortunate, as artificial oils have several negative aspects along with the good.

Artificial oil in the coat draws dirt. The stickier the oil, the more dirt will be attracted. Since dirt is the leading cause of mats, causing the hair to become dry, brittle and stuck together, any stickiness is unwanted.

Oiled coats often have a yellowish cast, especially on dogs with dry, porous coats. Heavy oil may require at least two shampooings. Sometimes a strong detergent will be necessary to remove all traces of the oil and dirt from the coat. This treatment can make the coat dry and brittle, and out of condition.

Despite these negative factors, some coats simply will require a helpful hand in the protective oils department; the easiest, and most effective way to oil down a dog is to use a water-dispersable oil. This may be mixed into water, and poured through the coat after the final, thorough water rinse. Lightly towel dry, then completely saturate the entire hair coat with the water/oil mixture. Finally blow dry the dog, as described earlier. Using this technique, the coat will be evenly oiled, head to toe.

Another method for oiling is to shampoo, apply creme rinse and towel dry, as described earlier. Then use a canned spray oil, spraying the entire damp hair coat. After spraying oil on the dog from head to toe, blow dry the coat, as above.

The dog is now ready to be "wrapped." The wrapping process involves separating the hair coat into sections. Each section is then wrapped and folded, using either plastic sandwich bags or waxed paper. Use small rubber bands to hold these "wraps" in place.

The number of sections is up to the individual to choose. Some people like large sections, other like many small sections. Sometimes the sections are split in half horizontally, thus forming two parallel lines of "wraps" down the sides of the dog. Use a steel comb to make parts and separate these sections.

Each section is held out, away from the body. The wrapping is folded lengthwise over the section of hair, making two to three lengthwise folds. This is then folded up, bringing the end of the length of hair upward, toward the body. This may be folded in half, and then in half again, or in thirds.

The rubber band used may be single or doubled, depending upon how secure the wrap is on the hair section.

These wrappings must be taken down, or unwrapped, brushed through and then re-wrapped, periodically. Here again, we must speak of

Take a triangle of hair, beginning at the outer corner of the eye, going upward toward the center part.

In preparing the head for topknots, conform the head hair to the dog's skull, maintaining center part from the tip of the nose to the occiput.

Use small latex rubber bands to make two topknots at either side of the center part on the head, using two even triangles of hair.

After securing both topknots with latex bands, determine whether they are even.

The topknots are then folded over to frame the side of the face. A latex band may be used to secure the topknots. Some people prefer to wrap a ¾ inch square piece of wax paper, setting paper or nylon tulle over the first elastic band, and hair, before folding over and securing with the second latex rubber band.

This photo shows a topknot using a wo paper wrapper on the left, and a plai topknot, using only rubber bands on th right.

If you are pleased with the look and the balance of the topknots, you may place on the bows. Individual bows may be tied on each topknot using ribbon or yarn. Bows also come ready made. These bows have either latex bands, tiny strings, pipe cleaners or twist ties to attach them to the horn of the topknot.

Ch. Joanne-Chen's Maya Dancer in wrappers.

Martin's Chanel-Cid models another method of putting the head in wrappers.

Ch. Aennchen's Pandava Dancer, modeling another way to wrap the coat. Being a male, there is more interest in keeping the rear and sides protected.

Here is a combination of wrappers and braids. Modeled by Ch. Martin's Michael-Cid and Ch. Su-Le's Golden Eagle, on the right.

301

the individual requirements of each dog and his particular coat. Some dogs will need their wraps down and put back up daily. For others, every other day is more than adequate.

When wraps are taken down, the coat may seem somewhat dry to the touch. The oil in the coat may have to be lightly refreshed. This may be done using a spray-on type oil, mentioned earlier.

If the coat is not put up in wraps, there is one basic rule to observe. Never groom a bone-dry coat. Always groom with some sort of lubricating agent, thus helping to decrease coat "drag." Coat drag is defined as resistance to the brush or comb going through the hair.

If you do not care to use a commercially prepared product, a light spray of plain water with a drop or two of a water dispersable oil added works well.

No matter how hard you try, matting will occur at one time or another on your Maltese. It is your job to separate the hairs forming these mats, suffering as little hair breakage and loss, in the process, as possible.

Saturating mats with a de-matting product may help. The water-dispersable oil and water mixture may help, as well as creme rinse and water solution sprayed into the mat.

Also useful for breaking down mats are mayonnaise and Vitapointe hairdressing. However, these two products are quite greasy, and the coat will require shampooing after their use.

After soaking the mats in one of the aforementioned preparations, the mats must be pulled apart, using your fingers and a comb. Begin at the outer ends of the mats, gently pulling them apart, combing out, increasing the length of your strokes each time. If this is done carefully, a maximum amount of hair will be preserved.

Special Care in Winter

Winter requires some very serious considerations, with regard to the good condition of the skin and coat of the Maltese. Central heating is indeed a great boon, in many respects. However, the very dry air may play havoc on your Maltese dog's coat. A room humidifier may be the perfect answer in the kennel or the home in the promotion of a healthy hair coat and good skin condition.

It is the winter months which will see even the best quality coats form mats which defy the most skillful removal.

Treating Irritated Skin

A Maltese may exhibit irritated skin for many reasons. Several soaps on the market, available from a pharmacist, may help alleviate a poor skin condition.

A particularly effective treatment for dry, flaking, cracked skin is glycerine and rose water. There is no prescription necessary for this preparation. It is available at any drug counter.

The procedure is quite simple. Bathe your dog as you would normally. Towel dry. Apply the glycerine and rose water to the dog's skin, full strength. A hair color applicator bottle will be helpful for this. Be certain to include the legs, ear leathers, under the chin and around the tail. Apply this solution to the skin twice daily until the skin returns to normal.

Never use the glycerine without the rose water added. Used alone, glycerine will act as a skin irritant. Use this solution diluted with water to spray on the coat for daily grooming during this period. It will take approximately two weeks for the condition to improve.

After the glycerine and rose water treatment is completed, switch to cottonseed oil. This may be applied to the skin using a cotton ball. The cottonseed oil is very greasy, but it is very necessary to the regimen. The oil will be rapidly absorbed into the skin.

If your Maltese shows signs of dry, scaly skin, perhaps a bit more fat added to the diet will be advantageous. Cod liver oil is helpful, the usual dosage being one half to one tablespoon per day.

Your veterinarian may recommend a shampoo to help alleviate the scaling skin condition.

Preparations containing high concentrations of linoleic acid will help the skin promote coat growth, as well. It may be helpful to include this vitamin in the diet.

The Pet Coat

If a Maltese is to be kept as a pet only, there is no reason for the owner to bother with the demanding rigors of show coat care. When a dog's show career has ended, keeping his show coat may be unnecessary work. There are several solutions to this situation.

If a Maltese possesses a fairly decent coat, it will not be that difficult to keep groomed. If the dog is the only one in the home, the fancier might appreciate his dog appearing in a bloom of glorious silk. It must be granted that a pet coat will never achieve the luxuriant mantle of the show dog. However, for pets around the home such coats are not needed.

It takes time to keep a Maltese coat in length. If this is desired, one should expect to devote one hour or slightly more, two or three times a week in grooming. The face should be washed and dried daily, especially about the eyes and mouth.

A dog kept in this manner will require a bath once or twice a month. Spray conditioners or a creme rinse and water mixture may be used to aid in grooming. However, it is highly advisable not to add too much artificial oil to the coat, especially if the dog is exposed to the filth of city streets, or the "natural" dirt of the great outdoors. This excess oil can turn your Maltese into a living dust mop.

The coat of the pet Maltese may also be cut or clipped. If the owner finds the longer coat difficult to contend with, scissors can shorten the hair to a more manageable length.

Electric clippers may be used to shave down areas of the body, to create an individualized look for your Maltese. A clipper with a #10 blade and a pair of scissors will be useful, or you may seek the assistance of a professional groomer.

Although shorter hair will require less care, remember that the Maltese is a white dog. He demands more care to remain fresh than a colored dog.

No matter what the length of coat, a Maltese must be kept clean and healthy. He should be fed a diet which will keep him in good tone with healthy skin and coat, bright eyes and the happiest of dispositions.

Eye Stain

Most authorities agree that heredity plays an important part in the amount of eye staining a dog will have. A heavy stainer is likely to pass on this condition to his or her get.

Keeping hair out of the eyes helps to prevent or cut down on staining. Two-inch gauze bandage may be used to roll around the topknot hair, fastened with an elastic to keep it up and out of the eyes. The gauze prevents the rubber bands from causing breakage. Nylon tulle may also be helpful. You can buy it by the yard and cut it into 2½" squares. Do not purchase the stiff nylon net, but the fine mesh nylon tulle.

Plain waxed paper or Sav-a-Wraps are good for this purpose. Some have found Handi-Wraps cut to size and Baggies useful, as well. Use a little spray of lanolin or mink oil on the hair before wrapping. These wraps must come down occasionally, the frequency depending upon the individual dog.

One must be careful with rubber bands not to catch any portion of the dog's body in the bands, as necrosis can set in. For growing short ends, braids may be helpful. Using some lanolin, mink oil or any conditioner, make two braids at the top of the head, catching up the fine hair. Use nylon tulle, waxed paper, or any of the materials discussed earlier to protect the ends and fasten elastics over them. Pigtails can be a cute touch to your Maltese.

One cause of weepy eyes is granular eyelids. These may be scraped by your veterinarian. Another very effective treatment for this condition is the application of copper sulfate, applied under the direction of your veterinarian. Some dogs may have this condition reoccur at intervals, so it needs checking periodically.

304

A good item to have in your dog's medicine chest is a 2% solution yellow oxide of mercury. This is better than mineral oil to put in the ey before bathing and for minor irritations. While cortisone and its derivativ effect almost miraculous cures in some eye infections, it should not be us indiscriminately. A product made for the human eye is ADAPT, a product made for contact lens wearers. It is helpful in eliminating eye irritation.

A preparation recommended in the prevention of eye staining is a mixture of boric acid powder and fuller's earth, in equal parts. Keep the mixture dry in a jar. After washing around the eyes with a very mild boric acid solution—one teaspoon to one cup boiled water—make a paste of the boric acid/fuller's earth mixture and plaster it under the eyes. It will dry very hard, and does a marvelous job in preventing stain.

If you have among your dogs one who likes to lick the faces of others, isolate the treated dog until the mixture dries. Renew every other day.

The fuller's earth/boric acid mixture can also be placed on the damp tear stained hairs and held in place by Desitin.

A warning must be made regarding the use of boric acid in treating tear staining. As mentioned earlier, the licking of the face of a dog so treated may be hazardous. This may be especially true when used on puppies which are still being licked clean by their mother. Dogs have died from ingesting boric acid; it can have an extremely toxic effect if consumed, so great care must be exercised in its use.

Desitin may be used alone, or you might try something not quite so messy as Desitin, such as Safari Stick, in white, or Clown White, which is the make-up clowns use. You can purchase it in stick form from the manufacturer, M. Stine Cosmetic Co., New York City. The product is called a lining color stick, white number 15. Opaque white lipstick is effective, in preventing eye stain, as well.

Veterinarians feel that many eye stain problems among white-coated breeds are associated with chronic, low grade infections involving the soft tissue around the eyeball. This chronic infection may produce swelling that interferes with normal drainage of tears away from the eye and may increase tear production. Therefore there is an overflow of tears from the corner of the eye onto the hair. The constant moisture and precipitated waste from the tears stains the hair under the eyes.

The name given to this infection is called "chronic follicular conjunctivitis." When a dog suffers from this problem, the sack of tissues surrounding the eye and the area behind the third eyelid may contain tiny follicle-like blisters, harboring germs causing the infection. The third eyelid is the small, wedgelike flap at the inner corner of the eye. Successful treatment of this problem involves the use of oral antibiotics, of which terramycin and tetracycline seem to be the most effective. These drugs should not be used in puppies which have not finished cutting their permanent teeth, as they can discolor the enamel. In addition to the oral antibiotics, an eye ointment containing terramycin or polymycin B can be used three or four times daily.

In extremely severe cases, the veterinarian may want to remove a tuft of lymphoid tissue from the area behind the third eyelid. It is also possible that the swelling of this gland may interfere with normal tear drainage from the eye. This tissue is comprised of much the same type of cells as in the tonsils, and just as in the case of bad tonsils, the tissue may harbor bacteria and thus be difficult to kill. This procedure was used quite frequently in the past, but with the advent of new and more effective antibiotics, the procedure now is often not necessary. It should not be inferred that antibiotics will solve all eye staining problems.

As with most infections, it is possible to spread the affliction from one dog to another. In a kennel situation, infection can spread like wildfire. One of the easiest ways to pass infection is by grooming. The common brush, comb or toothbrush used in grooming about the eyes may be guilty of spreading infection. Be certain to disinfect such tools between use on different dogs.

Ingrown eyelashes, anatomical defects in the eyelids and defects in the tear duct, which is supposed to empty excess tears from the eyes into the inner surface of the nose, may also contribute to the eye staining problem. Accurate diagnosis and frequent treatment is of prime importance.

All Maltese breeders are concerned with eye stain, and everyone seems to have a different answer to the problem. Many procedures for control of eye stain are yet to be uncovered. But, for the time being, there is more to be done for your dog's eye stain problem that just talking about it.

Ear Care

The dog's inner ear is a delicate structure which can easily become infected. This is especially true in the drop-eared breeds, such as the Maltese.

Suspect infection of the ear canal whenever your dog keeps shaking his head and scratching at his ears. Other signs of ear infection are tenderness, holding the painful side of the head down, redness and swelling of the skin folds in the canal, a purulent discharge and/or bad odor.

Common predisposing causes of ear problems are: soap, water, wads of hair, mites, allergies, and an excess wax buildup in the ear. A clean, dry ear usually will stay healthy.

Bacterial infections, which have been allowed to progress for a long time, produce extreme reddening and thickening of the ear canal. Infection is also the cause of considerable discomfort and pain. Such ears are difficult to cleanse without heavy sedation or anesthetic. In such cases, treatment will be prolonged. As a last resort, surgical intervention may be necessary

When a dog's show career has ended, keeping it in full
coat may be an unwanted task.   *M. Martin*

to open the ear, thus re-establishing air circulation and promoting adequate drainage.

The first step in the treatment of an external ear infection is to attempt to determine the cause. The next step is to clean the ears. If there is pus present, the ears should be flushed with a weak hydrogen peroxide solution or a surgical type soap. If there is an excessive wax buildup, a wax dissolving agent, such as Squaline, may be needed. After washing, dry the canal with a soft cloth or a cotton tipped applicator. Apply an antibiotic ear ointment, such as Panolog or Mitox. Apply to cleaned ear canal twice daily.

Some ear ointments come in containers with long nozzles which may be inserted into the vertical ear canal, while holding the nozzle parallel to the dog's head. Restrain your dog so that the tip of the nozzle will not accidentally lascerate the thin skin of the dog's ear drum. Squeeze in a small amount or a few drops of the ointment. As most infections also involve the horizontal ear canal, it is important that the medicine reaches this area as well. With your fingers, massage the cartilaginous area at the base of the ear to dispense the medicine.

In order to help keep the ear clean, excess hair is removed. This is easily accomplished with the help of a hemostat, available from either medical or dog supply shops.

A novice dog in this treatment may object, usually quite vigorously. It may require two persons at first, one person holding and one clearing the excess hair from the ear canal. As the dog becomes accustomed to this procedure, his objection and struggles will subside and ultimately cease.

Helpful Hints

Always remember that in striving for a splendid coat, if the gene responsible for length of coat is absent, no amount of preparations applied to the coat will bring about the desired length. Hours of anxiety, toil and trouble may well be for naught.

If, however, your dog does possess that special gene which will allow for a glorious silken coat, a great deal of trouble will be required to keep it healthy and strong.

A satin covered pillow is invaluable in keeping a Maltese in full show coat tidy. Such a pillow may be placed in the crate he uses at dog shows, and in which he travels. At home, a satin pillow in his bed will give excellent results. The satin is especially helpful to prevent matting.

Some dogs acquire nervous tics. This can be displayed in excessive licking of parts of the body and will cause affected areas to remain damp constantly. The condition also turns white hair red and is unsightly.

Especially a target of this excessive licking are the feet and legs. Sometimes a dog will even chew off quantities of hair.

Several products may be used to discourage this habit. They include cheap, smelly perfume from a dime store, Absorbine, Jr. and Bitter Apple, which is available from dog supply shops.

Dogs put up in "wraps" may transfer their nervous energy to the pursuit of pulling out these wraps. By applying the aforementioned products to the wraps, such behavior is quickly discouraged.

Again, in working toward the achievement of a superb hair coat, each dog will require its own special regimen, which you must ascertain by experiment. However, it is highly recommended that one always try out any new preparation on a small, inconspicuous area of the coat before applying it to the entire dog. What will work wonders for one dog's coat, may very possibly backfire, and create disaster on another.

11

Showing and Training Your Maltese

In CONSIDERING what goes into the creation of a top show dog, one must understand who and what a dog is. A familiarization with the instinctual and behavioral traits of the dog can be most helpful in the creation of a prime example of not only a Maltese, but a well-balanced dog, in general. There are certain key aspects in the personality of the dog, which if noted and taken advantage of, will help the breeder, owner or handler to achieve his ends.

Social Patterns

It is interesting to observe dogs in the meeting, for what it tells us about their rank and attitudes. What happens when two dogs meet? If the dogs are strangers, their hackles will rise. They will walk stiff-legged, until they are within sniffing distance of each other. Tails are held well up over the back, ears flattened. Both animals will emit deep-throated growls. As they slowly circle each other, one may begin to wag his tail slowly. This is a sign of dominance. This will usually conclude with both of the dogs wagging their tails, and going their separate ways. Sometimes the secondary dog will want to follow the dominant one.

On the other hand, if the first dog curls his upper lip, he has elected to fight. The second dog will either fight back or cower and run.

After waiting a time to make certain that the loser is not going to make a move, the victor in face down will urinate on any nearby object. This is, in effect, an act of dismissal on the part of the dominant dog.

Regarding show dogs, the dominant personality will usually be the one which shines out in the ring. He will be filled with self-confidence, and pride in his own being. However, there are always exceptions to every rule. We are at an advantage in dealing with a subordinate dog or bitch, as this knowledge will temper our approach and expectations of a Maltese.

Socialization

As important to the potential show dog as a good diet and proper grooming are proper social attitudes. These attitudes may be somewhat inherited. Mostly, though, they are learned. Both the potential champion and the homebody need to be socialized thoroughly. This social process, ideally, should begin in the whelping box, and continue for the life of the dog.

Proper socializing insures a well balanced, flexible animal, able to take all sorts of surprises in stride; such a dog will gait to thundering applause. He is the dog that can accompany you out for the Sunday paper, is trustworthy with youngsters, from whom you can take a bone, and a dog to whom you can comfortably offer a lasting place in your home and your heart.

Some traditional, and some not so traditional, thoughts on preparing your dog for any stressful or joyful situation that may come his way include allowing him to be handled. Of course, the other side to this is not allowing him to be handled. Your dog should be capable of being left quietly to himself, and be happy so left. A well-socialized dog is housebroken. He should be taught to feel safe, secure and happy in a crate, on a table or on a bench. Riding in the car should be an experience to which he looks forward. A dog should be taught to be happy with the idea of going somewhere. He should be fearless and secure in the company of strange dogs. Above all, a well-socialized dog is flexible, and will adapt well to any situation, positive or negative.

Stress

Beside external influences creating periods of stress, such as found in showing, stress may occur in a kenneled Maltese, as well. When dogs are kept in tiny boxes or small enclosures lacking anything to distract their attention and without a view of anything, save for a blank wall or ceiling, the dog will likely become a "spinner." Such a dog will run about in circles, chasing its tail, outside its cramped quarters.

For the owners of kenneled dogs, the question is, can they continue to keep their dogs confined to small, cramped quarters and boxes, and still expect their stock to remain "normal"?

Comprehension

Dogs do not speak very much English! As obvious a statement as that might seem, many people forget this very important fact when it comes to training their dogs. With time, dogs do come to understand certain key words, such as no, come, eat, its name and so on. In general, however, dogs communicate by noting your mood, the tone of your voice and your physical presence.

Your displeasure, regardless of what you may say, will be most apparent to your Maltese most of the time, because of how you say what you say. For example, you could recite the Gettysburg Address in an angry tone, waving your arms about. Your Maltese would, without question, get the message you were displeased.

Knowing this is important in understanding the psychology of dogs and their resulting actions about the home, and outside their familiar environments. When things are going well for you and your family, your dog tends to be happy. He senses the good times and will thus experience a feeling of security and well-being.

When things go poorly, your dog will sense this negative condition. He may react by moping about. He may be edgy, just as all the human members of the household.

A very important aspect of the dog's psychology lies in the fact that he is a pack animal. It is a very important part of his ancestral heritage. This aspect of the dog's make-up should be taken advantage of when training your Maltese to know what is expected of him. Knowing this is also helpful in guiding your everyday relations with your Maltese.

It is therefore important for the human handler to establish himself as the dominant leader of the pack. The family unit, the dog included, will become the dog's pack. Your Maltese may well decide that it can be top dog in the pack. This, of course, can be the start of serious trouble. A dog's behavior will be quite similar to that of a human child in this regard. A Maltese will push to see what it can get away with.

If you do not put your foot down and assert your leadership, the dog will move on to another level of disobedience. Establish ground rules early in a dog's life, and stick to them. Let your Maltese know what is right and what is wrong. Establish firmly who is boss in the relationship. Communicating honestly and forthrightly with your dog will save you both a lot of grief and enhance the relationship.

Dog Training Myths

You cannot teach an old dog new tricks. *Sheer bunk!* This myth was invented by the lazy human being who needed a good excuse for not learning new ways to do things. It does not really apply to dogs.

Puppies are too young to train until they are six months old. *Wrong!*

311

Puppies will acquire the most knowledge between the ages of six weeks through four months, since this is the time they learn most about adapting to the world around them. During this very early stage of their lives, puppies are housebroken, taught to come when called, to walk on a lead, to heel when off lead, to sit and stay, to retrieve, to swim, to stay in their own home environment and to perform trained tasks upon command. Show training and obedience training classes will rarely accept a dog younger than six months old. This is done mainly because of the younger puppies' great susceptibility to disease at this early stage of life. Another reason young puppies are usually excluded from such classes is due to their short attention span. This is especially true during group training.

It is therefore important for the individual dog owner to begin training early, during short intervals. For example, two or three minutes a day with an eight-week-old puppy is sufficient to show him what he will be expected to do. This may increase to five minutes at twelve weeks and ten minutes at sixteen weeks.

Parent animals teach their young by using punishment. It is the only way they know, and appears to have succeeded for thousands of years. The point is, punishment is a necessary part of teaching a puppy.

While it is true that punishment should be used, it should be used sparingly, and then only when better ways of solving a problem cannot be found. When it is used, it should be severe enough so the dog will be extremely hesitant to ever repeat the error again.

Light, repeated punishment can sometimes make the puppy believe that punishment is just an unpleasant part of life, to be ignored. He will therefore continue to repeat errors, and do things which will be incorrect and displeasing to you.

On the other hand, the use of reward, in the form of anticipated tidbits, can help to slow down and interfere with training, in some cases. The puppy may concentrate only upon receipt of the reward, and forget about the lesson to be learned. Often, the best form of reward for a job well done is plenty of praise and petting.

Evaluating Your Maltese

In evaluating a Maltese, it occurs that far too many breeders and fanciers are so busy looking for faults, they forget to notice the dog's virtues. A person who engages in this type of evaluation will certainly be the worst kind of judge. This type of evaluation is one of the most foolish mistakes a breeder or any member of the fancy can make. Rather, one should look closely at the standard. As you consider its requirements, consider your Maltese. If it appears he is a nicely balanced animal, in accordance with the standard, you might want to consider exhibiting him against others of his breed at organized dog shows. Be certain that the dog shows you attend are sponsored by reputable, reliable dog clubs. Most of these clubs will be affiliated in some way with AKC.

The Decision to Show

Whether or not you are going to exhibit your Maltese is one of the most important decisions you will ever make. An affirmative answer will most certainly open a new way of life for you. It will give you a new vocabulary and bring you many new friends and acquaintances.

Dog shows can be great fun, if one participates as a true sportsman. You must try to show your Maltese to his best advantage. Win or lose, you must keep the sport within proper perspective. Good etiquette and sportsmanship requires that the winning handler be congratulated.

Most important to remember is to always be good to your dog, even if he has lost in his class. This is true especially of the newcomer to the show ring. Remember that this is a new experience for your Maltese, as well.

A dog show is for dogs. The handler should wear comfortable, presentable, sensible clothing, suited to the sport. The Maltese should be fresh and clean for presentation. You should look forward to an enjoyable day exhibiting the Maltese of which you are very proud and happy to own.

At the dog show, stay with your dog as much as possible. It is best not to go off and leave your dog alone, unattended in his crate or carrier. This is especially important for a dog new to the dog show routine. He should feel comfortable at the dog show, and should not be left alone to become frightened and anxious. The dog show rightly belongs to the Maltese; he is the one in the spotlight.

In the pursuit of having a winner, begin by having an ideal mental image of that which is desired to be presented to the public. You must know your Maltese well. Be aware of what brings his best response, and what will keep him alert and interested. After your Maltese knows how to show, the use of bait, or a small edible reward, often helps keep his attention keen. Some dogs like to play just before entering the ring. This is a good practice. It may help to keep his spirit high. Such play will put the dog in a good humor, so he shows with his tail well up and his attitude attentive.

You may find that speaking in a soft tone to your Maltese while you are exhibiting him will be of great value. The Maltese has been bred for centuries to be responsive to the human will. This verbal communication with your Maltese strengthens his assurance that all is well. It may be useful while gaiting your Maltese, posing him on a table, or preparing him for a judge's inspection.

Ultimately, that which will get the best response from your Maltese you yourself will have to determine. The more you know about your Maltese, the more equipped you will be to handle almost any situation.

Since the picture of the Maltese in motion is invaluable, you must

Maltese judging at the Westminster KC show is always an impressive sight. In 1978, M▪ Frank Oberstar did the honors, selecting Ch. Oak Ridge Country Charmer (second from left

The proper socializing insures a dog which will gait to thundering applause. Ch. Stan-Bar's Spark of Glory at the 1982 AMA national Specialty.

A well-socialized dog will feel safe, secur and happy on a table. Ch. Noble Faith White Tornado at the 1982 AMA nation▪ Specialty.

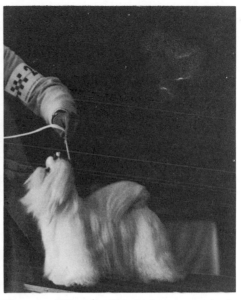

ur Maltese should be alert and interested. should always be paying attention to u, even when you are not paying attention him. Dee Sheperd and Ch. Bar None ccaneer.

The use of "bait" will help keep your dog's attention. Dee Sheperd and Ch. Bar None Sally Mae.

timately, you must draw the best response from your dog; breed judging at Westminster, 82.

determine at what pace your dog will give its best performance. Smooth, gliding motion is the desired effect. You, as handler, must move with your Maltese to achieve this visual image for the judge.

To do this, you may want to observe your dog in motion. Have someone else walk your dog on the lead. Have this person "move" the dog while you watch. In this way you may more clearly observe and analyze your Maltese's gait.

From the moment you and your dog enter the ring, you are both on exhibit. You must make every moment count. This will be the first strong impression and an important one. Walk proudly into the ring knowing you have a winner.

Confidence is the watchword. Believe in your dog, and in yourself. Move at the right pace. Direct all your attention to your dog. Do not look at the other exhibits entered while in the ring. In doing this, you will be getting a very potent message across to the judge, to the spectators and to your dog.

While in the ring, brush your dog only when you need to. If the Maltese looks great, excessive grooming may tend to detract from your dog. On the other hand, if the coat is not nicely in place, this will detract from the better qualities of your animal. Your own good judgment must be exercised at all times.

There are times when detractions may act in a positive way. For example, if your dog's posture is poor, you might try to detract from that by brushing the coat, while at the same time you are correcting the stance. It will be far better for you if the judge observes you brushing than to see the dog standing with poor posture.

If you are lucky enough to have a really good show dog, you can always depend upon him to "stack," or pose himself. If such is the case with your Maltese, do not be afraid to stand up and let the dog show himself off.

The Maltese should be walked, not run, on a loose lead, whenever possible. Sometimes a lead held taut will be necessary to better control the dog, for example, if he is not completely trained or has too many faults while gaiting. Sometimes a dog will become bored easily or tired. A lead held somewhat more tightly can help to prevent this from happening with some Maltese.

Never forget that you are working with a live animal, not a statue. However, while being exhibited on a table, the dog should be taught to remain quite still, especially while being examined by a judge. Be always attentive and ready to act quickly, always keeping your cool. With everything you do in the show ring with your Maltese, appear casual and act natural.

Work to make you and your Maltese a "unique" team in the ring. This will help your entry to stand out in the crowd. Do what is best for your own dog, and do it with "style."

316

You must decide at what pace your dog will give the best performance. Madeline Thornton and Ch. Sun Canyon Reach for the Stars.

In gait, a smooth, gliding motion is the desired effect. Ch. Aennchen's Soada Dancer.

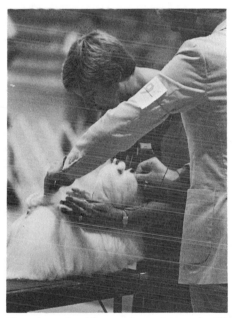

The dog should remain quiet and still, while being examined by the judge. Tim Lehman and Ch. Melodylane Raggedy Andy Luv.

Be certain to concentrate all of your efforts on those assets which make your Maltese most appealing. If he has a superb personality, let it glow in the show ring. If your Maltese possesses a great topline, body, neck, coat, pretty face, whatever, be certain the judge sees it.

Remember never to become anxious in the ring. The dog, as discussed earlier, can sense what you feel. Your confidence will extend to your Maltese. Do try never to allow a case of nerves to travel down the lead.

Be always courteous, to the judge, and to the other exhibitors. Remember that if it is not your day to win, there is always another show, and another chance.

Final Preparations at the Show

Just before entering the ring, you may want to freshen your dog's appearance, for optimum impact. One of the most frequently encountered problems at ringside is static electricity in the Maltese coat.

Commercially prepared coat oils can contribute to this condition. Most artificial coat oils are weakly electrically charged. Static electricity is amplified by the presence of these oils in the coat, especially during the winter months.

Exhibitors encountering static electric conditions in the coats of their Maltese are partially to blame for this condition. They have probably failed to completely wash out the protective conditioning oils used between shows.

Some exhibitors find that lamb's wool can help correct this condition. Lamb's wool may be wound onto the teeth of a metal comb, or around the pins of a steel pin brush, before using upon the coat. Static Guard, a product created for combating static electricity in clothing, may be beneficial in the Maltese show coat. Other suggested aids used in the control of static electricity include spray starch, a fine spray of borax, which will also add body to a fine coat, or Hair So New, which will also help soften a coarser textured coat.

To help maintain the line of your dog's part, a formula of two tablespoons of creme rinse diluted with about 16 ounces of water may prove helpful. This mixture may be misted lightly above the dog's coat, just before or after brushing. This will also help in preventing you from breaking or pulling out large amounts of hair in your comb or brush.

For a last-minute clean up, before entering the ring, baby powder works well. Some exhibitors like the effects achieved with cornstarch, as well as potato starch. A good idea is to combine both corn and potato starch in a 50-50 mixture. There are some commercially prepared canned spray on dry cleaning agents available on the market especially made for dogs. There are many human preparations which also work well. A word of

318

caution in use of these products. They may lead to excess static electricity in the coat.

White lipstick, set with a small amount of cornstarch will help to clear away unwanted eye stains.

We should insert a word of caution here. The AKC rules regarding dog shows state:

> No dog shall be eligible to compete at any show in the event that natural color or the shade of the natural color of the dog has been altered or changed by use of any substance, whether such substance may have been used for cleaning purposes, or for any other reason. Such cleaning substances are to be removed before the dog enters the ring.

Many judges are sticklers, and observe this rule to the limit. However, other judges have been known to recommend cosmetic aids. Care should be taken to show a judge what he or she likes best.

Summer Coolants

Outdoor shows can sometimes become unbearably hot, and your Maltese may suffer greatly as a result. Frozen shipping coolants, and coolants made to be frozen for use in cooler chests may be helpful to your dog in these conditions. They may be brought to a show, and wrapped in a towel. Your dog will stay somewhat cooler if he is allowed to sit on one. This is especially helpful when put at the bottom of the dog's crate at a hot, outdoor, summer show.

Down through the centuries, Maltese have been trained to be performers before the public. Pictured here is a Maltese *Pagliacci*, Tru-Luv's Sugar Plum of Al-Mar, bred by Marge Lewis and owned by Libby Rice.

In 1970, Puddin and Muffin, trained and owned by Betty Horney, performed at a Christmas party.

12

Obedience Training and the Maltese

THE MALTESE is a most likely candidate for obedience training, or any sort of training, in general. Despite his size, the Maltese dog possesses a great capacity to learn. This is fortified by the centuries-old instincts in the breed which make them want very much to please. In addition, the happy, outgoing personality is just one more positive aspect of the Maltese which makes him a good subject for training.

If you have never trained for the obedience ring, you might not appreciate the point of such an exercise applied to a Maltese. Many people associate obedience training with the large, unruly or sometimes aggressive dogs.

There is certainly little cause to fear that our Maltese will drag one down the street while out for a walk, brutally attack the mailman, jump on or knock down visitors or destroy your neighbor's property. The Maltese is usually so small and gentle in manner that it usually is quite an easy task to keep him out of what little mischief he is capable of.

Any dedicated, successful dog trainer, professional and nonprofessional alike, repudiates harsh and extreme methods of dog training. Rewarding the dog for what he has done right, rather than punishing him for doing wrong, is called positive reinforcement. This approach to dog training is far superior to any strong-arm tactic. The result will be a Maltese with a great willingness and joy and genuine enthusiasm on the part of both dog and master.

With regard to training for the obedience ring, there can be a great deal of pride and pleasure derived by working with your Maltese. If the Maltese becomes something more than a prop, more like a partner, a very special relationship between dog and trainer may very well develop. The obedience competition then becomes just so much icing on the cake.

As noted earlier, the Maltese is a very sensitive, highly adaptable dog. He is quick to learn and eager to please. He will quickly respond to his leader. The Maltese will thrive on discipline and take great pride in his accomplishments, no matter how small. They derive delight in expanding their intelligence. It is proven that dogs can and do become bored. An obedience-trained Maltese will certainly have little time for boredom.

In addition to possessing the mental capacity to be easily trained, the Maltese is aided by his obvious vivacious glamour and exuberance. The limitless energy and zest for life are easily channeled into obedience training.

Obedience Trials

If you find that you and your Maltese are enjoying the work, you may want to consider entering some obedience trials. The joy of showing a lovely, vivacious Maltese in the obedience ring is unique. Such training will take time, devotion and patience on your part. In addition, you will both face a lot of very hard work. The strains of bending and stooping may be fatiguing. However, the positive results will be gratifying.

It is rather evident that the Maltese shines in the breed ring. They can equally dazzle the obedience ring with their singular beauty and intelligence.

Maltese have proven themselves capable of winning the highest obedience honors in Utility and Tracking. It therefore becomes the choice of the master to what degree the training is pursued. This training may be the ultimate goal for exhibition purposes. Some Maltese have been trained to be performers before the public. Or the training might be simply to make a better companion of your Maltese. The possibilities are limited only by the owner's goals and desires.

Obedience trials were introduced into dog shows in the United States in 1933. The first licensed trials were held in 1936. Training Maltese for work in the obedience ring began in the 1940s and 1950s in the United States. An early enthusiast, who later became an obedience judge, was Mr. Herb Kellogg, who also served as president of the American Maltese Association. Mr. Kellogg was the first person to place a CDX title on a Maltese, Kellogg's Beau, CDX. This Maltese held CD titles in the United States and Canada.

Another early obedience enthusiast was Blanche Carlquist. She has the distinction of having owned and trained the first and the fourth Maltese in United States history to earn UD degrees. Her first, Luce's Missy Lucy of Villa Malta, earned her title in 1963.

Luce's Miss Lucy of
Villa Malta, CDX,
trained and owned
by Blanche Carlquist.

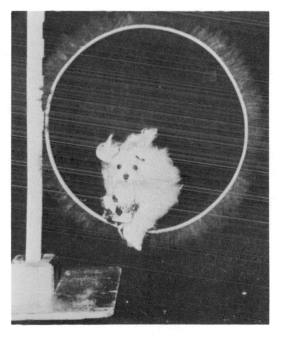

Obedience enthusiast
Blanche Carlquist's Caress
of Winddrift, UD, jumping
through a hoop in 1970.

The second Maltese to earn a CD degree was Muff of Buckeye Circle, owned and trained by Mr. and Mrs. Marsland. The third Utility title was awarded to Whispering Pines Sweet Jill, owned and trained by Mrs. Funk. Jill's record was enviable. She earned her CD, CDX, and UD titles in only 12 shows, making only one mistake in her CD work, and only two in her Utility work. The #4 title was awarded to Blanche Carlquist's Caress of Windrift, UD.

The enthusiasm for Maltese in obedience continued to gain popularity. In 1969, ten Maltese qualified for CD titles, one earned a CDX, and one was awarded a UD title. Among those Maltese were Exotic Mopsey of Richmore, CDX; Jamaican Gai Boy, CD; Markeith's Diamond Lil, CD and Miss Triss, CD.

By 1970, Markeith's Diamond Lil had advanced to her CDX degree. Others earning their UD degrees in 1970 included the #4 UD in United States history, Blanche Carlquist's Caress of Winddrift, UD. Other dogs earning their CD titles that year were El Towers Calafero, Cecil's Don Marconi Isle D' Malta and Zilla's Connie Thor.

Other earlier noteworthy names in the obedience ring include Marjorie Hoff's Bo-Margus of Kismet, CDX; Marilyn Richard's A-Cor Samaken, CD; Fife Shire's Madam Tina Sapovcheck, CD; and Aennchen's Moghul Dancer, CDX.

Kathy Clifton, from California, was active in the obedience ring for a time. Her Timmy Horrison, CDX, was noteworthy. Also most active in promoting obedience training for Maltese is Mary Lou Porlick, of Florida. Mrs. Porlick has served on the board of the AMA and is also active in the conformation ring. One of her first CD Maltese was Bobbelee Frosted Velvet. Velvet's daughter, Ch. Gulfstream Treasure, CDX, has the distinction of being the first champion Maltese bitch to earn a CDX title. The bitch was also awarded a Utility degree.

Also quite active in both obedience and conformation is Dr. H. Poggi of the Reveille Maltese. Dr. Poggi is proud owner of at least six champion CD Maltese.

Pam Brown, from Omaha, Nebraska, has been extremely dedicated to Maltese in the obedience ring, as have Faith Ann Maciezewski and Gay Latigo.

To see a Maltese dog in competition in an obedience ring is rare. To see one entered in tracking trials was unheard of until Joy's Mr. Feather arrived on the scene in 1974. He is the first Maltese to become a UDT in the U.S., Canada and Bermuda. "Mr. Feather," owned and trained by Carol Kollander, of St. Paul, Minnesota, became one of the doubtless few Maltese in the world to have earned a tracking degree in four countries. His titles include: American UD and TDX, Canadian OB Ch., UD and TDX, Bermuda CDX and TD and Mexican TD.

In 1979, at the 14th AMA Specialty show, held in San Mateo,

Primrose Chip O'Dillon proves that Maltese are smart as well as beautiful. He sports the CD and CDX titles, and is proudly owned by Marcia Folley.

Joanne-Chen's Gay Dancer, CD, trained and owned by Dr. Roger and Nancy Brown.

Brown's Dandi Dancer, CDX, trained and owned by Dr. Roger and Nancy Brown.

A 1969 portrait of Markeith's Diamond Lil, CDX, trained by co-owner Debbie Hill, co-owned by M. Keith.

California, obedience trials were held in conjunction with the specialty, for the first time since 1967. Gay Latigo was in charge of these efforts. Judge Merrill Cohen, who had passed on the regular conformation classes, also judged in the obedience ring. Mr. Cohen is approved to judge both conformation and obedience.

The entry was quite good, with seven in the Novice class (CD), six in Open (CDX), and three in the Utility classes (UD). Five entries were conformation champions, as well.

A high score of 193½ was earned by Sugar Cookie, CDX and Ch. Ginger Jake, CDX. In a run off, the winner was Ch. Ginger Jake, CDX, owned and trained by Faith Ann Maciezewski.

Of the 16 Maltese entered at that very special show, three qualified for a leg. They included Gill's Pappuccino of Jular's, Fantasyland's He's No Bug and R & B's Little Sonny Boy, CDX. Sonny Boy, CDX, is owned by noted obedience enthusiast La Vonnie Roach, of Omaha, Nebraska.

As noted earlier, the Maltese is a natural performer. More recently, here in the United States, the Maltese has been used to perform in one manner or another.

Betty Kern-Horney showed how adaptable the Maltese could be. She trained her two Maltese, Puddin Habeiby, CD (Joanne-Chen's Rajah Dancer × Waltzing Matilda), and Muffin to be quite extroverted showoffs. These Maltese performed every year from 1970 through 1976 at the New England Sportsmens' show. Before retiring from "show biz" this pair was quite a popular attraction, appearing at numerous shows and socials.

All the outfits and a decorated doll's baby carriage were created by hand by Ms. Kern-Horney. Ms. Kern-Horney mused on the time she accidentally permanently dyed Puddin green. This condition lasted for one year. Puddin died at the age of 15 years in 1982. Muffin was nearly 12 years of age at the time of his death in 1979.

13

A History of the American Maltese Association and Its Specialty Shows

THE FIRST purely American standard for the Maltese was established in 1906. This was done mostly through the efforts of Mr. M. Koerlin. He and his wife had worked hard to organize the first Maltese specialty club of consequence in the United States. The club, the Maltese Terrier Club of America, was organized in 1906.

This club eventually came to be known as the National Maltese Club and held its first specialty on November 30, 1917. The show, which was immensely successful, was held at the Waldorf Astoria Hotel in New York City.

By the end of the 1950s, there were two Maltese clubs. One, the Maltese Dog Club of America, had formerly been known as the National Maltese Club. Dr. Calvaresi, and mainly people owning dogs of his breeding were active in this group.

The Maltese Dog Fanciers of America were an active and vocal organization. Several AKC sanctioned matches were organized by this group; one was held on the grounds on Mrs. Virginia Leitch's kennel, Jon Vir, in Maryland. Another was held in New York City. Noteworthy early members of this organization included Mrs. Bertha Watkins, Ann Jones, Daisy Miller, Virginia Leitch, and honorarily Mrs. Agnes Rossman. Later, Mrs. Craig, Dr. Poggi, Mrs. Tinker, and Mr. and Mrs. Antonelli joined the roster.

The cover of the catalogue for the first AKC sanctioned match sponsored by the MDFA, featuring Ch. White Wings of Hale Farm, was designed by Ann Jones.

Best in Match was awarded to Mrs. Melgaard's Jon Vir's Love in a Mist by judge Agrippina Anderson.

By the 1950s, there was enough interest within the Maltese fancy to promote a national specialty show.

The American Kennel Club would not permit such a show without the sanction of an accepted parent club. Since there were two clubs extant, this was a point of great difficulty.

The year 1961 proved a momentous one for the American Maltese fancy. The highlight of the year came with a meeting of representatives of the Maltese Dog Club of America and the Maltese Dog Fanciers of America, at the Henry Hudson Hotel, in New York City, on the first Sunday in December. From this meeting emerged the foundation of the American Maltese Association.

The first officers elected included Dr. V. Calvaresi, president; Dr. Helen Shively Poggi, vice president West; Aennchen Antonelli, vice president East; and Tony Antonelli, secretary-treasurer. The first annual national meeting was held in conjunction with the Westminster Kennel Club show in 1963.

The newly formed club was quick to ratify and submit a new standard for the breed in 1963. This new standard was approved by the AKC in November of the same year.

In July of 1963, the new club held its first sanctioned B match at Pasadena, California. Bob Craig, husband of Eloise Craig, breeders of Good Time Maltese, officiated. Mado Reveille Nicholas, owned by Margaret Douglas, won this first match. The second B match was held in Santa Ana, California, with Ann Pendleton as judge.

The first A match was held on June 28, 1964, at the Louisville, Ohio home of Ann and Stewart Pendleton. Judge Maxwell Riddle officiated, taking Edward's Wee Holly to top honors. Ch. Scipio of Villa Malta, owned by Elvira Cox, was scored top winner at the obedience trial held in conjunction with the first A match.

In 1964, professional handler Wynn Suck judged at the second AMA A match, also held at the Pendleton home. He found his winner in Sun Canyon Matinee Idol, bred, owned and shown by Miriam Thompson. The winner of the obedience trial was Ch. Good Time terry Lynn, bred by Bob and Eloise Craig, owned and trained by Herb Kellogg.

AMA Specialty Shows and Winners

On June 11, 1966, American Maltese fanciers once again returned to Ohio, to attend the first American Maltese Association national Specialty, held in conjunction with the Columbiana Kennel Club show, in Salem.

Officiating judge Mr. William Kendrick passed on an entry of more than 50 Maltese, with few absentees. Ch. Co Ca He Aennchen's Toy Dancer was BB, handled by owner, Anna Marie Stimmler. Ch. Toy went on to place second in the Group that day. Ch. Aennchen's Shikar Dancer,

Brood Bitch class at the first B match held at Brookline Park, Pasadena, California. The winner was Sun Canyon Miss Tina, owned by Miriam Thompson.

At the second AMA B match, Ch. The Actress of Sun Canyon won the puppy 4-6 month class. Anne Pendleton is judging, Dr. Helen Schively Poggi is awarding the trophy.

owned by the Antonellis and Joanne Hesse, was shown to BOS by Larry Ward.

As noted, there was an astounding turnout of 53 Maltese at this show with entries in both conformation classes and obedience. There was a total of 14 champions entered in the specials class, with only one absent. In the regular classes, there were seven absent. One dog was absent in obedience.

The Maltese exhibited had traveled from as far away as California and Nevada. There was a good representation of dogs from the Mid West and Eastern areas of the country, as well.

Miriam Thompson's Sun Canyon Double-O-Seven was WD. Ch. Alpond's Sky Rocket was WB and BW from the puppy class. Sun Canyon Prelude, also owned by Mrs. Thompson, was RB.

Dorothy Tinker, of the Al Dor line, exhibited the winning brace, composed of Ch. Fairy Fay's Kapu and Ch. Fairy Fay's Figaro. Mrs. Thompson's brace placed second. Ch. Fairy Fay's Figaro won the stud dog class. Ch. Harlingen Dynamic, owned by the Pendletons, placed second in this class.

We thought it might be of interest to print here the written critique presented by Mr. Kendrick after judging the first American Maltese Association National Specialty.

It might be noted that the bitch classes were more heavily filled than the dog classes. There was a wealth of good bitches which augurs well for the future of the breed. Presentation was of a high order. Overall quality was such as to evoke genuine enthusiasm. Temperaments were of the typical outgoing sort which one associates with this delightful breed so filled with *joie de vivre*.

Passing then to the class for Puppy Dogs, Enrico, first, a standout and very forward, in lovely bloom for a puppy. Second to Alpond's Scamperino, pressing closely, and particularly well made behind with consequent good action. He had to be pegged back for his bite, not 100% at this stage of development. Third to Whispering Pine Sir Patrick. His mouth also gave cause for concern and his thin bloom left him at a disadvantage with the two above him.

A singleton in Novice, Anita's Snowhite Wee Kevin, was well schooled. He seemed longcast and his topline did not please.

Another singleton in American-bred, Sun Canyon Top Gun. His coat of fair length was without a suspicion of undercoat. He pleased in movement at both ends.

Sun Canyon Double-O-Seven, tiny and sound, captured first in Open. Second to Sun Canyon Starmaker, another good one, not so compact as the winner. Third to Eve-Ron's Timmi Too. In better flesh and presentation of coat he might prove one to reckon with.

Winners to Sun Canyon Double-O-Seven with Reserve to Enrico. The winner's extra good legs and feet, superlative condition and fine bone stood him in good stead here.

Nine answered in Puppy Bitches. First to Alpond Sky Rockette with a catalogue listing of champion. Very forward and in good flesh. Put down immaculately white. Remarkable coat length for a puppy. She moved with a purpose. Second to Cashmere's Maranna Dancer, of similar stamp, a shade smaller than the winner. Third to Al Dor High Hopes, very petite and with much appeal. Inclined to roach her loin. Fourth to Alpond's Wee Widget, another petite one with good in her. Schooling would help her.

Caricabu Pupee of Kismet, forward and charming, was alone in Novice. Her coat texture left something to be desired.

First in American-bred to Pendleton's Dreamy with second, and close up, to Sun Canyon's Sunshine Girl. Both petite, charming and typical. The winner's advantage in rib cage carried an exceedingly well prepared coat of ideal texture.

First in Open to Sun Canyon Prelude. Second to Stardom's Kawa Damura. Two high class bitches. The winner without the coat length of the second bitch, but what coat she carried was of ideal texture. The winner scored in neck and shoulders and especially in hind action. Third to Aennchen's Siin Dancer, another good one. Petite and compact. More preparation of coat might have helped. Fourth to Cecil's Donna Magi Isle D' Malta, petite, animated, and sound. Her coat texture not what we were looking for.

Winners to the winner of the puppy class with Reserve to the winner of the Open class in a close thing. The astonishing coat in length and texture for a puppy weighed heavily in the winner's favor. Both the Winners and Reserve satisfied in movement. Winners had an edge in neck but was not quite so level in topline as the Reserve. More forward thrust in the plume of the winner would be another asset.

Best of Winners to the bitch. She had too many guns in her coat and flesh for the dog to cope with this day.

Thirteen champions then answered along with the Best of Winners bitch to contest for the supreme honor. Truly a sight to gladden the hearts of all Maltese fanciers and lovers. A veritable queen, Ch. Co-Ca-He's Aennchen Toy Dancer, stood out immediately and was the eventual winner. In addition to her impressive breed character and personality, her coat, flesh, and general condition, all in top order, presented a combination seldom to be found in one package. We have no hesitancy in declaring that bitch in this form is a worthy contender for supreme honors in or out of the Maltese ring. She was most closely pressed by the bitch, Ch. Ludon's Issa, well off in all the essentials and closely approximating the ideal. This one with her second birthday in September of this year should have a brilliant future. Best of Opposite Sex to Ch. Joanne-Chen's Shikar Dancer, a rung behind both bitches, nevertheless stood out in dogs for his immaculate and proper coat, showmanship, and character.

The Maltese then journeyed to the West Coast for the second AMA National Specialty, held in Beverly Hills, California. The winner was found in Ch. Aennchen's Poona Dancer, co-owned by Frank Oberstar and Larry Ward. High obedience winner was Sir Soni Rava Reveille. The third Specialty was held in Pittsburgh, Pennsylvania, in 1968. Ch. Aennchen's

Poona Dancer again emerged victorious. The fourth Specialty was held in Chicago in 1969. Dottie White's Ch. Pendleton's Jewell won top honors that year, as well as taking them twice again in a row in 1970 and 1971. Jewell is the only Maltese to have won three consecutive AMA specialties.

Other American Maltese Association national Specialty winners include:

1972 - Ch. Joanne-Chen's Maya Dancer
1973 - Ch. Mike-Mar's Sirius of Revlo
1974 - Ch. Caramaya's Mister
1975 - Ch. Celia's Mooney Forget Me Not
1976 - Ch. So Big Desert Delight
1977 - Ch. Oak Ridge Country Charmer
1978 - Ch. Su Le's Jonina
1979 - Ch. Oak Ridge Country Charmer
1980 - Ch. Joanne-Chen's Mino Maya Dancer
1981 - Ch. Joanne-Chen's Mino Maya Dancer
1982 - Ch. Rebeca's Desert Valentino
1983 - Ch. Noble Faith's White Tornado
1984 - Ch. Myi's Ode to Glory Seeker
1985 - Ch. Non Vel's Weejun
1986 - Ch. Villa Malta's Chickalett

The AMA and Regional Clubs

On June 10, 1969, the American Maltese Association officially became an AKC member club. The AMA currently enjoys a membership of approximately 500 people, spread all across the nation. Members are also residents of Canada, Japan, Australia and Europe.

Under AMA jurisdiction, regional clubs may organize and become recognized. Following AKC approval and parent club recognition, they may hold specialties under AMA sponsorship, after paying the fee for additional specialties. These independent clubs may also seek AKC recognition as independent specialty clubs. To do this, local groups must hold qualifying matches and keep sufficient records, as required by AKC. These groups must also make all proper applications to AKC to obtain approval for all planned events. As of this writing, only one AMA member club, the Maltese Club of Greater Houston, has qualified to hold independent specialties.

One of the first member clubs of the AMA was the California Maltese Club, founded in 1965. This was a very active group comprised of many of those on the West Coast responsible for the formation of the AMA. In 1977, this Club was split into the Bay Area Maltese Club, located near San Francisco bay area, and the Maltese Club of Southern California, centered around Los Angeles. The California Maltese Club had published its own superb continuous publication, the *California Maltese Club Reporter,* for

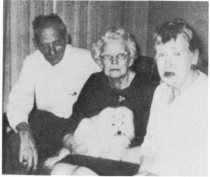

In 1969, at the AMA national Specialty, held in Chicago, Ch. Kaga of Khandes was named Puppy Sweepstakes winner and WD. Bred and owned by Dr. and Mrs. Roger Brown and shown by Mrs. Brown.

Pictured at the 1969 Chicago Specialty are Bob and Eloise Craig (left and center) and Margaret Douglas. The Maltese is Sir Jiminy Soni Reveille.

Ch. Co-Ca-He's Aennchen Toy Dancer, winner of the first AMA Specialty, 1966.

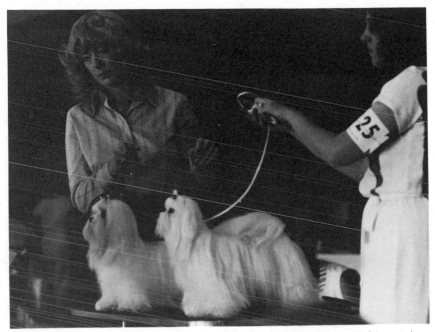

Pictured here are the WD and WB selected at the 1980 AMA national Specialty. Ch. Bar None Sally Mae was also named BW (right), bred and owned by Michelle Perlmutter. Ch. Joanne-Chen's After the Lovin (WD) is owned and shown by Sue Kuecher (left).

"A Special meeting of the Maltese Dog Fanciers Association." A cartoon which appeared in the May 1924 issue of *Pure-Bred Dogs Gazette.*

Ch. Pendleton's Jewel won the fourth, fifth and sixth AMA Specialties in 1969, 1970 and 1971.

many years, beginning in October 1965, and ceasing publication in December 1981.

This publication, originally known as the *Maltese Gazette,* had for several years been the only Maltese publication in the United States prior to the formation of the American Maltese Association, and its official publication, the *Maltese Rx.*

Others of the earlier Maltese branch clubs included the Potomac Maltese Fanciers, the Florida Maltese Club, which in 1972, changed its name to the Maltese Club of Greater Miami, at the request of AKC, the Maltese Club of Southern Florida, the South West Maltese Club, which is now known as the Las Vegas Maltese Fanciers.

The Evergreen Maltese fanciers existed for some years in the Pacific North West. At this writing there is a current attempt to revive this group of fanciers.

The Metropolitan Area Maltese Association is an active group of Maltese fanciers located in and around New York City. This is one of the few current member clubs of the American Maltese Association.

The New England area is represented by the Central New England Maltese Club.

Several of these clubs, including the Bay Area Club, the Metropolitan Area Association, and the New England Fanciers have had the opportunity and pleasure of hosting national Specialties.

The usefulness of clubs cannot be overrated. It is one of the surest ways for a mass dissemination of ideas and information. They enable the implementation of national Specialties, which, in effect, give the fancier the opportunity to see what other breeders have produced. This is most beneficial for breeders in gauging their stock against that of their peers.

On the debit side of the issue, clubs may also be very negative forces. When an organization ceases to truly be representative of its membership, great harm can result in the form of biased judging, nonrepresentational decision making, the arbitrary exclusion of certain members and their ideas and ideals, and biased efforts to exact changes in the standard for the breed. It therefore becomes the prime responsibility of the membership of any organization or society to keep close watch on the workings of their club and its officers. One should always feel free to express one's opinion. Always exercise your right to vote. Above all, be certain the organization benefits you. Take in all the ideas and information offered to you. If there isn't enough, ask for more.

337

14

Anecdotes

FOR CENTURIES, the Maltese has been the subject of prose, sculpture and painting. Indeed, much of our knowledge of the physical appearance of early Maltese is due to the work of early writers and artists. In this regard, we are fortunate that the Maltese is primarily a breed of the aristocracy, for they were the people with the funds to support the artists in times past. Naturally, all things which touched these aristocrats' lives were readily available as subject matter.

At times, the Maltese inspired, even if not actually being incorporated into the artist's work. One of these was the noted 19th century authoress, Ouida. In the historic town of Bury St. Edmunds, where England's Magna Carta was first drafted, Louisa Ramé was born. Because this child's attempt to pronounce her name was "Ouida," it became her nickname. It would eventually come to be one of the most famous names in literature. She used that name on all of her stories, novels and letters.

Ouida moved with her mother and grandmother to London. Later, she left London for the Continent and spent most of her life either in or near Florence.

Although Ouida was a most prolific and successful writer, she did not have the slightest idea of good economy. She died in absolute poverty, too proud to appeal to her friends. Ouida counted some of the most distinguished and noteworthy people in the world at the time as friends.

After her death, Ouida was laid to rest in the English cemetery at Bagni di Lucca, Italy. An anonymous friend commissioned the Italian sculptor, Guieseppe Vorfini, to design and build her tomb. It has a reclining figure of Ouida at its top, with a Maltese at her feet.

One of Huldah's paintings, *Winter in the Park,* featuring a Maltese Dog.

Portrait of the authoress "Ouida," holding her beloved "Puck" in 1878.

Woman in raspberry costume holding a Dog, by Mary Cassatt. Hirshhorn Museum, Washington, D.C.

In the town of her birth, in England, friends had a beautiful monument erected in her honor and memory. The design consists of a square column with medallions of Ouida on two sides, and figures of justice and sympathy on the other two sides. Around the column is a drinking fountain, with a low trough on either side for animals to drink from.

The inscription thereon was composed by Earl Curzon of Kendelston. It read, "Born at Bury St. Edmunds, January 1, 1839. Died at Via Reggio, Italy, January 25, 1908. Her friends have erected this fountain in the place of her birth. Here may God's creatures, whom she loved, assuage her tender soul as they drink."

Ouida not only loved her own dogs, but all dogs and all animals as well. She was a founding force in the Italian SPCA.

While Ouida herself lived an unblemished life, the characters she created were not necessarily persons of virtue. In her time, young people were forbidden to read her books.

There have been many dramatizations of her works. Most famous of these is *Under Two Flags*. Child star Jackie Coogan appeared in the silent film adaptation of her novel, *A Dog of Flanders*.

Ouida was above all a dog lover. An 1878 portrait shows her with her Maltese "Puck" in her arms. It was Puck who supposedly wrote the novel bearing his name.

Mary Cassatt (1844-1926) was an outstanding American painter and artist, working primarily in France. She became an important part of the modern art movement which included such artists as Cezanne, Renoir and Manet.

In 1901, Ms. Cassatt executed a pastel drawing of a woman in a raspberry costume holding a Maltese. Although several other small animals appear in other of her paintings, this appears to be the only work she did which included a Maltese.

Another highly noted American artist, most active during the 1940s and 1950s, was Huldah. Her paintings resembled in style, color and technique, those of the renowned French painter, Renoir.

Hulda lived in New York City during most of the creative period of her life. She was born in Dallas, Texas, and studied art at the Grand Central School of Art and at the Art Student's League, both in New York City. She spent four years in the private classes given by Robert Brackman at Carnegie Hall. She studied for six months with Nicholas Lakis, as well.

Her professional painting career began in 1940. Her work was exhibited at the Howard Young Gallery and at the *Salon Des Artistes Français,* in Paris, every year for several years. The first year she exhibited there her works were awarded honorable mention.

Many of Huldah's works included the Maltese. This dog was modeled by a Maltese owned by a friend, Irma Blood of New York City. The model was a littermate of Gay of Villa Malta, owned by Ann Jones, an early

Maltese Dog Fanciers Association and American Maltese Association secretary.

The Maltese has been used in theatre work, as well as film. Maltese were used in the film *Mary, Queen of Scots,* in which one was seen accompanying her to the block. In London, a Maltese named Teena played *Flush,* in *The Barretts of Wimpole Street,* a production housed in the Globe Theatre. She was a constant lap companion, while onstage, of Miss Marjorie Blake, the acresss who assumed the role of Elizabeth Barrett Browning.

The Maltese Before the Public Eye

As in ancient times, the Maltese continues to receive admiration from the general public. He has been used in television commercials quite frequently, as well as in fashion shows, newspaper and magazine advertisements, on greeting cards, and on business cards. He has been the subject of newspaper articles and has been featured on television programs. Considering this dog's great inherent beauty, he is likely to continue receiving public attention.

The Maltese and Famous Personages

For centuries the Maltese dog has been considered a dog of the aristocracy and those of genteel society. This tradition continues to this day. A true renaissance woman is mistress to two lovely Maltese, bred by the author. They are Aennchen's Tattva Dancer and Aennchen's Safai Dancer. These lovely little Maltese were acquired by the noted philanthropist and benefactress of the arts, Miss Alice Tully. Miss Tully is particularly noted for her great contributions to Lincoln Center for the performing arts, in New York City. There stands Alice Tully Hall, devoted to the performing arts, especially chamber music. Within Alice Tully Hall is located one of the finest custom built organs constructed in modern times. Miss Tully is an ardent admirer and great benefactress to the cause of animals, as well.

Other noteworthy personalities who are owned by, or have been admirers of the Maltese dog in their lifetimes include Liberace, a pianist and stage performer of great note, who owns a Maltese bred by M. Hohs of Ohio. Rosemary Clooney, noted popular singer, has owned Maltese for several years. She received her first from Dr. Calvaresi's Villa Malta Kennels. The late television personality and night club comedienne, Totie Fields, was mistress to several Al-Dor Maltese. Singer-actor John Davidson has been a Maltese owner, as has actress Lee Remmick. Noted actresses of stage and screen, Miss Shirley Booth and Miss Mona Freeman, have owned several Maltese. Actress Mia Farrow, while married to singer

341

A high fashion model holding a Maltese
owned by Mr. C. Deraita.

Liberace and his Merry-Ho Maltese puppy.

Frank Sinatra, acquired a Maltese. Other celebrated entertainers that have owned Maltese are Tallulah Bankhead, Edward O'Brien, Helen O'Connell, as well as the late Gary Cooper who owned Maltese of the Yelwa bloodline.

The Maltese and Christmas

The Maltese and Christmas seem just naturally to go together. Perhaps it is because he is white, as white as the driven snow—another Christmas natural. Perhaps, too, it is due to his joyful, spirited, outgoing personality. This certainly is in keeping with the spirit of the Christmas season. Needless to say, his elegant looks and demeanor are in keeping with many aspects of this holiday as well.

For whatever reason, the two blend wonderfully well together. Many Maltese fanciers have taken advantage of this charm. Most notable have been Aennchen and Tony Antonelli, who each year designed a new Christmas card featuring the Maltese.

Mrs. Dorothy Tinker, of the Al-Dor Maltese, has sent out some of the most delightful Christmas photographs featuring her Maltese. She has done this for many years.

It seems likely that Maltese and Christmas will continue to be a tradition celebrated for many years to come.

The Maltese as a Watch Dog

Despite their extremely small size, Maltese are known to be superb watch dogs. This proved to be of great benefit to the late Italian journalist, Miss Chiara Pisani.

Miss Pisani was especially noted for her interviews with the famous and wealthy, including the late Shah of Iran, Marlon Brando and Charlton Heston, among others. She was often accompanied by her pet Maltese, Aennchen's Kara Dancer, on trips to the Continent. Kara has had the distinction of joining her mistress for dinner in some of the finest restaurants in Europe.

Kara is a litter sister to Ch. Aennchen's Hindi Dancer, owned by Dr. and Mrs. Roger Brown. She is also mother to Ch. Aennchen's Shiko Dancer and Ch. Aennchen's Stela Dancer.

Kara and Miss Pisani made news when it was reported in the *New York Times* and the *New York Daily News* that Kara had protected her mistress' townhouse from a burglar. The thief had broken into the first floor living room of the multi-story dwelling, during the dead of night. Kara sounded the alarm from her mistress' second floor bedroom suite. She would not stop the commotion, causing Miss Pisani to be awakened. Miss Pisani was a sportswoman of note. She took hold of a nearby rifle, and went downstairs to find the thief at work. The thief tried to escape out the rear garden, only to be shot and wounded by the excellent markswoman,

343

Santa visiting Am. & Can. Ch. Moppet's Bolero of Normalta.

A striking Christmas portrait at the home of Annie Kanee.

344

Two puppies in a cradle.   *M. Martin*

One of the youngest champions on record, Ch. Aennchen's Savar Dancer.

Miss Pisani. The thief was stopped in his tracks and the authorities called. Little Kara was the great heroine, and so touted by the newspapers. Kara, who attained fifteen years of age, was given to the author upon the death of Miss Pisani.

Maltese Hair Products

The dog's hair has been used for many years to make yarn which has been woven and knitted into articles of clothing, such as socks, shawls and scarves.

With the shortage of woolen yarn caused by the Second World War, a plea for animal hair suitable for yarn making was issued by the British Government. Maltese hair was suitable for making operation stockings and bed socks for wounded soldiers, due to its white color.

Taking the idea from the British plea for animal hair, Miss Ethel Monroe, of New Orleans, collected the hair from her Maltese dogs and pet Persian cats. From this hair, she had several very attractive coverlets woven.

She was most noteworthy within the fancy as a result of these efforts.

This tradition is carried on today, more for esthetic reasons than due to actual need. Mrs. Barbara DiStefano has been experimenting in the use of various kinds of animal hair in spinning home-made yarns.

Using the Maltese coat, she has been able to spin some very fine, silky yarns. These yarns are then knitted, crocheted or woven into a variety of articles, all of which are soft, warm and delightfully serviceable. These include coverlets, scarves, and so on. Mrs. DiStefano has found that yarn spun from the Maltese coat takes on color from natural dyes quite well. In addition, the natural shade variations of the natural color coat are quite attractive. Hand spinning yarn is quite time consuming, however, it is worthwhile when the quality of the furnished yarn is considered. Mrs. DiStefano may be contacted at Box 15, Brady Road, Warwick, New York 10990.

She can provide the details for the amount of hair needed in preparation for making yarns for any number of items. It seems an intriguing prospect to own a sumptuous sweater knitted of champion Maltese hair.

Noteworthy Facts

Some interesting sidenotes regarding the Maltese dog are presented here for your consideration.

The average Maltese litter will usually have one or two puppies. Four and five in a litter are not unheard of. However, litters of more than five puppies are quite rare. Several such litters have been reported; one was

346

Mrs. DiStefano with her spinning wheel, and some scarves and shawls woven from the Maltese hair coats.

Miss E. V. Monroe, sitting on a coverlet woven from Maltese dog and Persian cat hair. Before her are a few "contributors."

owned by Gloria Busselman of Pen Sans Maltese. She reported a litter of seven puppies whelped in June of 1969. Six of these survived.

Preceding Mrs. Busselman's litter of seven was a litter of seven puppies, reported by Rose Sloan of Kismet Maltese in 1961. All survived.

Mrs. C. Kreveneck of Golden Valley, Minnesota, reported the largest litter recorded to date, in 1964. There was a total of eight whelps, including three males and five females! All survived.

The Maltese certainly would appear to be capable of being a prolific little producer, in light of this information.

The youngest champions of record would appear to be tied by Mary Hechinger's Ch. Sun Canyon Drummer Boy, who finished at seven months. Also finishing on his seventh-month birthday was Ch. Aennchen's Savar Dancer, owned, bred and shown by Mr. and Mrs. J. P. Antonelli. Also noteworthy, finishing at eight months of age was Ch. Charlie Brown of Al-Mar.

The American Maltese Association instituted an award system for recognizing Maltese dogs and bitches which have proven themselves valuable to the breed by producing champion offspring. The idea for this award was suggested by Joyce Watkins of Marcris Maltese. It was adopted by the American Maltese Association after receiving approval from the American Kennel Club.

To be eligible for the MALTESE MERIT AWARD, a dog must have sired at least five champions, and a dam must have whelped three champions.

Owners of Maltese which have accomplished this may apply to the AMA on approved application forms.

If approved, the dog so awarded will receive a certificate indicating his or her recognition of merit to the breed. In addition, any Maltese so awarded, may add the letters MMA following his or her name on all documents.

Following is as complete a list of the recipients as possible, from the information available at the time of this writing.

Dogs awarded the Maltese Merit Award appellation include:

> Ch. Nyssamead's Jonah of Tennesa
> Ch. Marcris Love and Kisses
> Ch. C & M's Camero of Villa Malta
> Ch. Infante Mystic Caper
> Ch. Mike Mar's Ringleader II
> Ch. Al-Dor Little Rascal
> Ch. Couer-De-Lion
> Ch. Joanne-Chen's Maya Dancer
> Diavolino of Villa Malta
> Ch. Non Vel's Weejun of Carno
> Ch. Eve-Ron's Snokist Cherub
> Ch. Aennchen's Raja Dancer

Ch. Aennchen's Shikar Dancer
Ch. Aennchen's Siva Dancer
Ch. To the Victor of Eng
Ch. Su-Le's Blue Jay
Ch. Su-Le's Roadrunner
Ch. Su-Le's Sandpiper
Ch. Salterr Gloryseeker
Ch. Fremont of Valletta
Ch. Fairy Fay's Figaro
Ch. Al-Dor Randy, CD
Ch. C & M's Valentino of Midhill
Ch. San Su Kee Star Edition
Ch. None Such of Midhill
Ch. Joanne-Chen's Mino Maya Dancer
Ch. San Su Kee Showoff
Ch. Fantasyland Bugalewey
Ch. Gayla's Piccolo Pete
Am., Mex., Int. Ch. Mac's Apache Joray of Eve Ron
Ch. Su-Le's Bluebird
Ch. Maltacello's Romeo
Ch. Caramaya's Mister
Ch. Aennchen's Shiko Dancer
Ch. Aennchen's Soomi Dancer

Bitches awarded the Maltese Merit Award include:

Lester's Lilly Lady Cecil
Ch. Cotterell's Luv of Tennessa
Marcris White Cascade
Marcris Happy Holly
Joanne-Chen's Mini Maid Dancer
Bobbelee Frosted Velvet
Joanne-Chen's Sheeba Dancer
Ch. C & M's Tiny Moonglow
Sun Canyon Mell-O-Dee of Love
Bali Hai's Misty Pebbles
Ch. Lady Saphronia Reveille
Ch. Russ Ann Petite Charmer
Primrose Raggedy Ann
Ch. Eve-Ron's Jendi from Oak Ridge
Ch. Aennchen's Puja Dancer
Ch. Su-Le's Robin of Eng
Ch. Su-Le's Jacana
Ch. Inge of Winddrift
Ch. Vicbrita As Always
Boswell's Tinkerbell
Ch. Aennchen's Pompi Dancer
Aennchen's Siimi Dancer

350

The Love of the Breed

by Joyce Blake Watkins

This is what it means to me.
The pride of owning one or more of these elegant
    animals.
The respect you have for someone else's Maltese.
The good sportsmanship you display in the ring
    when losing those all important points.
The loving care you give your dog when keeping it clean,
    well groomed, well fed and free of vermin.
The joy of having a new litter and watching them
    develop.
The getting up every two hours to feed newborns
    when your bitch is unable to.
The tears you shed when you have done all humanly possible
    to save an adult or puppy and it has been in vain.
The turning away of a prospect for a puppy when their
    children are unruly.
The help you are willing to give to another person
    in the breed.
The foolhardy selection of a weak puppy for your
    stud fee, in hope that you may save it.
The compassion you feel for another's loss of their
    pet.
The anger you feel when any Maltese is abused.
The thrill of seeing pups you bred in the show or
    obedience ring
The contempt you have for puppy mills.
The knowledge that your Maltese thinks of you as
    his very own God and you think of him as a member of
    the family.

BIBLIOGRAPHY

ALL OWNERS of pure-bred dogs will benefit themselves and their dogs by enriching their knowledge of breed and of canine care, training, breeding, psychology and other important aspects of dog management. The following list of books covers further reading recommended by judges, veterinarians, breeders, trainers and other authorities. Books may be obtained at the finer book stores and pet shops, or through Howell Book House Inc., publishers, New York.

BREED BOOKS

AFGHAN HOUND, Complete	Miller & Gilbert
AIREDALE, New Complete	Edwards
AKITA, Complete	Linderman & Funk
ALASKAN MALAMUTE, Complete	Riddle & Seeley
BASSET HOUND, Complete	Braun
BLOODHOUND, Complete	Brey & Reed
BOXER, Complete	Denlinger
BRITTANY SPANIEL, Complete	Riddle
BULLDOG, New Complete	Hanes
BULL TERRIER, New Complete	Eberhard
CAIRN TERRIER, Complete	Marvin
CHESAPEAKE BAY RETRIEVER, Complete	Cherry
CHIHUAHUA, Complete	Noted Authorities
COCKER SPANIEL, New	Kraeuchi
COLLIE, New	Official Publication of the Collie Club of America
DACHSHUND, The New	Meistrell
DALMATIAN, The	Treen
DOBERMAN PINSCHER, New	Walker
ENGLISH SETTER, New Complete	Tuck, Howell & Graef
ENGLISH SPRINGER SPANIEL, New	Goodall & Gasow
FOX TERRIER, New	Nedell
GERMAN SHEPHERD DOG, New Complete	Bennett
GERMAN SHORTHAIRED POINTER, New	Maxwell
GOLDEN RETRIEVER, New Complete	Fischer
GORDON SETTER, Complete	Look
GREAT DANE, New Complete	Noted Authorities
GREAT DANE, The—Dogdom's Apollo	Draper
GREAT PYRENEES, Complete	Strang & Giffin
IRISH SETTER, New Complete	Eldredge & Vanacore
IRISH WOLFHOUND, Complete	Starbuck
JACK RUSSELL TERRIER, Complete	Plummer
KEESHOND, New Complete	Cash
LABRADOR RETRIEVER, Complete	Warwick
LHASA APSO, Complete	Herbel
MASTIFF, History and Management of the	Baxter & Hoffman
MINIATURE SCHNAUZER, Complete	Eskrigge
NEWFOUNDLAND, New Complete	Chern
NORWEGIAN ELKHOUND, New Complete	Wallo
OLD ENGLISH SHEEPDOG, Complete	Mandeville
PEKINGESE, Quigley Book of	Quigley
PEMBROKE WELSH CORGI, Complete	Sargent & Harper
POODLE, New	Irick
POODLE CLIPPING AND GROOMING BOOK, Complete	Kalstone
ROTTWEILER, Complete	Freeman
SAMOYED, New Complete	Ward
SCOTTISH TERRIER, New Complete	Marvin
SHETLAND SHEEPDOG, The New	Riddle
SHIH TZU, Joy of Owning	Seranne
SHIH TZU, The (English)	Dadds
SIBERIAN HUSKY, Complete	Demidoff
TERRIERS, The Book of All	Marvin
WEIMARANER, Guide to the	Burgoin
WEST HIGHLAND WHITE TERRIER, Complete	Marvin
WHIPPET, Complete	Pegram
YORKSHIRE TERRIER, Complete	Gordon & Bennett

BREEDING

ART OF BREEDING BETTER DOGS, New	Onstott
BREEDING YOUR OWN SHOW DOG	Seranne
HOW TO BREED DOGS	Whitney
HOW PUPPIES ARE BORN	Prine
INHERITANCE OF COAT COLOR IN DOGS	Little

CARE AND TRAINING

COUNSELING DOG OWNERS, Evans Guide for	Evans
DOG OBEDIENCE, Complete Book of	Saunders
NOVICE, OPEN AND UTILITY COURSES	Saunders
DOG CARE AND TRAINING FOR BOYS AND GIRLS	Saunders
DOG NUTRITION, Collins Guide to	Collins
DOG TRAINING FOR KIDS	Benjamin
DOG TRAINING, Koehler Method of	Koehler
DOG TRAINING Made Easy	Tucker
GO FIND! Training Your Dog to Track	Davis
GUARD DOG TRAINING, Koehler Method of	Koehler
MOTHER KNOWS BEST—The Natural Way to Train Your Dog	Benjamin
OPEN OBEDIENCE FOR RING, HOME AND FIELD, Koehler Method of	Koehler
STONE GUIDE TO DOG GROOMING FOR ALL BREEDS	Stone
SUCCESSFUL DOG TRAINING, The Pearsall Guide to	Pearsall
TEACHING DOG OBEDIENCE CLASSES—Manual for Instructors	Volhard & Fisher
TOY DOGS, Kalstone Guide to Grooming All	Kalstone
TRAINING THE RETRIEVER	Kersley
TRAINING TRACKING DOGS, Koehler Method of	Koehler
TRAINING YOUR DOG—Step by Step Manual	Volhard & Fisher
TRAINING YOUR DOG TO WIN OBEDIENCE TITLES	Morsell
TRAIN YOUR OWN GUN DOG, How to	Goodall
UTILITY DOG TRAINING, Koehler Method of	Koehler
VETERINARY HANDBOOK, Dog Owner's Home	Carlson & Giffin

GENERAL

AMERICAN KENNEL CLUB 1884-1984—A Source Book	American Kennel Club
CANINE TERMINOLOGY	Spira
COMPLETE DOG BOOK, The	Official Publication of American Kennel Club
DOG IN ACTION, The	Lyon
DOG BEHAVIOR, New Knowledge of	Pfaffenberger
DOG JUDGE'S HANDBOOK	Tietjen
DOG PEOPLE ARE CRAZY	Riddle
DOG PSYCHOLOGY	Whitney
DOGSTEPS, The New	Elliott
DOG TRICKS	Haggerty & Benjamin
EYES THAT LEAD—Story of Guide Dogs for the Blind	Tucker
FRIEND TO FRIEND—Dogs That Help Mankind	Schwartz
FROM RICHES TO BITCHES	Shattuck
HAPPY DOG/HAPPY OWNER	Siegal
IN STITCHES OVER BITCHES	Shattuck
JUNIOR SHOWMANSHIP HANDBOOK	Brown & Mason
OUR PUPPY'S BABY BOOK (blue or pink)	
SUCCESSFUL DOG SHOWING, Forsyth Guide to	Forsyth
TRIM, GROOM & SHOW YOUR DOG, How to	Saunders
WHY DOES YOUR DOG DO THAT?	Bergman
WILD DOGS in Life and Legend	Riddle
WORLD OF SLED DOGS, From Siberia to Sport Racing	Coppinger